Last Days

To Margo Timmons,

Adventure begins with the
first step...

John Roshelley

12-20-91

Last Days

John Roskelley

STACKPOLE
BOOKS

Copyright © 1991 by John Roskelley

Published by
STACKPOLE BOOKS
Cameron and Kelker Streets
P.O. Box 1831
Harrisburg, PA 17105

Printed in the United States of America

10 9 8 7 6 5 4 3 2 1

First edition

Text design by Tracy Patterson
Maps by Dee Molenaar

Library of Congress Cataloging-in-Publication Data

Roskelley, John.
    Last days: a world-famous climber challenges the Himalayas'
Tawoche and Menlungtse/John Roskelley.
        p.   cm.
    ISBN 0-8117-0889-6
    1. Roskelley, John.   2. Mountaineers — United States — Bibliography.
3. Mountaineering — Himalaya Mountains.   I. Title.
GV199.92.R67A3   1991
796.5'22'092 — dc20
[B]   91-12872
                                                                    CIP

*To Chris Kopczynski, Kim Momb, and James States.
And to the many others who shared with me
the adventures of the rope.*

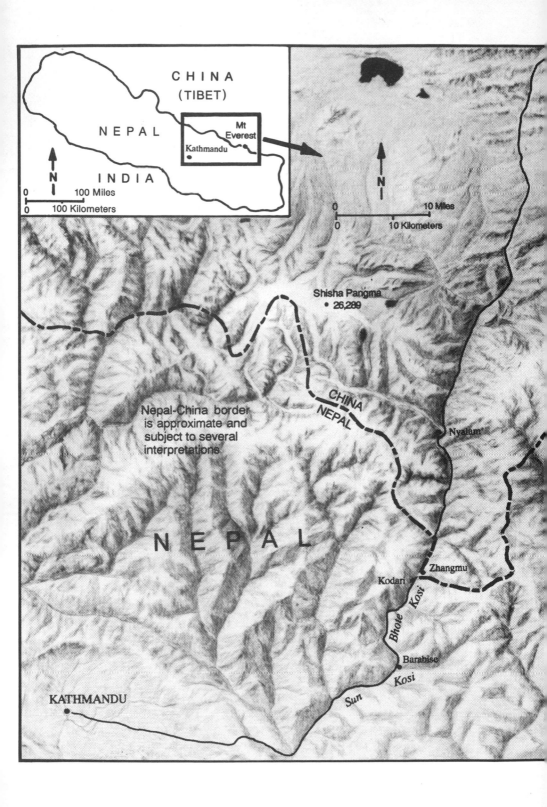

CHINA
(TIBET)

NEPAL

Mt
Everest

Kathmandu

INDIA

N

0   100 Miles
0   100 Kilometers

N

0   10 Miles
0   10 Kilometers

Shisha Pangma
• 26,289

CHINA
NEPAL

Nyalam

Nepal-China border
is approximate and
subject to several
interpretations

NEPAL

Zhangmu

Kodari

Bhote   Kosi

Barabise

Kosi

Sun

KATHMANDU

CHINA
(Tibet)

Tingri

Tsang Po *(Brahmaputra)*

(by jeep)

(by trail)

Phusi La
17,753

Dazhang

Rong Shar Chu

Chuwar

Changbujian

Cho Oyu
26,750

Rongbuk valley

ri Shankar
,405

Menlung Chu

Menlungtse
23,560

CHINA

NEPAL

MT EVEREST
29,028

Lhotse
27,890

Tawoche
21,535

Pheriche

Makalu
27,825

Ama Dablam
22,494

Namche
Bazar

Kosi

Arun

valley

Dudh

Lukla

© D. Molenaar, 1991

TAWOCHE
21,535

VIII

VII

VI

II

Tawoche I

Glacier

TAWOCHE
showing route
up Northeast Face

Tawoche
21,535

Cholatse
21,129

Lobuje
20,161

Panorama from above Pheriche

1

gaunt·let \ˈgȯnt-lət\ *n* A perceived challenge from a mountain that releases the hormone "test-your-own," creating instant brain-lock. See "sexual conquest."
(*Roskelley's First Climber's Dictionary*, 1991)

"DON'T EVEN THINK about it," Tawoche rumbled to me in Mountainese, guttural tremors punctuated with rockfall and avalanche understood and heard solely by mountaineers with weak knees and rucksacks full of excuses. Whoever said climbers had intestinal fortitude?

Besides, it was too late. Destiny was destined. My eyes followed the contours, gullies, and buttresses of the face from bottom to top as if it were a twenty-dollar topless dancer in a Texas bar. I didn't miss a move.

Tawoche's face was a true "Pig" worthy of the honor bestowed upon it by the comparison. Years back when I was a youth brash as a thunderstorm and bear-cub foolish, "Pigs" were peaks like Robson, Chephron, Edith Cavell. Climbs capable of creating impromptu illnesses cured only by beer and pizza back in Banff.

I never said "Pig" to their faces. Oh, no. No more than I would walk unroped on a glacier or have lunch under an icefall. Even during the brain-dead years of my youth I always whispered "Pig" to my partners if we were near the peak as if commentating at a golf tournament. And never, ever, before my attempt.

So out of curiosity I answered Tawoche, "And why not?" (on

the edge of adding "Pig" but catching myself). "You're just another mountain with an ugly face."

"Because you're not the first and you won't be the last," Tawoche replied.

I couldn't argue that point. It was right. Like a bird of prey, Tawoche perches above a river of Everest pilgrims. A river that floods its banks spring and fall with summit hopefuls who can and will stand upon Everest's crown—given enough Sherpas and bottled oxygen.

In all these years of passing beneath this massive, unclimbed, untouched wall, why haven't these Everesters climbed Tawoche's wizened Northeast Face? **The Face.** How is it these hopeful conquerors of the earth's highest summit, these men and women strong as yaks and determined as ants, have passed beneath Tawoche's face and not thrown the gauntlet?

Because Tawoche spoke to them, too.

"I'll be back," I warned it, faking just the right Austrian lisp to emulate Arnold Schwarzenegger's cyborg, the Terminator. Then, in typical early vintage Roskelley, added ". . . Pig."

But I whispered it.

George Orwell's predictions of the fictitious "Big Brother," who would surreptitiously watch us forever, never came to pass in 1984 other than in our imaginations, but my Tawoche did. Tawoche took a small corner of my mind, haunted it, and relentlessly challenged me to return. I worked out with The Face, ate with The Face, envisioned it when my mind needed escape, even saw it in my dreams. I climbed it, was rescued from it, died on it, and yet never left Spokane.

In 1984, two years from my first encounter with Tawoche, I looked upon an empty spring. I had a choice: get a job or go climbing, which wasn't really a choice at all. Joyce, my half-time wife and full-time supporter, expected, no, demanded of me to migrate to the Himalayas each March and September for the same reason a duck goes south in the winter—to avoid the cold. In my case, the cold shoulder. "Do something, John, you're driving me nuts."

Joyce needed those two or three months' relief to rebuild the nest, take a deep breath, stand back, and come to grips with being hitched to a high-pressure system.

"Joyce," I began, "I have my eye on a little peak in Nepal this coming spring. Can you hold down the fort while I take a month to knock if off?"

"I could rebuild it," she thought, but tactfully said, "I'll manage. Have you got any money coming in?"

Wives are raised knowing how to pull the first verbal punch, set you up, then cow-kick you in the ribs. It might be inherited, but I suspect that as little girls they learn it playing house. Maybe there are written lessons that come with their first Barbie and that mouse, Ken. It's probably on video by now.

Joyce was just digging. She knew I was on a monthly retainer with Du Pont's fiberfill division. Up until falling into that safety net I was making the official climbers' salary—the same as, but not more than, what a good pachyderm makes with Barnum and Bailey's Circus.

"Sure," I replied in my "What the hell do you take me for, a bum?" voice.

Official permission granted from the Boss, I requested a permit to climb Tawoche from the Nepalese Ministry of Tourism. It was as easy to get as a bad cold. After all, it wasn't as though I were asking for season tickets to the Seattle Seahawks games. The Ministry hadn't sold that one in years.

According to my sources in Kathmandu, there had been no known attempts on Tawoche's Northeast Face since I bravely threatened it verbally in 1982, feet safely planted in Pheriche, with no plans to go back. Oh, I wanted to. But desire can dig a lot deeper than the doing. Yet even back then, standing below that face with only a drop of a thought to return, I was caught in a moment of hesitation, and self-doubt eased its way into my thoughts like the long fingers of a coastal fog. Could I? Would I? Hell, should I?

The world's best climbers—and those who think they are—
trek the Khumbu Trail gawking at Ama Dablam, Thamserku,
Lhotse, and Everest pointing out previous routes and future possibilities. Few come back, much less follow talk with ingenuity and
boldness.

Then comes Tawoche's triangular face. It stands apart as the
valley doglegs northwest as if to say, "Let me show you our fly-
weight champion of the Himalayas, Tawoche." Climbers point out
the obvious line slicing the center of the face, a cleft as deep and
exposed as an infected sword scar on a pirate's cheek. Geologists
call it a fault, climbers call it a dream.

On either side of the iced center line are painted cliffs of
metamorphic gneiss, crackless, overhanging voids of pink granite
shot through with massive swirls and dikes of black diorite. Evidence of ledges appears as horizontal snow stuck to the walls,
looking like a flock of white seagulls amidst a dark and threatening
sky.

There's a route or two "out there" away from the center. Nothing direct. The kind of route you would have to fight your way up
rather than flow with. A line such as the one your car would take if
you took your hands off the wheel. Gneiss creates that. It's not like
the bold directness of granite with its systematic joints that follow
a track as if laid for a railroad. Gneiss leaves you hanging, wondering about continuity, seeking alternate direction. Sometimes there
is none.

Even from the bar in Pheriche, a wind-strewn grouping of
rock hovels set among a patchwork of summer potato fields,
Tawoche challenges the climber's drunk or sober ego. Seen
through a smoke-stained bisquine window popping in and out
with the evening wind, The Face comes alive, distorted and ani-
mated as if dancing to the long-distance static on the radio, which
never stops playing Nepal's most recent love songs. The Star beer
flows down throats parched by the ever-constant wind and rising
altitude, supporting wild talk and wilder ideas—until morning.

"Still there," some hung-over one says. "And here I thought it
was just a bad dream."

There, looking up at what Emilio Comici could give as an

example to his classic line, "I wish some day to make a route and from the summit let fall a drop of water and this is where my route will have gone," climbers get the "Word," Tawoche's Word. They shake their heads, dodge another fresh yak pie, and walk on to make another ascent of Everest.

I wanted that Face.

I can't tell you for certain why I climb, but I know why I wanted that Face. It is my time to leave the sport. Maybe not completely as if turning off a water spigot, but time to finish off with a bang and get out while I'm still at the top of my game, still physically and mentally sharp, still feeling that spark within me that has pushed and driven me for twenty-five years of mountaineering.

Tawoche is legacy material. A monument, so to speak. A spectacular route, dead center up an impossible-looking face, unavoidable by my future peers on their way to make another ascent of the world's highest peak.

Now, to climb The Face I knew someone had to be two-thirds loco and one-third drunk or totally ignorant of the objective. No sane individual would agree to, let alone admit to, challenging the Northeast Face. So selecting a qualified, bona fide climbing team was like trying to find a lost ten spot down on New York's Forty-second and Broadway at noon. Damn near impossible. But a few ideas came to me just shy of being as original as the quantum theory of relativity.

I went through all my possibilities and past climbing partners. My old dog, Sam; Kim Schmitz; Ron Kauk; Rick Ridgeway; Lou Reichardt; Jim States; Chris Kopczynski; Kim Momb; Jack Tackle; and on and on. It was a list you wouldn't want at a social party, but then again, most of them would have made Who's Who in American Mountaineering.

I began the elimination procedure based first on intelligence. That criterion removed Reichardt and Sam on the first cut. Both were too smart. Those employed, whether successfully or not, made the second cut. This eliminated Ridgeway, States, Tackle, Kopczynski, and a dozen more. Family ties canceled a few others.

Those who were left had obvious detrimental hang-ups. Schmitz had taken an eighty-foot free-flight in the Tetons and cratered onto a ledge. He was out unless some miracle-worker surgeon could remove his shattered tibias and fibulas and reattach his feet to his knees. Knowing Schmitz he'd soon be climbing 5.11 again in no time.

Kauk was a shoo-in after our climb of Uli Biaho in Pakistan in 1979, but more recently his commitment was questionable. He was to have joined me on Aconcagua in Argentina that winter, but the day before departure I called him and he canceled. His girlfriend was going to have a baby.

"Well, we'll only be gone three to four weeks, Ron," I said. "When's the baby due?"

"This week."

"Why didn't you think about this sooner?"

"I just found out."

So I was on the verge of thinking solo when Jim Bridwell popped into mind. The "Bird Man," as he is known in Yosemite, had in recent years proven himself to be a superb alpinist. Beginning with his ascent of Cerro Torre, one of the world's most sought-after big walls, Bridwell had gone on to climb two Alaskan ogres, the North Face of Kachatna Spire and the East Face of the Moose's Tooth. In 1982, thirsting for a taste of high altitude, he, along with Ned Gillette and Jan Reynolds, made the first American ascent and first winter ascent of Pumori, a difficult pyrimidal peak a stone's throw west of Everest.

Bridwell was hot and obviously not just a warm weather, California rock jock as many thought, but an experienced mountain man with few to zero qualms about saving his hide for bingo and a bed pan at a rest home. Besides, I knew him from prehistoric climbing days: Yosemite, 1969.

The "Bird" had to have been born with forty-year-old wrinkles furrowing his face and belly-button hair. No way did he start out as a child. When I first met Bridwell in Yosemite in the late 1960s, I just naturally figured he was part of Yvon Chouinard's or Royal Robbins's generation. A good decade or two ahead of me.

He looked worn and weathered like an old oak stump. It wasn't until years later I found out he was only four years older than I.

Bridwell is to Yosemite what Babe Ruth is to baseball. He broke every record on every climb in the Valley. I vividly remember watching Bridwell and Mark Clemens, one of his many partners, work on the first ascent of New Dimensions, a preseventies horror climb in the Valley. Bridwell looked as though he had only 1 percent body fat. His skin was a transparent film over blood vessels and meat that pulsated and expanded whenever he moved. Bridwell was a walking example of a medical textbook figure for the human musculature. I was no couch potato, but stood in awe of what living on cigarettes, coffee, climbing, coffee, working out, and more coffee did for the body. Did I want to look like this? Yes. Did I want to live like this? No way. So I returned to Washington State University and finished my junior year. Thanks, Jim.

Bridwell's reputation was punctuated with fables and outlandish legends that were captivating, though sometimes highly improbable. His fame had borne publicity and, along with it, controversy. Why? I never asked. He was always joking and seemed a likable fellow to me. Yes, he was into the hippie lifestyle of the California sixties — wild clothes, cosmic books, long hair, brown rice, free love, and antiwar sentiment, which wasn't my scene. But he always treated me with respect and kept his extravagant ways in check. If there was anyone alive who knew more about big walls, he wasn't of this earth.

I got Bridwell on the phone. "It's a classic. You'll love it," I said.

"I saw it two years ago on the way to Pumori," he replied.

"Damn. So you don't want to go?"

"Sure. It looks great to me."

P.T. Barnum was right. There's a sucker born every minute.

"I'll send you a blow-up so you can get reacquainted."

I never did. Bridwell was treed and I figured there wasn't any sense in pulling off the dogs and losing a partner by exposing Tawoche's ugly mug again. His wife, Peggy, told me he was so excited he left home and went climbing for a week. "Ask him on a few more, will ya?" She sounded like my wife.

For some reason I wanted three climbers on Tawoche. Same as if I wanted two cups of coffee, or five gallons of gas instead of a full tank. There wasn't anything specific in my mind that said, "John, take three because. . . ." It just was.

I decided to break Roskelley tradition. If I couldn't find an American who wanted that Face enough to suffer financial ruin and divorce, it was time to look internationally. Japan.

Japanese climbers were eating up routes in the Himalayas and Karakoram faster than I can choke down a plate of sushi. Their teams rivaled herds of sheep in number, had more equipment than Komatsu, and were better financed than Sony. They're organized, clean, and polite, and eat healthier camp food. Ever been on an American expedition? The two cultures are worlds and an ocean apart in the fine art of successful, cooperative ventures. If I were into predicting the future, one sure bet would be that our children will be eating squid with chopsticks before we can pitch our forks and spoons into another closing landfill.

I know two Japanese supermen, Naomi Uemura and Naoe Sakashita. Uemura was (past tense) Japan's hero adventurer who climbed Everest with the first Japanese team in 1962, dog-sledded to the North Pole solo, dog-sledded across Northern Canada solo, rafted down the Amazon from its headwaters to its mouth solo, and had other incredible adventures before disappearing on Mount McKinley while attempting the first winter ascent — solo. Uemura was the only real hero I've ever met.

Enter the samurai. Sakashita should have died. Didn't. Should have again. Didn't. So I decided to let fate have another shot at him. He had already climbed K2 by the North Ridge and Kangchen-junga via the North Face. What I didn't know about were his ascents of Jannu North Face in 1976 and Annapurna II, and his climbs in the Alps. He had to have balls as big as a bull elk's, even though he was typically Japanese: around five foot two, with glasses, built the way a good pole barn is built — sturdy.

Sakashita could probably run circles around Bridwell and me. The circumference of his thighs matched that of my waist and, although his muscles were not as defined as Bridwell's, when

Sakashita moved a lot of hard lumps rolled and moved with him.

Sakashita hid a Mr. Hyde personality behind the Japanese manners and continual smile. He reminded me of a lion in the bush not yet hungry. There was a calm–before–the–storm feature in his black eyes that told me to ignore his politeness and reserve. When the prey was visible, this cat would be hungry. Tawoche would become life itself, subsistence, not just a climb. Sakashita's eye had been on Tawoche years before. We were his first excuse to go for it. He wanted the first ascent of The Face and it was either go with Bridwell and me or perhaps lose that opportunity.

Sakashita said *hai* too enthusiastically for someone who had seen The Face before. I was tempted to ask him his statistics, such as number of partners on his teams, percentage that returned . . . those kinds of questions. But, not knowing Japanese etiquette, I stuck to the more traditional approach: "What? Where? When?" With tradition guiding our relationship, we organized food, finances, and equipment through the mail, relying on his one visit to his employer, Chouinard, in Ventura to fine-tune our arrangements.

By early April we were as eager to set foot on Tawoche as a pack of lions on a fresh kill. A redneck, a Bridwell (the only way to describe Bridwell), and a samurai. A group as unlikely as *The Hobbit*.

2

fail·ure \ 'fā(ə)l-yər \ *n*   A state of mind result-
ing from a decision based on common sense
rather than emotion.
(Roskelley's First Climber's Dictionary, 1991)

"SPECIAL AGENT THOMAS. Bureau of Alcohol, Tobacco, and Fire-
arms. Please step off to the side."

As if I had a choice. The overweight, six-foot, prematurely
balding Thomas had me gently but firmly beneath my triceps,
directing me to an empty corner near our departure gate. Bridwell,
who was right behind me as we were about to enter the jetway
leading to our Thai flight, was in the same predicament. The agent
who cornered him was the height of a California redwood and not
a cottonball short of two hundred pounds.

One thing was clear: whatever Agent Thomas was after was
because somebody wanted Jim or me to take a fall. This was a
setup, through an anonymous tip. Thomas and his buddy knew we
were flying Thai International Airlines that morning and were
waiting at the departure lounge like a pair of vultures. They had
planned our search and seizure to the second — while we were still
in U.S. federal authority, yet showing our boarding cards to an
international flight.

"Empty all your pockets, pull your belt, and take off your

shoes," Thomas instructed as he bird-dogged through my carry-on and camera gear. "How much U.S. currency are you carrying with you?" he asked, as he frisked my arms, torso, and legs. A more thorough job could only have been done on Bo Derek.

"Not enough," I replied, grinning.

Thomas was not amused.

"Nine thousand three hundred and forty dollars."

"It's a federal offense to carry more than five thousand dollars cash on your person off U.S. soil unless a permit is applied for in advance. Do you have that permit?"

"Uh-oh," I thought. "No, but I'm carrying expedition funds for the two of us, me and the guy you have over in the other corner."

I knew Bridwell had at most several hundred dollars cash in his possession. Thomas could stick me on a technicality, but would he?

Thomas told me to stay put and he and the other agent walked off to one side to confer, while Bridwell and I looked at each other across the departure lounge and shrugged our shoulders. A Thai airline official joined the agents, and by the way he pointed and looked at his watch, I was sure we were holding up the fully packed and boarded flight. The pressure was on the agents to make the arrest or let us board.

"Okay," Thomas said, handing back my passport, wallet, and ticket. "Have a nice flight."

"I hope, Bridwell," I said once on board the plane, "that whichever 'friends' of ours set this up haven't contacted every customs department from here to Nepal."

Sakashita met us at Tribhuvan International Airport in Nepal. Right out of the chute I began wondering if I were capable of keeping up with this Japanese version of Speedy Gonzales. He arrived several days before we did to arrange for a post-Tawoche, two-man, alpine-style attempt on Ama Dablam's South Face. The two peaks sit adjacent to each other in the Khumbu. Sakashita expected an easy, quick, and inexpensive secondary approach for

Ama Dablam. His Japanese partner planned to meet him sometime in early May. I, however, felt pushed just to get the Tawoche climb off the ground.

We were joined by three trekkers from Spokane; our Sherpa sirdar, Ang Nima; and our cookboy, Dorje. The team boarded a Royal Nepal Twin Otter for a sixty-minute flight to Lukla, a highland Nepali village catering to the lucrative trekking and mountaineering trade.

Lukla had quickly grown out of livable, buildable space like a seven-year-old boy grows out of his jeans. Below massive, vertical granite walls, Lukla-ites terrace steep hillsides for sites on which to erect stone hotels that will accommodate hundreds of tourists, hippies, mountaineers, and their Sherpa staffs.

During peak tourist seasons, April to May and September to October, Lukla serves as a hundred-cattle corral for a thousand cattle. Rest housing, campsites, even food are as scarce as good help. While rhododendrons color the upper hillsides, raging torrents carve deeper into the gorges, and the Himalayas cut a swath of white through a deep blue sea of sky, tourists, trekkers, and expedition climbers eager to reach Kathmandu arrive in Lukla for the one-hour flight back to civilization only to wait days, sometimes weeks for good weather and a scheduled flight to arrive. Normally passive human beings stuck in Lukla have been known to resort to bribery, verbal abuse of Royal Nepal Airline Corporation (RNAC) staff and each other, or even fisticuffs to grab a seat on the next available flight back to Kathmandu. Why study monkeys in a cage when Lukla is available?

If it weren't for the mud, mangy curs, scrawny chickens, stench of sewage and rotting vegetables, and countless slimeballs that suck off the tourist trade, Lukla would be pleasant. But during the tourist season it's just another Talkeetna, Alaska, without a decent bar or toilet.

Mountaineers are at the top of the social ladder in the Khumbu, which speaks for itself. In our own countries we're mostly considered antisocial parasites into our "own thing." Of course, there's a bit of truth to that. But in the Superdome of the climbing world—the Himalayas—mountaineers gain a kind of dignity, a purpose, like bankers in a bank or doctors in a hospital. We look important, almost official, just by number alone. Zopkios and yaks toil along the trail, laden with stenciled waterproof boxes that proclaim destinies such as "1984 Everest South-southwest via the Right Side Expedition"; and porters carry European plastic drums locked and cabled and taped, fireproofed, waterproofed, nonbreakable, and biodegradable reading "1984 Lhotse Do or Die Expedition" with the name of a famous mountaineer scribbled in indelible ink across the top. These caravans of transport sometimes stretch along the trail for miles, pushing trekkers and local traffic to one side of the narrow path as if to say, "We're here to smother that peak into submission with gear and garbage." And they do.

Tourism for the sake of "getting into the culture" or "enjoying the mountains" disappeared with the first rupee payment to a local for a bowl of rice. It was like sticking grain in front of a horse. Sherpas knew right away there was gold in those Vibram soles walking past their old huts and, like the born traders they are, reaped the benefits. Enterprising families turned their homes into lodges, restaurants, and stores. Fathers, brothers, and uncles hired on as guides, cooks, cookboys, and trek leaders. Junk and inherited trinkets around the house became "artifacts" and tourist fodder soon to be exhibited on a coffee table or credenza in some million-dollar Berkeley mansion to proclaim to guests that the owner "was there."

Sherpa and Tibetan families are as tight as two-hundred-knot rugs. It's as hard for an "outsider" like a Limbu tribesman or low-land Bhotia to break into the trekking/mountaineering business as it would be for an Irishman to become part of an Italian crime family. A lot of this has to do with expeditions that hire their Sherpas from businesses in Kathmandu catering to tourism. Through years of successful Himalayan mountaineering, the name "Sherpa" has become synonymous with "guide." Ignorance follows misunderstanding. The Sherpas keep the business "Sherpa" and the tourists expect it. It's as if other Nepali tribes can't start a fire, erect a tent, or walk on anything but level ground.

My experience has been different. The strongest Nepali that ever ran for wood or packed a load for me was a Limbu. He squeaked into the game through the back door by marrying a Sherpa girl and living in Sherpa country.

Our two base-camp Sherpas for Tawoche were hired through a trekking agency in Kathmandu. Ang Nima is my lucky charm. I always request him. He isn't flamboyant or charismatic like many sirdars. He doesn't even speak Ricardo Montalban English or summit 8,000-meter peaks. But Ang Nima is a worker—he predicts what needs to be done and does it, gets the right price for food and fuel and pays for it, and eagerly carries loads if I need him to without my feeling as though I'm asking a fly fisherman to use bait. Ang Nima selected Dorje as cookboy. That was good enough for me.

The Everest trek can be walked in several days all the way from Lukla to base camp, where you would promptly drown in your own body fluids and die of cerebral or pulmonary edema, or it can be done at a more "got nothing to do" pace that allows your body to acclimatize safely. We took the more prudent method and arrived in Pheriche after six days of dodging trinket stalls near every village and avoiding instant Americanization advertised along the trail, from "hot water" to "peach cobbler." The Khumbu trek is the Nepali equivalent of a trip down Pacific Coast Highway 101.

Unluckily for us, neither earthquake nor erosion had reduced Tawoche's Face to an easy scramble. It was still there, leaning toward the valley as if chastising a young child: "You're back? Ha!"

Yes, it was laughing in my face and neither Bridwell nor Sakashita seemed to understand Tawoche's particular dialect of Mountainese. Sakashita, whose samurai instinct was in attack mode, failed to pay any attention because a samurai fears only fear itself. Bridwell, an alpine war veteran himself, needed a closer look. His last image of Tawoche had been under favorable winter circumstances. Now it was spring. I sensed he may have shared a few of my doubts, although he stoically showed none—except by smoking his unfiltered Camels until they burnt his fingers. Tawoche must have said something to him.

The village of Pheriche is twelve bodies short of becoming a ghost town. If it weren't for the fact that trekkers and expeditions had to pass through on their way to Everest, no one would live there.

Pheriche marks the end of tourist amenities — if it's not beyond them. One of my personal hells would be to have to live in Pheriche for eternity. I would take up religion to avoid that. A few seasonal rock huts, a hole-in-the-wall Sherpa store, two trekkers' "hotels" with bedbugs (at no extra charge), and the Himalaya Rescue Association hospital sit atop moraine debris like an oil spill on a frozen lake. An endless wind worries the few scrub bushes and junipers as it's sucked into the equatorial heat of India from Tibet's frozen plateau through a toothless gap in the Himalayas called the Lho La (*la* means high pass).

A few days spent at our base camp in Pheriche packing loads and acclimatizing made climbing on Tawoche something to look forward to. Our approach was as easy as walking to the base of El Capitan in Yosemite. We crossed the river on temporary wooden poles, zigzagged up the grassy slope below the peak on yak trails, then located and excavated a flat, sandy campsite for advanced base just below the terminal moraine from the glacier below The Face. Two days later we moved to advanced base to begin carrying our climbing gear to the bottom of the wall.

To get to the wall from our advanced base camp I figured straight. Straight from point A to point B. None of this skirting here and floundering there. The glacier looked smooth as a baby's rear and free of crevasses. There were no complaints or alternate suggestions from my companions.

We roped up hard onto the glacier as we climbed over a rise and beside a crevasse. I took the lead, skirted the monster crevasse we hadn't seen until over the rise, and was angling back toward the wall when the earth and sky turned table and I dropped abruptly into the bowels of the glacier. The covered crevasse was spindly, but wide enough to make me feel as though I were being eaten by a shark. I wouldn't have felt so uneasy if the rope had stopped me, but we were parallel to the crevasse when I dropped, and I managed to brace myself in the opening before plunging another one hundred feet.

Sakashita joined me after I clawed my way out. "I fell into a crevasse on Annapurna and broke my leg," he said. "Very scary."

"Yeah, I'll bet," I replied between breaths. "Did your partner pull you out?"

"Ahhh, no. I was solo."

"Oh."

People like Sakashita come out of a broken box marked "Do Not Open if Damaged." How could anyone decide to travel on a glacier solo? Especially in the Himalayas.

We dropped off the glacier after deciding that point A to point C then to D then to B looked safer and quicker. Bridwell took the lead and gave our little party a simulated "choo-choo" look as he puffed away endlessly on Camels, sending a foul smell down the rope as if the smoke knew where to go.

Five thousand feet above, the sun's morning rays hit Tawoche's frozen summit; then, as if fast-forwarded, the orange light crawled down The Face, a Northeast-east-east more sun-facing than North-facing Face. Then, slowly, like a spring shower, the wall came alive with the z-z-z-zing and w-w-w-whir of rockfall and the battlefield odor of cordite.

We stopped a hundred yards from the center of The Face—at a safe distance to listen and watch the deluge of destruction, but close enough for our senses to absorb the danger and convince our determined minds that an attempt was suicide. This face was a winter-only route when days are short and the sun catches the wall for only a few hours at most.

Big rocks, little rocks, no-way-are-you-going-to-survive rocks showered The Face without pause. Our discouraged faces were so long we couldn't even buckle our helmets. Traveling half-way around the world; months of training; days of preparation; thousands of dollars—to trek to the base of Tawoche. The climb was suicidal. Not even Sakashita wanted to get any closer. That said more to me than all the rocks beelining down the wall.

We bagged it. Sewed it up and left the route. I could hardly look Bridwell or Sakashita in the eye. Even though I knew our decision was the correct "mountaineering" one, it didn't ease the disappointment or guilt I felt around my partners. Not until we separated and went our own ways would my self-criticism wane and time begin to heal the frustration.

Sakashita wanted the summit by any means, even if this meant climbing the original ascent route. I'm not like that. The route is more important. Once that's gone, I'm mentally gone, incapable of turning my force to another.

For a peak with a central location and an easy approach along a major trek route, Tawoche had few suitors. Considered a difficult 6,000-meter peak to climb, it was first attempted in 1963 by a joint American-New Zealand-Sherpa team. They reached a point within two hundred feet of the summit.

The first ascent, an illegal climb of the peak, was made in 1974 by a five-man French team led by Yannick Seigneur. All five made the summit. But there was one small problem: the unauthorized ascent of the 4,600-foot Southeast Face was not taken lightly by the Nepali Ministry of Tourism. The team members were later fined six hundred dollars by the government and restricted from climbing in Nepal for four to seven years.

The second ascent, using the same Southeast Face and Ridge, was later made by a joint Japanese-South Korean expedition in winter of 1985–86. After a Japanese member fell 2,400 feet to his death, the Japanese climbers, who had reached an altitude of 19,000 feet, left the mountain to the Koreans. The Koreans fixed over 5,000 feet of rope before placing Heo Young-Ho and Ang Phurba Sherpa on the summit on January 12, 1986.

I didn't want an ascent up an innocuous gully on Tawoche, but for Sakashita's peace of mind, Bridwell and I joined him on an alpine attempt on a northeast gully situated along the tentacle like East Ridge. Knowing how confusing navigation directions are in the Himalayas, I wondered if this route was that taken by the other teams and misnamed. [Author's note: Lowe and I found old fixed line in this gully on our descent.]

The weight of my pack the morning of our alpine attempt

would have dropped a mule in its tracks, yet my heart and soul felt
heavier. After several large rocks flew by us in our gully and the
sun turned the ice to a knee-deep slush, I gave up. I couldn't force
myself to climb Tawoche just for the sake of a summit. Bridwell
joined my mutiny and together we pressured poor Sakashita into
descent, using his upcoming attempt on Ama Dablam as a means
for him to save face.

Bridwell and I returned to the States. Sakashita went on to
make the second solo ascent of Ama Dablam via the Southwest
Ridge. Tawoche maintained its position as the most awesome unclimbed face in the Himalayas.

3

Jeff·Lowe \ jef-lō \ *n* A cyborg machine, disguised as a human, that is capable of ascending any of earth's geologic features.
(*Roskelley's First Climber's Dictionary*, 1991)

FOUR YEARS LATER Tawoche was still on my mind. Not seriously as in 1984, but as an occasional fill-in to the lapse at the end of a climbing conversation: "If you get the time, let's do Tawoche." Statements that gave the listener the impression I was hard at the game, climbing the big stuff. It was a facade. They didn't take me seriously. And I took their "Hey, yeah, let's do it" the same.

I was staring at the terminal screen on my computer, inputting sales data, and feeling kenneled and ready to dig for freedom, when the telephone rang. It was Jeff Lowe.

Jeff's company, LoweCo, was under contract with my consulting firm, American Sports Group, to sell a line of outdoor clothing manufactured for Remington Arms. Sales were not going well. Neither was my relationship with Remington. Jeff and I both suffered from a bad case of climbing nostalgia, remembering what hard-ass mountaineers we used to be and knowing what slab-ass businessmen we were becoming.

"Why don't we bag this working bit, Jeff," I big-talked out of frustration, "and the two of us go climb that ugly wall on Tawoche?"

"When should we leave?"

Okay, I thought, I've played this before. "It's got to be this winter," I suggested. "There's too much rockfall in the spring."

"Let's do it," Jeff said.

This wasn't ego talking or wishful thinking. Here was "Pack up, we're gone" type talk. Jeff committed himself fully to the project we set for January 1989. When the phone went dead so did my enthusiasm. It was ten years since the last time I climbed a wall like Tawoche's, and for the past two I was kinked over and ground-tied with a debilitating back injury from logging. "What the hell," I figured, "I've got to get back into the game or get out. Tawoche will make my decision for me."

We had several months to raise ten grand, develop specialized clothing for winter weather, and convince our wives we weren't over the hill for this type of climb. Maybe Janie, Jeff's wife, was convinced, but Joyce was worried. Neither Jeff nor I had climbed seriously for several years, and it had been fifteen years since our last climb together — Peak XIX's North Face in the Russian Pamirs.

There was tension between Jeff and me in Russia in 1974. It wasn't hot-and-cold obvious or something said. More like a couple of unfamiliar hunting dogs let loose in the same piece of cover — a lot of bush-peeing and butt-sniffing gets done before the birds feel any threat. We were competitors. Two of the best in a sport riddled with perfectionists, individualists, and intense athletes.

Jeff had confidence. Confidence in his ability, confidence in himself. It may have come from downhill ski competitions in which he excelled or from having climbed since he was too young to remember with his dad and brothers. Whatever it was, Jeff was bold within himself and didn't need others to bolster his ego. His courage came from experience and training, not from what he could carry in his pack.

I first learned of Jeff's ascents through word of mouth. When someone's the subject of conversation, I know they've reached the top of the heap. Jeff was on top years before my name was bantered

about in climbing circles, and he is still there. The rest of us come
and go like a cloudy day.

The climbing community has a communication system as so-
phisticated as that of a maximum security prison—word travels
fast, but not accurately. Lowe can climb a new waterfall one day,
and climbers throughout the world know about it the next. The
fifty-foot first ascent may come out on the other end a five-
hundred-foot horror, but at least Lowe's name is attached to it.

One winter in Banff, Alberta, word spread through the Canadian climbing scene that Lowe was coming to climb several of the
unclimbed Canadian Rocky waterfalls. Lowe never left Colorado.
The waterfalls he supposedly was after were attacked unmercifully
until climbed by Canadians who feared Lowe would knock them
off. His reputation alone is enough to get things done.

I first heard of Lowe when he completed an ascent of El
Capitan's North American Wall prior to my ascent in 1971. At that
time it was considered perhaps the hardest big wall climb in the
world. His name came up again that year when I found out he
climbed the East Face of Chephron in the Canadian Rockies
around the same time I did. I knew he was good. I didn't pay much
attention to many climbers, but I started to listen and watch for
Lowe's name. It was always there attached to a first ascent of this or
a first "free" ascent of that.

Lowe's a lizard on rock, yet his reputation begins and ends on
ice and alpine walls. He's so damn good at the whole sport that
the rest of us are extinct on the lips of our peers. Solo, solo in
winter, alpine walls, Himalayan faces, Karakoram rock ridges—
Lowe can climb more ways than there are routes. American alpinists like Jeff—"all-around cowboys," I call them—are so rare they're
shoo-in candidates for "endangered species" status.

Jeff is built like me: wiry. The two of us are about the same
height, five foot ten, although I think he stands a little straighter;
are the same weight, 145 pounds, give or take a few beers; and have
the same alpine background. Uncle Sam even drafted both of us for
Vietnam and reluctantly ended up giving each of us 1-Y status for
the same reason—bad backs. It's ironic that two of the healthiest,

strongest, most driven mountaineers in the world should flunk the army physical. How embarrassing.

With so much in common, we still wouldn't pass for brothers. While in the Pamirs in 1974, Jeff wore his flaxen-colored hair shoulder-length à la Gen. George Armstrong Custer (before the Sioux gave him a haircut) and sported a matching-colored, well-trimmed handlebar mustache. Tanned and muscular, Jeff can crank one-arm pull-ups in the morning and still do 5.11 rated climbs all afternoon. I've only done one rated 5.11 in my life, and it was downgraded several years later.

Jeff and I branched on opposite sides of the tree of life. He grew up liberal, a self-proclaimed hippie of the sixties and early seventies, Volkswagen-vanning and climbing throughout the West. I evolved just the opposite, growing up in Spokane's lumber, mining, and wheat farming community—conservative, perhaps too narrow minded, and basically "redneck."

After the Russian Pamirs trip Jeff and I matured, slowly enough I'm told. God only knows where those hard-nosed opinions went that were so important to us back then. Even our tunnel-vision attitudes opened up. Not a full crack, maybe just a cra--, but enough for us to realize that it's easier to follow the streambed than to keep busting over the bank. Rather than our changing the world, we changed. Neither Jeff nor I were wild with the wind anymore. We married two lovely ladies, absorbed mortgages and credit cards, had children, and committed the ultimate statement: became employed. After fifteen years, Tawoche-time, our circle of understanding was complete. We could be friends.

Lowe and I joined together in the Pamirs because of fate. Gary Ullin's death during the first attempt on Peak XIX left the rest of "Mash," the original four-man team, lacking interest in finishing the North Face. While Bob Craig and John Marts, the remainder of the original team, made safer plans, Lowe and I teamed up. We were a bread-and-butter team. We knocked off the North Face safely, completed the finest new route in the Pamirs that summer. I regret that I never pursued his company after the Pamirs. But that changed in 1989.

Tawoche Northeast Face; 6:30 A.M., February 1, 1989

Something was out of place. Makalu, to the east, looked different, as if it were wearing a see-through nightie. As a matter of fact, the entire Himalayas looked a bit misty. And yet there wasn't a cloud in the sky. The morning sun's 93-million-mile rays that streaked across Tibet were setting the higher summits on fire. But this morning I was looking at it through different eyes.

I covered my right eye. Jeff was a blur ten feet away. The valley below, Pheriche, even the peaks were edgeless, indistinct. My left eye was in constant fixed-focus as if covered with Vaseline. Cerebral edema.

There was no mistake. I tried blinking like an owl, slow and deliberate; fluttering my eyelids like hummingbird wings; even pressing hard against the cornea and rubbing furiously. Nothing. My iris was pin-pointed and stuck as if rusted solid.

This wasn't the first time. Caught in a storm on Mount McKinley's Cassin Ridge in 1981 with Jeff Duenwald, I experienced problems with both eyes. We were a day's climb of the summit, only two thousand feet short, the difficulties overcome, when hurricane winds and zero visibility forced us to bivouac on a narrow ice ledge.

Waiting inside our small tent on the second day of the storm, I went blind. It was as if someone had removed my eyes for repair. A minute later my sight reappeared, but slowly, as if rising from deep water. For the next two days we were trapped and unable to climb up or down, and my vision changed from night to day, day to night every few minutes. Any exercise or movement quickened the process.

On the fourth day the storm dissipated. Descent was our only option. Duenwald felt uncomfortable placing anchors, so I rappeled first using our only rope, a 165-foot, nine-millimeter. On descent we spotted an old, fixed eleven-millimeter rope, scavenged that, and removed former climbers' anchors to use for our own. As I went blind every few minutes for forty-five to sixty seconds, I stopped, hung on, and waited for my sight to return. While hammering in anchors I did the same, swinging madly at the piton as my sight died, then waiting patiently for it to come alive again with color and images. In three days we rappeled the Cassin Ridge. Quick descent to a lower altitude solved the problem and probably saved my life.

I was less desperate on Tawoche. Jeff Lowe and I were one day onto the wall, hours away from safety, yet potentially minutes away from defeat.

Two-man teams are subject to crisis defeat. Injury, death, illness, even a drop-from-the-sky "I don't want to go" attitude change can turn a reasonable climb into a short trek home. It's what makes Himalayan alpine-style ascents as rare as sightings of snow leopards. Solo is possible but beyond the talent of all but a few mortal climbers on a difficult, unclimbed alpine Himalayan wall like Tawoche. Possible but unlikely.

The alpine method is worth the madness. Both Jeff and I are Himalayan veterans with numerous experiences on both big, un-wieldy expeditions and lightweight alpine-style climbs. There is no question where we stand. We will climb alpine-style, a skeleton climb of minimum gear and personnel climbing from bottom to top without fixed camps or ropes, and face a low-percentage suc-cess rate before bludgeoning the peak into submission using staged camps, Sherpas, and bottled oxygen. The route and method of ascent are more important than simply standing on top by any means. It is commonly acknowledged that seeking summits by any means is for Alpine Club members everywhere who require con-versation fertilizer.

I knew the blur in my one eye was just the beginning. There was one choice to make. Descent. My edema was mild, almost unnoticeable at this point. But to continue and hope to recuperate was out of the question. The only sure cure for high-altitude dis-ease is an immediate descent of considerable altitude. The more altitude loss, the better.

Descent, though, was not my problem. It was telling Jeff. This time it wasn't the mountain or the money or my teammates. It was me.

Why me? Jeff's history of high-altitude problems was worse

than mine on Himalayan climbs. Where did I make my mistake? It had to be because of our flying separately to Lukla. During the initial flight to Lukla, Jeff's plane landed before weather closed the strip to my aircraft. I returned to Kathmandu. Rain and cloud shrouded the upper Himalayan valleys for the next week. I sat in Kathmandu at 4,500 feet while Jeff was in Lukla at 9,200 feet becoming acclimatized to the higher elevation. Upon my arrival seven days later, we set off for Tawoche for a quick—in my case, too quick—ascent. I needed more time to acclimatize.

There was no use going this way and that with it like a big pine tree in the wind. Jeff had to know.

"Jeff, I've got a mild case of cerebral edema."

He rustled around in his hanging tent, fought the zipper down to shoulder level, and peeked out. "How do you know?"

"I can't focus my left eye," I explained. "I must not be acclimatized properly."

Jeff acted as if I had asked him whether he wanted Cheerios or Wheaties for breakfast.

"Well, what do you think?" he replied. "We could sit here for a day and see if you improve or drop to Pheriche and wait there for three or four days."

"I think I should drop," I said. "Chances are I won't get better up here."

"You're probably right. Let's leave everything but a few necessities here. Our three ropes will get us to the glacier."

Jeff took my admission easily without making me feel guiltier. Had he contributed to my own self-condemnation, the climb might have ended there at only one bivouac up the wall. But with experience and aging came understanding. He hid any disappointment he felt, bolstered my damaged ego, and directed his energy into a clean, safe descent to the glacier in three rope lengths. We left our climbing gear hanging from the wall at our high point for our return—if I could return.

Tawoche was testing us. Actually, our age was the real culprit. This wasn't the first time success seemed to be disappearing with the speed of a falling body. Several months prior to departure, Jeff and I were asked to appear in a magazine ad for Nike All-Conditions Gear, a new line of specialized outdoor clothing. The ad was to be shot outside of Las Vegas.

Several days before departure I lifted a bale of hay and pulled a lower back muscle, reinjuring my back. The muscle spasm tilted me sideways like an old ridge-top Sierra juniper. I pumped aspirin and muscle relaxants as if they were popcorn and stayed flat on my back until departure for Las Vegas. But it didn't help.

I was supposed to meet Jeff, the photographer, and the Nike staff at the Las Vegas Airport. My flight arrived on time. Theirs didn't. Five hours later I was still standing, unable to sit in fear of not being able to stand again.

Once everyone arrived we rented cars and drove to our hotel several hours outside of Las Vegas. I went to bed. Sometime during the night I tried to make it to the bathroom, stood up, then fell over. Unable to get back up, I crawled on my hands and knees eye-level with the porcelain. "How am I going to shoot a climbing ad in the morning?" I thought. But what was really on my mind was, "How am I going to climb Tawoche in one month with this severe back problem?"

Jeff was having problems with his back, too, having had a ski injury the week before. Both of us looked as though we were in our nineties, better suited for wheelchairs than for climbing one of the world's most difficult walls. We were the joke of the ad shoot. Two of America's best mountaineers and neither of us could climb for the ad. The final ad photo was taken leaning on each other in front of red rocks lit by a morning sunrise, because that was as far as I could get from the car.

With the help of generic cortisone, easy workouts, and rest, I recuperated feeling similar to an old tractor—I worked, but a breakdown was imminent.

Seattle; January 9, 1989

Too soon it was Tawoche-time. Jeff, his wife, Janie, and their three-month-old baby girl, Sonja, met my wife, Joyce, our six-year-old son, Jess, and me at the Weston Hotel in cold, rain-soaked Seattle two days before departure for Tawoche to purchase gear and pack.

Organized, well equipped, and almost financed, Jeff and I kissed our broods good-bye and took our seats on Thai Flight 1201 to Thailand. I wasn't the John Roskelley who had climbed Gauri Shankar and Uli Biaho a decade before. Far from it. The fire was there, sure enough; it was just that the fuel was wet and hard to start. But one look at Jeff, with his quiet "let's get it done" attitude, and I felt the fuel begin to burn.

I had questions of myself that needed answers. If for no other reason than peace of mind as my life as a Himalayan mountaineer wound down, they were necessary. Tawoche would give me those answers.

4

trek \ 'trek \ *n*   A journey through time.
(*Roskelley's First Climber's Dictionary*, 1991)

KATHMANDU IN MIDWINTER is a Himalayan jewel. Winter purifies
the city, suppressing months of layered dust and cleaning the air,
and brings a patience to the Nepali people missing throughout
the other seasons. Masked for tourists spring, summer, and fall,
Nepal's capital city plays the character of a crowded, polluted, and
filthy metropolitan slum whose inhabitants live hand and foot off
the tourist trade. As winter's low, midmorning rays of sun filter
through the old city's narrow streets, life is renewed and the city
awakens like an ant nest disturbed by a foot. The air is sweet before
the dust is scattered by human, animal, and motorized movement
and the Himalayas, magnified by their winter coat of freshly fallen
snow, loom over the city.

Kathmandu is cold and damp on January mornings, the same
as it was at the bottom of the lead-zinc mine where I worked as a
kid. Moist cold, the kind that gnaws through clothing and seeps
through the soles of my shoes to numb my toes. I just couldn't get
warm. Not until the sun was ten o'clock high and the mist had
dissipated did the sun heat the earth and warmth return. Until then

I hunkered in front of the Houstons' kerosene heater jealously hogging the unit's BTUs and hoping no one else would get out of bed and want to share.

Jeff and I took residence (hoping for only as long as a bird stays on a wire) at Robin and Pat Houston's house outside the city. Their hospitality had a medicinal effect on our emotional well-being, which always needs repair soon after leaving our families, and their superb cook, Chindra, added to our fortyish waistlines. The Houstons were permanent residents in Kathmandu until 1990 and, like most Western families in foreign lands, were used to small expeditions camping in their spare rooms and hallways. It's a small touch of home for those of us who are uprooted for months on end and provides a chance for them to learn what's happening to friends in the U.S. On comfort and convenience such as our stay at the Houstons', the difference between success and failure lies.

The Houstons' residence was a recent bonus. For years I used the Reads' Kathmandu home as my personal staging ground for major expeditions as well as a few minor ones. Al Read, former manager of Mountain Travel, Nepal, and his former wife, Jennifer, absorbed countless expeditions into their home. I was a frequent guest, somewhat like a tick bird on the back of a rhino, taking advantage of their old walled-in estate, which shut out the noise, dust, and reality of Kathmandu during the tourist seasons. Their front yard was the site of many equipment packings, parties, and quiet interludes. I attribute much of my "success" to staying at the Reads' and the Houstons' homes, where the food was safe to eat and the stress of expedition life disappeared at the veranda as the Reads' houseboy or the Houstons' cook would greet me with "Namatse, John sahib" and a cold Star beer.

Royal Nepal Airlines schedules daily flights into Lukla most months, January being no exception. The trip takes sixty minutes, but clouds, snow on the runway, or even winds can delay, eliminate, or turn back flights from the takeoff at Kathmandu to within sight of Lukla. If the pilot decides it's too risky to land, he turns the plane back to Kathmandu. This can happen for days at a stretch.

Far be it from me to complain about an aborted flight. While

flying into Lukla in 1982 on a windy April morning to attempt
Cholatse, I realized that it's safer to climb than fly in the Himalayas.
The flight was pretty mundane for fifty-five minutes. Below us
were the fertile hills and valleys of Nepal terraced and farmed on
every square inch of ground that wasn't cliff or running water.
Generations of dividing land holdings among a man's sons and
then their sons and so on have created plots so small that some of
the women's hips are bigger than the farms. Along the horizon, the
Himalayas speared the first fat clouds growing minute by minute
in the sunless valleys.

Among the peaks was Gauri Shankar, its West Face, jagged
and tall, thrusting broad shoulders along the Tibetan border daring
all those hard men and women climbers flying to Lukla to "climb
me if you can!" and laughing at them as they flew by. I climbed that
face in 1979. Led sixty-six of the seventy roped pitches. Gauri
Shankar and I got along despite the steepness of the route and bad
weather. I felt comfortable with our route, and the mountain never
showed us its anger. As I flew by and gazed at that route, I wondered how our team of mismatch, five Americans and five Sherpas,
succeeded. The Gauri Shankar team was like a bunch of horses that
never worked with each other before being thrown onto a hitch:
there was a lot of pulling, but not in the same direction—until the
end. I guess that's when it counted the most.

A young, thin flight attendant, one of those Nepali girls I
want to roll into my arms and hug to death, dressed in a skintight
sari, passed out water and hard candy then sat down in back to
read *The Rising Nepal,* the king of Nepal's equivalent of *Pravda.*
Gauri Shankar and its Tibetan sister, Menlungtse, disappeared on
the horizon as the plane neared Lukla. Everest was already hidden
in cloud.

The sixteen-passenger Twin Otter dropped over a high pass
into the Dudh Kosi gorge (*kosi* means river). Far below, the gush-
ing white water roared steeply toward the plains of Nepal, draining
several of the largest glaciers in the Himalayas including the
Khumbu Glacier on Everest. Lukla at 9,300 feet was soon visible
perched on a morainal shelf almost a mile above the river. Then the
excitement began.

Lukla's airstrip is sloped somewhat like a playground slide at a McDonald's restaurant. The low end of the runway drops abruptly into the gorge and is being eroded away. The top butts into a cliff. Somewhere on that postage stamp of grass and gravel the pilot has to drop his plane in one piece. He gets one final approach.

Gazing down the aisle and through the cockpit, I watched as the pilot nosed down and cut power. I had a video-game perspective of the landing and felt like a red-tailed hawk diving for a mouse. All I could see was grass coming toward the nose of the plane at terminal velocity and at an impossible angle to pull up from, and the silhouetted hands and arms of the copilot frantically grabbing controls. I tightened my seat belt, braced my legs against the metal bar on the floor, and stiff-armed the seatback in front of me. The plane nosed in like a duck hit hard with No. 4 lead shot.

At the last second before impact I heard more throttle and watched the pilot bicycle-pump the wheel until the nose inched up to horizontal (but not enough for the slope of the strip); then we hit front wheel first, bounced, straightened, bounced again off all wheels, and taxied up the runway lined with a battered fuselage and other sundry plane parts.

I turned to the stewardess after peeling my fingers off the fabric and asked, "Is that a typical landing?"

Her eyes were as big as my boots and from the looks of her sari she should have shot those underarms with a whole can of Mennen for Big Sweat. She replied, "That was an unusual landing," then got up to clean her sari or hand in her resignation. That was seven years previously. Time enough for those pilots to have practiced plenty before I had to face that landing again.

Jeff and our Nepali liaison officer, Mr. Chetri, flew in a chartered Otter hired by our agency to transport our gear to Lukla. Because government regulations allow only one foreigner to ride a charter, I took the regularly scheduled flight ten minutes later with our Sherpa staff. In that ten-minute period Lukla became socked in because of clouds, and our pilot turned back to Kathmandu. I didn't see Jeff for a week.

This wasn't a problem. If I had been with someone other than Jeff I would have worried that this week-long interruption of our plans would have destroyed our drive. But not with Jeff. I went to the airport each morning, waited for the cancellation, took a taxi to the Annapurna Coffee Shop for cappuccino, then back to the Houstons'. On the sixth day the weather in Lukla cleared. Our two Sherpas and I flew into Lukla landing smoothly as a duck on quiet water.

"I thought you might have climbed the face by now," I said, stepping off the plane. "Are you still up for it?"

"It's been great!" Jeff replied. "Just read and relaxed. I haven't done that in months."

Within an hour of landing, our sirdar, Tenzing (no relation to Tenzing Norgay, who, with Sir Edmund Hillary, made the first ascent of Everest in 1953), organized our gear into ten zopkio loads and we were on the trail for Namche Bazaar.

The Khumbu had changed dramatically in the five years since my last visit. Like noxious weeds along a slash road, rock and timber guesthouses and restaurants offering everything from pancakes to apple pie had sprung up along the trail to Everest. The growth outside the border of Nepal's spectacular Sagarmatha (Everest) National Park rivals what has been done to famous resort towns in America.

Our small, lightweight expedition passed unnoticeably through Phakding, Chumoa, and other small villages along the route. The megabucks expeditions with their armies of climbers, Sherpas, and porters are slowly going the way of dodos. Our Western attitudes are changing to reflect the trend toward modern alpinism and, of course, protection of the environment. We're on the comet's tail, but still light years from catching up with the Europeans' futuristic style and routes. American alpinists are still tainting the air with archaic expeditions. It's time we got with the program.

The big expeditions are white elephants created by Himalayan veterans of years past keeping their hands in the game through organization and leadership or by purely summit-oriented climbers. Their attitudes are fixed. The younger generation of alpinists organize smaller, more environmentally sound expeditions. This reflects the change in alpinism throughout the world.

The route has become more important than the summit, the style more significant than success.

On the second day, January 23, our expedition reached Namche Bazaar. Jeff's Sherpa friends were not surprised to see him back. This was Jeff's fourth trip in winter to the Khumbu, and he was fast becoming a legend even among the hardened Sherpa expedition veterans as "the one who climbs in the cold."

We were no longer in the "lowlands." Namche Bazaar at 11,300 feet sits within a steeply terraced amphitheater facing south two thousand feet above the confluence of the Dudh Kosi and the Bhote Kosi. A natural spring below the main trail is Namche's source of water and, recently, up to twenty-five kilowatts of hydroelectric power — enough for several low-wattage lightbulbs per home, but not enough for electric heat. Charcoal and wood serve as the only sources of heat for cooking and providing warmth. With the daytime air temperature hovering around a moist, bone-chilling twenty degrees, it's hard to get comfortable unless the sun shines and the temperature warms to sweater weather, provided there's no breeze.

I thought it was cold in Kathmandu. I was wrong. It's cold in Namche. Cold as in nose-tingling, finger-numbing, leave-me-alone-hunkered-in-my-sleeping-bag cold. No way was I going to survive one night on The Face at these temperatures. Do you think I had second thoughts? Those little creatures were eating me from inside out. I was cold in Pasang Kami's Guesthouse. Cold at dinner. Cold everywhere. I wondered if Robert Redford, who had stayed here several years before, had complained of the cold. Or Jimmy Carter and his army of CIA men. What did they think? They probably never complained of the cold, but then they weren't here in winter.

"You're going to have to find yourself another sucker, Jeff," I said, crowding the guesthouse charcoal heater, a former five-liter vegetable-oil can used to burn the few slivers of charcoal that Pasang Kami's wife rationed like booze to a gathering of alcoholics. "How in the hell will I survive on The Face when I'm freezing my ass off crowding this tin candle like Batman?"

"You suggested this."

"I did? Well, even I can be wrong."

"That's nice to know."

I whined enough that Pasang's wife and kids kept the charcoal coming and the coffee hot as Jeff and I prepared for the next leg of our trek. I found it warmer outside the guesthouse than in when the sun was shining, but the typical afternoon clouds had us hunting for more charcoal burners and down jackets long before nightfall.

Now was the time to acclimatize properly. Not at Pheriche. Not on The Face. Both Jeff and I on past expeditions had experienced the headaches, nausea, lassitude, swelling, frozen extremities, and other symptoms of high-altitude disease. Both of us are familiar with how pulmonary edema (PE) and cerebral edema (CE) decompose the victim from the inside out, flooding the lungs or skull, cheating the body of oxygen, and leisurely executing the victim, many times without his or her knowledge. Farther along the disease's course, the body's alarm system wails and announces, "Whoa, restrict blood flow to the hands and feet and get more oxygen to the heart, lungs, and other organs." The hands, feet, and brain become numb, conscious thought slows, then stops. The victim drops into a coma. It happens fast and immediate descent is the only cure.

Therein lies the enigma. Descent takes exertion. If the victim stays perfectly still, it will take time to fall into a coma and die. If he exerts himself, the fluid flooding the cavity accelerates and death arrives quickly. So once the victim starts to dress, puts on his boots, and descends, it had better be fast because he's racing Death and Death is holding the time clock.

We weren't into that "hurry-up-let's-get-this-expedition-over-with" stage yet. Both of us had cleared the slate back home. Jobs were on hold, home repair was in the Yellow Pages, the wives, kids, and assorted dogs, mules, and horses would fend for themselves. Until we finished Tawoche or it finished us, Jeff and I were here to stay. Four weeks, six, eight, it didn't matter. What mattered was our attempt, and only bad weather or the difficulty of the route could force us to back off.

Inch-thick hoarfrost covered the vegetation and rime ice paved the trail as Jeff and I hiked through the fog toward Tengboche Monastery early the following morning. Strange pinhole marks in the ice led us to two Japanese trekkers wearing crampons on the trail to avoid slipping and falling into the Dudh Kosi thousands of feet below. Not a bad idea. I sometimes mischaracterize all Japanese as pure samurai, people who would starve to death, take a plunge, anything before losing face. Then I run into guys like these two who won't even walk an icy trail without crampons. There's no pattern.

It was certainly practical to use crampons on that path, but I would rather die skating off the trail before putting them on. I mean, how would it look if Jeff and John were caught in the act by some American trekkers? Next thing we'd know, photos and a complete story on our "Attempt to Walk the World's Most Dangerous Trail" would be sent around the world by Liz Hawley and Reuters News Service. Uh-uh. But during the two-thousand-foot descent into the Dudh Kosi gorge, a descent reminiscent of the Olympic bobsled course in Calgary, I almost changed my mind and put them on.

We walked upon the blackened, charred, and destroyed remains of the Tengboche Monastery ("Great High Place," 12,700 feet) just before noon. Several days before our arrival, a fire started by an electric space heater or stove coil within the monastery gutted the two-story wood and stone gomba. The twenty-two-kilowatt hydroelectric power system was installed for the monks in 1988, paid for by a fund-raising effort in America. Until then, the monastery had survived more than one hundred years without a major fire. The destruction took less than two years from the introduction of modern technology.

Jeff and I climbed through the wreckage examining burnt remains of ancient hand-printed books, prayer wheels, clay images of gods and goddesses, and other religious paraphernalia, each of us absorbed in the significance of the loss of such relics to the Buddhist religion. The night of the fire several trekkers staying in a guesthouse close by and some of the monks saved most of the monastery's treasures and religious artifacts, but the loss of the monastery to Buddhism must be the equivalent of Christianity's losing the Vatican. Plans to rebuild the famous landmark and religious center were already under way, as evidenced by the king's helicopters flying dignitaries into Tengboche daily with potential financial donors.

Jeff and I were on the trail to Pheriche by 7 A.M. through the now bare and colorless rhododendron forest near Tengboche. A musk deer, surprised by our sudden arrival, bounded through the thick forest and deep snow for fifty feet, stopped, and warily watched us pass by. The deer is endangered throughout its Himalayan range because its musk, found in a small orifice near the animal's urethra, is a valuable commodity in the scent shops of the Far East. For a tiny animal the size of a cocker spaniel and as harmless as a koala to be destroyed so some horny guy in Hong Kong can get a psychological bigger erection seems the height of human idiocy. It's too bad the Man upstairs didn't give humans the breeding season and animals twelve months of sex. Maybe we'd accomplish something other than thinking about ways to enhance our libidos. The Nepalis use guns and dogs in areas outside Sagarmatha National Park to hunt the musk deer.

In 1978 as I walked out from my attempt with Kim Schmitz on Jannu's North Face, I surprised two Nepali dogs circling a small, tusked, male musk deer perched and trapped on a cliff. Bounding up the trail toward his barking dogs and me was a hunter with an old flint musket. I threw down my pack and ran up the hillside toward the dogs, picking up and heaving several rocks at them and chasing them away from the deer. The dogs turned their attention on me, barking and growling, but continued to back off. I soon had them on the run. The musk deer took the opportunity to leap off the ledge and disappear into the forest above.

The hunter ran at me in a rage. He screamed in Nepali, pointing at his dogs then at where the deer had run. My interference had cost him the thousands of rupees that the deer's musk was worth. The yelling didn't bother me. At a certain decibel level my ears overload and go deaf as if on a circuit breaker. Years of listening to Joyce, I guess. It was the musket I was worried about. The hunter acted as though my musk would substitute nicely and might bring more rupees. At that thought I angrily yelled and walked toward him with a look that said in universal language, "Get out of my way before I wrap that antique piece of garbage around your neck." He backed off mumbling in the same language something about a yak's patoot, I'm sure, but by this time I was in control. I picked up my pack and walked away as he called his dogs and began climbing up the trail in search of his missing quarry. At least the little critter had another chance.

Farther along the trail, Jeff and I spotted a small herd of Himalayan tahr, goatlike animals with long, chestnut brown hair, feeding along the banks of the river, climbing cliffs, and jumping to and from snow-covered boulders like our North American mountain goats. We left them in the cold shade and walked across the bridge spanning the Imja Kola to the sunny eastern slope. Ama Dablam's massive South and Southwest faces cut the Himalayan skyline like a gigantic quartz crystal on sky blue velvet.

Jeff had climbed the "regular" South Ridge route with an American team in 1979, then returned several days later to solo a difficult new route, also on the South Face. The walk through the Khumbu River valley toward Everest may as well be a Jeff Lowe Hall of Fame from his successes among the local peaks. Only the South Face of Nuptse has thwarted him on two attempts. I wouldn't bet against Jeff's making good on that face someday, too.

As Jeff photographed Ama Dablam, I spotted two large tahr males below the trail. The 150-pound animals with their twelve-to fourteen-inch horns were moving slowly, feeding on the bunch grass growing along the cliffs. I gave chase into the gorge until they finally stopped, curious as to what kind of animal would be following them so quickly on their terrain. Little did they realize it was a *Homo sapiens Roskellius,* which is short on speed but long on cliff climbing. Once I was into position across a gully, the curious tahr stopped and stared. Time for me to motor-drive several rolls of film through my Nikon as they fed and watched, then walked and leaped from one hummock of grass to the next. Tired of my dogged approach, they bounded off along the river's edge where even I couldn't follow safely without hardware and rope.

The Khumbu River valley doglegs northwest at Ama Dablam. Eons ago, during the last ice age, the Khumbu Glacier from Everest and Lhotse cut south toward Cholatse and Tawoche, where it was forced to turn southeast underneath Nuptse's and Lhotse's South walls, finally to butt heads with a second massive glacial system coming from Makalu in the east. Both turned southwest toward Namche Bazaar. Ama Dablam was cut cleanly on the north, west, and south sides leaving vertical walls and knife-bladed ridges of pink metamorphic gneiss shot with massive dikes of black diorite. The glaciers left their rubble of boulders upon retreat to Everest. Centered amidst this accumulation of morainal debris is the summer pasturage village of Pheriche.

Among all these magnificent peaks, winds build through the interchange of warm and cool air. They're funneled through the throat of the Pheriche valley like water through a dam spillway. The winds aren't bad as the valley turns south toward Tengboche as if they dissipate among the ice and rock of Ama Dablam. They're not even that bad at Everest base camp. But in Pheriche it blows like the fat lady sings—long and hard.

The Himalayan Rescue Association Hospital is the only decent building in Pheriche. It has windows, a wood stove, a kitchen area, bedrooms, and a caretaker. It even has solar-powered lights and stereo system. This was our base camp. Jeff knew the physician in charge of the building and while in Kathmandu asked for and received permission to use it. We couldn't have hoped for a better base camp while waiting for our attempt on Tawoche.

Despite the cold, wind, and blackened, iceless route on Tawoche, our chances of success were inching past the one-in-a-hundred mark I overextended us early on. For the first time in weeks my thoughts crept into the optimistic gray zone. Not clear-cut white as in "We're going to climb that thing," but close to it. One look at The Face told me the odds weren't exactly in our favor, but with a few beers tucked away and the stove crackling juniper I upped the odds for us to summit to one in fifty. And that was optimistic.

"What do you think the odds are of our getting up that thing, Jeff?" I asked after several days in Pheriche.

"Fifty-fifty," he wagered.

Same old Jeff. I would have given those same odds for one of us to die along the route. But I wasn't about to say it.

5

Sher·pa·ni \ shər-'pä-nē \ *n*   A lot of fun in homespun.
  (Roskelley's First Climber's Dictionary, 1991)

"HOW'S THE HEAD?" Jeff asked.

That question started every morning since Jeff and I had dropped off The Face, as surely as our French roast was brewing in the kitchen of the Himalayan Rescue Association hospital. The state of my eyes monopolized the first five minutes of conversation. By then we were well on our way to stuffing ourselves with scrambled eggs à la Tenzing, Nepali baked beans, Sherpa chapatis layered with jam and peanut butter, and more coffee as only a couple of experienced Himalayan vets could do.

"It might just be these eggs, Jeff, but I'm feeling damn good."

That was a fact, at least that I felt well. After I first arrived in Pheriche, I experienced swelling of the fingers and around the eyes and some dizziness, like the kind of head trip that comes from drinking too much cheap wine. While I lay in bed the room would spin around, sometimes in both directions, but once I was up and moving, the disorientation and personal carnival ride evaporated. I didn't consider these to be symptoms of cerebral edema. They were too subtle. I chalked them up to oxygen deprivation, strong coffee—anything but face reality.

As I became acclimatized, the wooziness left and didn't return.

The days spent at advanced base and above helped. Only my next trip on The Face would tell me how much.

"If the weather's good tomorrow," I said to Jeff, "let's go for it."

The weather was stable. A high-pressure area in Tibet served as an effective blockade to potential storms from India and southeast Asia. Daytime temperatures hovered in the mild upper twenties to upper thirties. The wind, a steady ripper better suited for racing for the America's Cup, scoured the narrow valley at freeway speeds in the afternoon, but commonly died during the night. During our first attempt we had noticed that the ridge to the north effectively blocked the valley wind. While the Himalayas were quiet, it was time to climb.

Our arrival in Pheriche nine days earlier on January 25 had not made Pheriche's list of happening events. Unlike most expeditions passing through, the only major stir we raised was more dust and dry yak manure into the air than usual. I felt guilty calling our trip an "expedition." A "Tawoche Twosome" maybe, or "Pair against Tawoche," but not expedition. The few trekkers that wandered to and from Everest Base Camp were huddled in the only trekkers' guesthouse, within arm's reach of the pot-bellied wood stove ordering thermoses of Sherpa tea and snacking on the staple trek food, Nebico biscuits. A few yaks glanced in our direction but lost interest. This was winter. Flapping to attention, though, were Pheriche regulars, the Himalayan goraks, oversized crows that sixth-sensed a change of diet as we unlocked the hospital and occupied our base camp.

Jeff and I had the binoculars on Tawoche before Tenzing could stoke the stove with scrub juniper and ceremoniously place hot tea in our hands.

"It doesn't even look like the same face to me," Jeff said. "Where's all the ice?"

I glanced over his shoulder at a sixteen-by-twenty-inch color photograph of The Face taken in April 1984, then up at the real thing. "You're right," I replied. "Good thing you brought your rock shoes."

"What do you mean? Didn't you bring yours?"

"Hell, no," I said. "I'm a mountaineer and it's a well-known fact we don't climb rock."

The locals should have named Tawoche "Chameleon Peak." The only resemblance between the photo and peak above us was the skyline. The Face was cavernous, black as the goraks that glided around the hospital. What little ice remained was thin and rock-pocked as though it had survived a bout of smallpox. Many of the snow eyebrows in the 1984 photo were gone. Those that remained seemed small and far from our intended route.

"Forget about running up that center ice gully," Jeff uttered from behind the binoculars. "And I'd have thought there would be more ice in winter."

It was our experience that mountains put on their thickest coats in winter. The Face should have been frozen solid. But with the mild fall and even milder winter, this Himalayan giant six miles from Everest more resembled El Capitan in Yosemite.

We packed accordingly. Between Milky Ways and tea, Jeff and I spread our twenty-by-twenty-foot plastic tarp on the lee side of the hospital, unpacked our Cordura duffles, and separated gear.

We didn't just separate, we eliminated. It used to be so simple when I was eighteen years old and poor. I had one pack, one pair of boots, one pair of crampons, and so forth. Now my basement at home looks more like a Recreational Equipment Co-op store than some of the stores do. Of course, none of it can be left behind. "What if I break a crampon? What if I drop an ice axe? What if . . .?"

Our expedition was thin from the start, but Jeff and I were still fat with gear-a-mania. We packed eleven duffles of food and gear at the Weston Hotel in Seattle before leaving. At the Houstons' in Kathmandu, we eliminated extra food, hardware, and clothing. In Namche Bazaar, we "stored a bit more." In Pheriche below the point where we had to start carrying loads, Jeff and I got pure anorexic.

My backcountry skis stayed bagged and taped in the hospital. There wasn't enough snow on the slopes to our advanced base to cover the yak dung, let alone ski. Jeff wasn't convinced, however, and took his along. We eliminated half the ice screws, the bolt kit, several specialized tools, most of the rope, some pickets, and some gas cartouches. Every time one of us looked up at The Face, another piece of gear or package of food found its way into the "leave" bag.

As we pitched each piece of gear, we quoted some famous person who had said, "Weight is our enemy." Our expedition was pencil thin in no time with that quote. Almost too thin. Our mental scale of judgment tipped between thin and too thin, risky and just plain suicidal.

It was then that Jeff quoted our favorite actor, Robert Redford, from one of his best movies, *The Natural:* "Tawoche's Face is the 'best there ever was, best there ever will be.' " With this thought, we stopped eliminating paraphernalia and, like rice vendors in a Nepali bazaar, tossed back into our "go" pile a few pitons and slings to balance the scale between too much weight and not enough for success. We called it good.

How much food to take is always a dilemma. It has to be carried. Too much and you feel like a loaded C-130 on a short runway; too little and all you do is think of food and what you should have brought. Sitting in our offices in the States, Jeff and I guesstimated twelve days on The Face. Twelve days! What kind of a fairy tale were we living? Once the reality of The Face loomed over us, eight days looked like the maximum. That decision eliminated bags of food and gas cartouches.

"We'll give hauling a chance," Jeff said, "and if that doesn't pan out we'll have to carry the loads by pack up fixed ropes."

I agreed. We weren't about to use a mechanical winch, which some large expeditions had used in the Himalayas before with mixed results. Besides, Jeff and I weren't into eliminating problems, just overcoming them. Better muscle than machine in this case.

With a goal of eight days, we packed accordingly. Each of us had his own hanging stove, cookset, and food in his pack. On a wall like Tawoche's, the chance of bivouacking close together and sharing a stove was as remote as getting to the top without a storm. House calls to the other guy's bivouac were out. Once into our bags, we were buried for the night. The food was plastic-bagged into one-day units of candy bars, freeze-dried fruit, oatmeal, drinks, soups, dinners, and miscellaneous "gut food" for calories. Either Jeff or I would heft the final product and pronounce it light or "you'd think we were climbing Everest." With that, a candy bar or two would find its way in or out of the sack. Once the cream was skimmed off, we came within a few pounds of fighting weight.

I bought our mountain food in my hometown of Spokane with the same amount of care I put into purchasing a lotto ticket: I made it quick and cheap. I threw in the basics like oatmeal and Cup-O-Soup, added candy such as M&Ms, and succumbed to cashews and a few other goodies. What I considered to be my tours de force were the microwave dinners in their own packages. Not only were they easy to prepare—just boil them in our pot, package and all—but they actually tasted like real food. Granted they were a bit heavier than freeze-dried, but I didn't feel like a balloon—all gas and ready to rise—after eating one, either. Despite Tenzing's cordon bleu cooking, I was eager to start eating Western.

I lifted one of the final loads. "Tell me, Jeff, are there two of us or six?" The total weight including personal gear looked to be around three hundred pounds.

Jeff moved on the problem as only an experienced Himalayan veteran knows how. "Let's have it carried to advanced base and decide there."

That was fine with me. Tenzing had put the word out in the Khumbu Valley for several porters to help us ferry the loads to our advanced base at 16,000 feet. As long as Jeff and I didn't have to carry all the gear to advanced base by ourselves, there was no need to make a hasty decision.

A couple more days at the hospital, and an ascent, even an attempt on Tawoche, was going to be history. Jeff and I were too comfortable next to the wood heater listening to everything from Bach to Tracy Chapman and reading from the well-stocked library to venture forth "into the jaws of death, into the gates of hell." Maybe we could call this a photoreconnaissance and satisfy our sponsors with that.

The cold night wind gusting through the valley could have frozen the ears off a polar bear. Inside I stoked the small homemade wood stove with another branch of juniper, settled back onto the daybed, grabbed another handful of popcorn, and continued to read. I felt like a pampered gladiator on the verge of my first battle.

"Did you hear giggling? Girls giggling?" I asked.

Jeff's eyes, hidden behind the glare of his eyeglasses, inched over Robert Ludlum's *The Bourne Identity* and looked toward the door. "Yep. What do you think Tenzing's up to? Think he'll share?"

"Would you?"

The giggling turned to whispers on the cold side of the door, which opened slowly to reveal two pretty young Sherpanis characteristically holding their hands over their mouths to suppress continual giggling.

"I think I'm in love."

"You've been saying that all the way in," Jeff replied. "Which one?"

"Doesn't matter. I love them all."

Tenzing followed the girls in as they entered, stood by the wall, giggled, pointed out something about us, and whispered and giggled again and again. We were dissected, vivisected, point-a-sected, and whisper-sected without even knowing what was being said. But Tenzing was laughing.

"Okay, Tenzing, what's this all about?" Jeff asked.

"These two girls and two others from Dingboche are our porters," he replied with a grin as wide as a waxing moon. "All the men of the village are tending yaks."

No doubt Tenzing did this to embarrass our male chauvinist egos. Hiring four Sherpa girls aged sixteen to eighteen to carry our loads to advanced base would burst an ego bubble any day. But it would be fun. And being Sherpas, they were strong and willing.

Originally from Kham in eastern Tibet, the people known as Sherpas settled in the Khumbu and Solu valleys among the Himalayan peaks sometime in the mid sixteenth century. Sherpas, or "people from the east," are one of many tribes throughout Nepal, but the only one that lives permanently in the higher elevations.

At elevations up to 14,000 feet, Sherpa families till the glacial soil to plant potatoes, buckwheat, turnips, and other short-season crops using yak-drawn, single-shear plows made of wood. Each spring, animal dung and human waste fertilizer is shoveled into dokas, large reed baskets, and removed from the lower level of the Sherpa home, which serves as a winter stable and woodshed. It is then dumped on the fields and plowed under. All work is done by hand or with animal help because of the steeply terraced, small plots typical in mountainous terrain. In Nepal the land dictates ancient ways.

Farming and raising herds of yaks, naks, zhums, and zopkios are no longer the only sources of income for a Sherpa family. Trekking, tourism, and working for expeditions have supplemented the families' incomes and in many instances replaced farming completely. Sherpas own the Khumbu. All hotels, restaurants, trekking firms, tourist shops, and tourist amenities are Sherpa family businesses or Sherpa co-ops. For a group of people to be such shrewd businessmen and still be considered totally honest is an extraordinary compliment to them.

I have never heard a negative word spoken about a Sherpa. The Dorjes, Pasangs, Ang Nimas, and others I've climbed with or hired are always banker honest, pleasant as a warm day, and harder working than a team of yaks. As difficult as this is to admit, I felt at times on some expeditions that if I needed rescue the Sherpas, and not my American teammates, would be the first to my aid.

Using Sherpa girls as young as twelve as porters is not uncommon. In fact, after experiencing porter dissension on my expedition into Jannu in eastern Nepal in 1977, I swore I would hire Sherpanis from then on. My young Sherpani porters not only worked harder than the men, but arrived in camp earlier, never complained, and made my day the richer by just being girls.

Sherpa females, young and old, have a tough life in an unforgiving world. From morning to night, from the time they can walk until they die, a Sherpani's work is never done. I've seen girls six years old and even younger carrying porter loads of wood, fifty pounds or better. On the other end of life, I've wondered at the tireless dexterity of an eighty-year-old woman sitting and weaving cloth all day long. Having stayed in Sherpa homes for days, I am amazed at the extent of their chores, not for pay or to improve life, but simply to exist day to day.

A typical day for a Sherpani starts early, long before first light. The sleeping quilts are picked off the floor, the cookfire embers are coaxed into life again, tea is made, and the family is fed. The chickens, yaks, and sundry other animals are fed, milked, pastured, and watered. Then it's back into the kitchen to wash, cook, and clean house. Much of the day is spent helping the men plow the field, plant crops, or fertilize. On other days, wood is cut and fetched by doka from miles up the valley. By nightfall, while the men discuss the day's events, the Sherpani cooks, cleans, and after everyone else is fast asleep, goes to bed.

In 1989 I stayed for four days in a Sherpa home in Ghunsa in eastern Nepal and received a different perspective on their culture and intimate life. Like American girls, the young Sherpanis talk and dream with close friends. They're touchers, intimate people who are not inhibited about showing affection. Peer relationships among young girls is vital because these girls, at least in remote villages, are not allowed to date. And if they were, where would they go?

Late one night in Ghunsa, after I had eaten and gone to bed in my tent, I heard excited woman-chatter entering the house near where I slept. Soon afterward, I heard rhythmic chanting and pounding on the floor. I had to investigate and returned to the house. Seven young Sherpanis were lined up arm-around-waist in the center of the room, dancing by pounding their feet to a beat similar to that of our Native American music. They carried the tune without instruments, by chanting in a singsong way.

The girls were having a great time, laughing and giggling, poking each other, and making fun of each other's dancing. But I noticed that the mother of one of the girls was sitting off to one corner and never joined in. It was then that I realized I was seeing one of the few things in life a Sherpani has a chance to enjoy before being married off to live and work for the rest of her life in her father-in-law's home: an intimate association with her pals.

Our Sherpanis appeared at the hospital before daylight. I

could hear them in the kitchen giggling again. While we ate breakfast they took turns sneaking peeks at us chowing down on Tenzing's culinary masterpiece. I peeked back, feeling that peculiar
tinge of magic that quickens my heart when I'm around young
girls in a teasing mood. They were pretty in a healthy way with
their burnt cheeks on deep brown skin and those secretive ebony
Asian eyes that have the depth of a Himalayan midnight sky. The
kind of down-on-the-farm girl that one would marry, not Vogue-
ish or synthetic makeovers. They were excited, too. Here was potential adventure with a couple of fair-haired, blue-eyed Americans, and these girls weren't one bit intimidated by our perceived
wealth in contrast to their poverty.

The girls were dressed for the wind and cold. Under traditional homespun, ankle-length jumpers and brightly colored
silk blouses, each girl wore wool pants and hand-me-down
expedition-issue long underwear. A long, finely knit shawl for the
head; black, high-top Chinese tennis shoes that looked like P.F.
Flyer clones; and a short, black wool jacket completed the outfit.
None of them wore gloves or probably ever did.

If there ever was a finer morning in the Himalayas it was
before the time of man. I had to walk fast just to feel a breeze,
and the only clouds were those that came from our mouths as
our warm breaths hit the crisp, cold air. Ama Dablam, Lhotse,
Cholatse, Thamserku, and Tawoche bit the blue sky as sharply as
the teeth of a great white shark. Again and again I questioned my
sanity for even being here.

"Who's the old fella with the prayer wheel?" Jeff asked Tenzing.

"He is the head lama from Pangboche Monastery," Tenzing
replied. "He has come a long way this morning to give prayers for
your safe journey."

Tenzing set a cloth on a table outside the hospital, while Lakpa
brought out the wicker basket chairs. When the seating was finished, the offerings were placed on the table—a plate of uncooked
rice, a basket of chapatis, apple slices and candy, and a jug of chang,

the Sherpa rice beer. With sweet-smelling juniper burning on the
rock wall in front of Tawoche, we gathered around the table for
chanting and prayers by the lama. At certain interludes we all
grabbed pinches of rice and threw them into the air. The whole
service took a half hour.

The sixtyish-looking lama was poor. He had on a ragged,
discolored, maroon Tibetan tumbu robe; an ash-colored Tibetan
jacket; homespun black pants; Chinese tennis shoes; and an old,
fur-lined, Chinese-print Tibetan hat, which he wore cockeyed as a
drunk might wear a baseball cap. Coming from a small, insignifi-
cant monastery in a poor village such as Pangboche, the lama was
destitute. Lamas subsist on gifts from farmers and villagers, who
are taught through Buddhism that there is a higher position in the
afterlife and return to earth for those who are generous. By the
looks of our lama, the people of Pangboche were destined to return
as worms.

In 1982 I walked through Pangboche on my way to the Gokyo
Valley and Cholatse from Pheriche. It was a pretty village across
the Khumbu River gorge from its wealthier, more famous cousin,
Tengboche Monastery. Significantly, the smaller Pangboche Monastery holds two of Nepal's most interesting artifacts: a yeti hand
and skull.

I'm skeptical, to say the least, when it comes to the tale of the
yeti, but my curiosity got the best of me. While touring the monastery I asked to see the "animal" parts. A Tibetan nun opened a
velvet-lined box, and inside was the complete bone arrangement of
a very long-fingered simian hand. What simian I wouldn't venture
to say.

The skull was another matter. It was similar to half an oblong
coconut, but thinly layered with reddish hair. Whatever that skull
belonged to must have found it difficult to wear a hat.

I don't know whether the lama was safeguarding us while we
were still alive, guaranteeing us a higher entry level in our next
life, or both, but we made his trip to Pheriche an overwhelming
success judging by all the goodies in his sack as he bid us farewell.
We waved as he departed for Pangboche, spinning his hand-held

prayer wheel and weaving back and forth down the trail, slightly inebriated from finishing off the gallon of chang purchased for the occasion.

Our Sherpanis were waiting patiently, hefting various loads to judge their weight and balance and select the best to carry. Tenzing obviously had an eye for beauty: there wasn't a bad flower in the patch.

Advanced-base gear needed to be carried first. Jeff told Tenzing which bags were to go, and the girls each punched and kneed a soft spot on one side of the load, looped a yak-hair tumpline around the bag, squatted beneath the head strap, and stood up. The girls did the "porter jig" to arrange the lumps and bumps in each bag, made the usual comments for sympathy — "much too heavy; much too big" — then, laughing and talking, speed-walked from the courtyard.

We were across the river and onto the hillside as a wind picked up and the sun delivered a much-needed dose of warmth. I was feeling slow and lethargic and a bit woozy, hardly competition for Jeff's energy. As he slowly disappeared up the slope toward Tawoche, I crawled even more slowly upward, enjoying the girls' ribald jokes translated admirably by Tenzing despite his limited grasp of English.

The girls were just having fun. I enjoy the flirting and teasing associated with Sherpanis. It's a social game with them and not intended to be taken seriously, although premarital sex is not considered a sin and illegitimate children are common and readily accepted by their society.

I know several Westerners who have slept with Sherpanis while in Nepal and found the experience a rare treat, if only because neither party was looking for a commitment — the couple just considered it a fun time. But fun can get carried away. While trekking into Kangchenjunga in eastern Nepal in 1989, I learned that the one-year-old son of a very pretty Sherpani in Ghunsa where we stayed was the result of a night's pleasure with a famous British climber. Indeed, there was a strong resemblance to the "gentleman" in question.

Personally, I enjoy their humor up close and love them from a distance. First of all, I'm married, and neither Joyce nor I is that open-minded. Second, as pretty and sexy as some of them are, and I admit to breaking my heart over at least two of them, they are culturally different. They lack medical and dental care, and personal hygiene is practically unknown. Perhaps the biggest deterrent (besides Joyce's left fist) is the acrid smell on their clothing and bodies from smoke and yak ghiu, a clarified butter. I can't stand yak ghiu.

As clouds appeared and the wind rattled over the rocky ridge, I put my Polarplus pile over heavyweight Thermax long-handles over Nike Lycra running gear and added shelled mitts and Gore-Tex this and that, finally creating my own Hawaii. The Sherpanis were wearing their traditional dress that has seen century after century come and go and has kept Tibetans and Sherpas just as warm as our modern synthetics and drier than our windproof-waterproof-everythingproof breathable performance fabrics — and they certainly seemed more comfortable to me.

Advanced base was just a fifteen-minute hike from where the Sherpanis dropped our loads. Iced boulders up a steep, loose gully and frozen creeks spilling from the Tawoche Glacier prevented them from continuing.

"Tenzing," I said, "tell the girls they did a great job and send them down. We'll take the loads from here."

They quickly wrapped their heads in shawls, jammed their cold hands inside their jumpers and against their breasts for warmth, and ran down the pasture slopes for Pheriche. Tenzing and I continued on in search of Jeff and advanced base.

The campsite was sandy and barren of snow when we arrived. Fresh glacial water flowed beneath a six-inch-thick ice layer on a nearby stream. Jeff was on the cliffs above getting a better look at the route. When he returned, we pitched the tent and secured the loads from goraks and marmots.

"The Face looks a lot better up close," he said. "Not quite as vertical as it looks from below, but as steep as any face I've been on."

I had been at the base of the wall in 1984. Any steeper and The

Face would hang so far valleyward it would shelter Pheriche from snowfall.

Tenzing helped me pitch our dome tent, while Jeff built a small rock latrine along the moraine. Once our camp chores were completed, we loped down the two thousand feet of forty-five-degree summer yak pasture back to Pheriche. As long as the weather held and it didn't snow, future carries to advanced base promised to be a pleasant workout.

Jeff, Tenzing, and I moved to advanced base several days later after one more partial carry aided by two of the young Sherpanis. Leaving the comfort of the hospital was not as difficult as I thought. As cold as it became at night at 16,000 feet, I felt warmer living outdoors during the day and in a tent at night than inside the drafty cold of a stone building. More important, advanced base was on the lee side of Tawoche's North Ridge. Without the continuous valley wind, winter climbing in the Himalayas was almost civilized sport. Not quite, but almost.

6

re·treat \ ri-'trēt \ *n*   An intelligent and prudent course of action taken upon viewing Tawoche from Pheriche.
    (*Roskelley's First Climber's Dictionary*, 1991)

OUR FIRST ATTEMPT ended less than three hundred feet above the glacier. I didn't expect such a small favor so early, but if I'd had my choice of where to get sick it was here. There was a chance I would recover from the cerebral edema and make another attempt, but what if . . . ? Poor Jeff. He'd been through this scene in the Himalayas several times with other partners and as the victim himself. Whatever Jeff was thinking about our chances, he was keeping it hidden.

The cerebral edema caught me on the blind side, so to speak. The climb started as smooth as glacier-polished granite. Our scramble to the base of the wall was safe and short. We eliminated more gear at advanced base to reduce weight. The weather was lambish at a time of year when weeks of snow were the norm and the red snake inside the thermometer stayed coiled in the bottom bulb, rarely raising its head to zero. Even our backs were feeling strong, as if the thought of climbing did more good than our normal breakfast of aspirin and pain killer.

Within a half hour after leaving advanced base and scrambling over morainal debris, Jeff, Tenzing, and I roped up to cross the

Tawoche Glacier to the foot of the wall. Crevasses appeared as a glacial wink here and a bigger yawn there, but they were open and obvious, allowing us to pass without a threat. The Face stared down at us, looming taller and wider then I had imagined, seeming to encompass the three of us within its two large, armlike ridges and draw us in to itself like three iron filings to a great magnet. All was quiet.

The closer I got to the center of the wall, the faster I climbed. I wanted to hug the base and get underneath something. There was no telling when a barrage of rockfall or car-sized chunks of ice would pit and scar the surrounding snow cone that was already a cratered moonscape. The slope steepened determinedly as we reached the avalanche cone. Without waiting for a belay, I cramponed up the cone, over the slightly hidden bergschrund, and into the safety of rock overhangs. Jeff joined me as I set up a belay and brought Tenzing to the wall.

I knew this section of wall. It was one of the few spots with a crack and gully system that broke the lower overhanging band. Jeff and I had glassed the wall for hours the past few days. We knew the wall was tight, typical of metamorphic gneiss. There were too few cracks down low. Once into the main crack system, a deep cleft right of center sporting a cleavage Dolly Parton would be proud of, we could count on reasonable belays and bivouacs. But that was one thousand feet above protected by slabby, rounded, crackless-looking rock that was bent on replacing the "a" in ascent with "de."

Taking the first pitch on an unclimbed, unattempted face is a ritual rivaling a halfback's getting the football on the first play of the season opener. What happens here can determine the success of the team. Flounder and pitch one might be the extent of John and Jeff's Tawoche history.

Jeff wanted the pitch. I wanted him to have it. For nearly twenty years I led more than my share of rope lengths, many times entire climbs or the most difficult sections. But it had been years since I had been on a climb like this. I'm like a '48 Plymouth that's been sitting for decades in a back pasture. More than a bit rusty. I had confidence — in Jeff. Mine was thin skin over thick doubt. I needed to touch the rock, feel gravity give way, hang awhile in my slings, and feel air beneath my feet. I didn't want to disappoint Jeff before we had our "sea legs," and I wanted the team to feel good right off the snow. I didn't put up much of an argument when Jeff asked if I minded if he took the first lead.

"Well, darn, I was looking forward to it, but go ahead." I managed to sound disappointed. "Watch your topknot," paraphrasing Jeremiah Johnson, our movie hero.

Just as I knew he would, Jeff returned the salutation, "Watch your'n."

If it weren't for the catchy lines from our favorite movies, Jeff and I would have been a dull couple. As it was, we knew them all as though we had written them.

Jeff tightened his helmet, adjusted his ice tools, checked his harness one last time, then carefully took a few steps toward the crack. "Here we go."

"Give her hell," I said.

I sat down on my pack completely protected by the overhanging lip at the base of the wall. Preclimb butterflies were finally landing in my stomach. We would find out soon enough whether the wall would be safe, dangerous, or just plain "let's get the hell out of here."

Jeff was fiddling and a-diddling trying to make up his mind whether to try free climbing the blocky lower section or use his specially designed étriers, three-step ladder stirrups with metal footsteps for ease of use with crampons. With all the hardware, ice tools, slings, and clothing, just walking over to the crack was a chore. He pulled out the étriers and went to work.

Like me, Jeff hadn't climbed in more than a year, and there was a lot of unprintable mumbling for the first fifty feet. But as though he were sweating WD-40, he worked his way into fluid motion. A Friend here, a piton there, and the rope slowly moved through my figure 8. At one hundred feet he was out of sight. His haul line resembled a guy wire from a telephone pole, the way it swung into space beyond my belay.

I was like a little kid on his first day of school. In my anxiety I yelled up questions for Jeff as if he didn't have enough to do. "How's it look? Why are you stopping? What's going on? How come you're breathing so hard?"

"Jeez, Roskelley, ease up. You'll know soon enough." After a while I did.

Close to a full lead up the rope Jeff stopped, set up his belay, and yelled for me to jumar. I fastened my jumars and slings to the rope, followed the rope with my eyes, then glanced down at the sunlit valley and Pheriche. I thought, "Where are my brains? What am I doing? I've got kids, a farm. I'm too old for this shit." Nevertheless, I couldn't yell up at Jeff "This is insane!" like I wanted to. Outwardly I displayed a lion's attitude, but the real me wanted to scream "Uuunnncle!"

Nothing is harder than leaving the ground on a rope that stretches like a rubber band. I worked hard, putting my weight on the rope for five minutes before bouncing off the ground, slowly spinning to the beat of a second hand, first glancing at Tenzing, then the valley, then the rock, then back to the everlasting grin on Tenzing. I could see it in his eyes, "Here are two fools."

Like Jeff, it didn't take me more than a few minutes to fine-tune my movement, adjust my sling lengths, and develop a rhythm. Slothlike, I moved up the wall to join him at the belay.

I really didn't want the next pitch either. It looked reasonable — nice cracks, a few loose blocks, ice runnel in the center. I just didn't feel at the top of my form yet. But I didn't say anything. And Jeff didn't offer to lead the pitch for me.

Our first belay change was a Laurel and Hardy affair. I entered the belay on the wrong side. Jeff was still sorting gear. The haul line was tied over the lead rope. I was scared of the next lead and was putting runners over my neck first, hardware second. Jeff was stripping off clothes.

"Well, this ought to be interesting," I said, more to myself.

I led upward. Magic. As soon as my hands and feet hit the rock and I was on the sharp end of the rope, my fears evaporated. I was once more in control. Jeff and I could do this climb.

I ended the pitch one hundred feet from Jeff hanging in slings beneath a small roof alongside the main crack, which bulged with a frozen waterfall. It was either shorten the lead to a hundred feet or find myself belaying in the gully and potential debris zone. I apologized to Jeff as he arrived at the belay.

"Hey, use your judgment," he said. "It must be good if you're still alive after all these years."

Standing in his étriers, Jeff acrobatically strapped on his crampons for the next pitch, a narrow chimney filled with ice. I had yet to move or jerk around on any of my anchors like Jeff was doing and winced as visions of anchors popping and both of us flying past Tenzing to crater into the glacial ice below entered my mind. Jeff wasn't worried. He jerked and leaned, stepped and slipped as if the anchor would never come out, and I soon learned to forget about the danger and do the same. We had to test the anchors, approve them in our psyches, and get on with it.

Jeff was in fine form and showed me why he was famous throughout the world for mixing it up on ice and rock. A few minutes after arriving at my belay he was gone. I watched him front point in the narrow gully to a bottleneck as the two side walls narrowed. Climbing as smoothly as a quiet brook, Jeff switched from ice to rock, stemming between the two walls with his legs until he was forced to use his étriers over a small roof.

I was into the climb now. The butterflies were gone, and so was my self-doubt. As Jeff had said several days before when I voiced a hesitant thought, "Don't think of the wall in its entirety. Think of it as one pitch at a time."

I concentrated on this thought as if my sanity depended on it. The wall above was gone. Only the next 150 feet of rock and ice mattered.

"We're there!" I heard Jeff yell.

A half hour elapsed before I joined him on a thin stance thirty feet below a future bivouac site. There were pins and nuts poked and slotted everywhere possible, but they all added up to not quite bombproof. This was it for the day. We had intended to "explore" the route, descend to advanced base for more gear, and start up the wall the following day.

"Let's use the three-hundred-foot haul line as a rappel rope and jumar back up on it in the morning," Jeff suggested. I looked at the eight-millimeter rope a spider would have turned up his nose at, but as long as Jeff went first, what the hell.

After dragging, coiling, and attaching our climbing ropes to the belay along with hardware and nonessential tools and gear, Jeff set up his rappel gear and disappeared over the roofs below. I watched the anchors for any sign of failure, thinking maybe I should disconnect myself from the whole mess just in case it all went. But I didn't. After all, Jeff wouldn't do such a thing. Would he?

Jeff and Tenzing were waiting for me at the base of the rope. Minutes after my arrival we climbed down off the avalanche cone and walked back to camp. The sun was gone from the basin and with it the daytime warmth. To stay warm we packed our wall loads for hauling on the route. Weight was still a factor. It would take all three of us to carry the food, stoves, butane cartouches, sleeping gear, and extra clothing to the foot of the wall in the morning. How Jeff and I would get it up the wall from there was anybody's guess.

Jeff, Tenzing, and I shouldered fifty-pound loads for the two-hour walk to the base of the wall the next morning. The pressure to perform was off. The urgency we had felt the previous morning to touch the wall, to experience a bit of void beneath our feet, was relieved. This morning we leisurely left camp hoping we would not return again. If all went as planned we would descend the less technical East Ridge from the summit. Advanced base would be eliminated by Tenzing while we were on the wall.

Jeff and I planned the day precisely. We intended to jumar to our high point, work out a hauling system that would take as little energy as possible, and bivouac nearby. Getting ourselves up the wall would be easy. It was the two hundred pounds of ballast in the form of provisions and gear that worried us.

"I suggest we teach the two prettiest Sherpanis how to jumar and let them bring the loads while we lead."

"Don't be ridiculous, Roskelley," Jeff replied. "We should take all four."

Jeff was always one step ahead.

Jeff went first, jumaring the ropes to our high point of the previous day. It was his job to set up a haul system using jumars and his body weight to hoist the loads up the wall. Both of us were experienced big-wall climbers and experts at hauling heavy loads, but often it is the terrain that dictates which method of gear hauling is used rather than experience and technique.

Tenzing and I watched helplessly as the first duffle inched up the wall 40 feet and snagged below a roof. Jeff, hauling from anchors 150 feet up, couldn't budge it. I attached our second bag to an extra haul line and left it sitting on our snow ledge with Tenzing. Dragging the haul line, I jumared to the stuck bag to help Jeff pull it over the roof and onto the slabs above. By this time the game of golf was looking better even if I had to carry the golf cart on my back.

One hour disappeared faster than our enthusiasm. By the end of the second hour Jeff and I were exhausted, discouraged, and convinced this wasn't going to work. Hauling was out of the question.

With hauling an impossibility, we decided to carry the loads up the wall on our backs. This was no great revelation. It was always in the backs of our minds. But packing eight days of food, camp gear, personal gear, and climbing equipment onto and into two Lowe Expedition packs was the equivalent of stuffing a genie in a bottle. Besides, the weight of each load was close to, if not bursting over, the century mark. Try standing in étriers balanced spiderlike on a springy rope, lifting and swinging onto your back over a hundred pounds, then jumaring up vertical, sometimes overhanging, rock and ice. If this climb happened two thousand years ago we would be a Bible story somewhere between David's slaying of Goliath and Moses' parting of the Red Sea. It was going to be that difficult.

I helped Jeff haul our two loaded duffles to his stance, then continued on to our anchors at the tops of our lines. It was my turn to strain uselessly trying to haul the loads. With Jeff jumaring alongside shoving, pulling, cursing, and lifting the haulbag, I finally raised it to my stance. I thought I detected a fleeting whimper for mercy coming from Jeff, but I was wrong. It was coming from me.

"I'll drop down and disconnect the other bag," he said. "Then I'll stay with it until you get it up."

"Jeff, we've got problems," I announced as if he'd been at a health spa and was ignorant of our situation. "We'll never make it at this rate."

He knew that. He also knew that carrying the loads would have to start the next day. It was too late to change systems this day.

By 4 P.M., the bags were at the top of the ropes; Tenzing was a distant dot nearing advanced base; and we were still thirty feet short of a potential bivouac spot.

Jeff belayed me up the short icefield to where it butted against rock. I put in five good anchors, strung the rope between them, and began pulling up ropes, duffles, and anything Jeff attached to the haul lines.

By the time we and all our gear were in one spot we felt as though we had just completed the Ironman Triathlon. But we still weren't through.

Jeff took the top left side of the kitchen-sized, sixty-degree icefield and began hacking a platform with the pick on his ice hammer for a place to stand, sit, or lie down. I did the same on the right side ten feet away. We worked like a couple of nineteenth-century lumberjacks chopping down a sequoia. After an hour and a half, the ice platforms were shoulder-width and six feet long, big enough to spend the night on, small enough that we didn't wear out our desire or our muscle.

My platform was still on the small side, but I intended to sleep in my Porta-ledge, a hanging hammock similar to an upside-down army cot with straps on the top side instead of legs on the bottom. I hadn't used this big-wall contraption since Uli Biaho in 1979 simply because it was awkward to set up, heavy, and cumbersome, and had a tendency to flip to vertical with me in it if I so much as rolled my eyes. But it beat standing in slings for ten hours if Jeff and I didn't reach a decent bivouac site one or two nights on the wall.

I was wrestling my hammock into submission trying to get it to flatten along the wall when Jeff pulled his one-point hanging bivouac tent from his duffle. Ten minutes later he was inside his giant golden chrysalis, sheltered, comfortable, protected, trying hard not to glance over at me and my misery. I was jealous.

My hammock wouldn't work. Like me, it was too old to work smoothly. I packed it into its tubular stuff sack, hefted its twelve pounds, and without so much as a Hail Mary tossed my hammock into the darkening void. It was the first victim, but not the last, to get a free flight off the wall in our continuing program of weight reduction. But from then on, I had to find a natural ledge or a spot to build an ice ledge. Only Jeff would have the option to bivouac without a ledge.

This was the cold time of year to be on a Himalayan wall. There were two hours of the sun's warmth in the early morning from 6:30 to 8:30. After 8:30, the sun rotated behind the wall's northeast ridge and disappeared, leaving the face in cold shadow. Heat-loosened rock and ice mercifully stopped falling as the sun dropped below the horizon, but with it went the radiant warmth of the day.

A plunge in temperature is the evil of darkness. I was still setting up my bivouac at dark. Fingers of icy cold penetrated gaps in my climbing clothes, sweat-soaked from laboriously chipping a small platform in the concretelike ice. I improved my ice ledge to accommodate my foam mat, sleeping bag, and duffle. It didn't look too bad when I was through.

Jeff's hanging stove was purring steadily next to his tent before mine was out of the bag and ready to go. Feeding ice to the small pot was as time-consuming as feeding a child and just as continual. Just when I was comfortably snuggled into my sleeping bag with my bivouac sack firmly pulled over and drawstring tight, the stove would boil in anticipation of more ice.

Two cups of cocoa and a cup of soup, and I was ready for dinner. That's when I found out why Jeff was angrily mumbling to himself in the dark ten feet away. My "tour de force" microwave dinners in their own dishes were too big for the cup-sized pot necessary to work with our hanging units. It wasn't life or death.

The problem was simply solved by heating half of the plastic dish, then flipping it over and cooking the other end. More movement in and out of our bags with arms and heads than necessary, but nothing vital—yet.

We poured the boiled water from heating our dinners into our quart water bottles, not only for quenching thirst during the night, but also initially as hot water bottles for our feet. Throughout years of expedition climbing, this small act before zipping myself in for the night is the day's single most important event. When my feet are toasty warm, my world becomes a spot of nirvana. Where I'm at or what's ahead doesn't matter. I turn into a lion cub on the Serengeti with not a care beyond my next feeding.

I shut the stove off, inchwormed deep into my sack, and draw-stringed the bivouac sack tight around my head so that only my eyes, nose, and mouth were open to the cold air and the billions of stars in the Himalayan sky. The wall rose in leaps of black broken by pearly eyebrows of starlit ice above me. I knew now what it felt like to be a lost dog on the San Diego freeway during rush hour. How many baseball-sized rocks or chunks of ice above me were ready to pop loose after eons of thawing and freezing and erosion? It would only take one. We were perched at the bottom of a funnel. Anything breaking loose from far above would find its way to us. I moved closer to the wall and underneath the foot-deep roof above me and eventually drifted into an uneasy sleep.

The following morning I noticed my eye wouldn't focus—a form of cerebral edema in its infancy. Jeff and I bailed off the route early that morning and spent the better part of the following week in Pheriche in hopes I would recover enough to return to Tawoche's wall. Personally, my hopes were shattered of ever climbing The Face.

7

com·mit·ment \ kə-'mit-mənt \ *n* The suicidal act of exposing oneself to objective danger.
(*Roskelley's First Climber's Dictionary*, 1991)

ALONE AND TRAPPED with my own thoughts of what lay ahead, I
walked away from Pheriche for advanced base camp for our second
attempt. When I'm troubled, I need to be on my own. Thinking
requires quiet and a lot gets done when I'm not using my mouth.
Tawoche wasn't my trouble; my health was. The hike assured me I
had the strength; the thinking put the climb in perspective.

Cerebral edema was at the top of my thought list. Would it
return? I felt okay, but no better than before. In one more day I
would be back at our first bivouac. The answer was only hours
away. If the edema returned after a night on the wall, my dream
of climbing Tawoche's Face would disappear with the morning
light. And along with Tawoche, perhaps my career as a Himalayan
climber.

For Jeff it was a different chapter. Jeff's a superb soloist. Confident, meticulous, a perfectionist. He likes working out a route's
problems by himself. It adds another dimension to a sport that has
more facets than a prism. Soloing Tawoche's wall was on his mind.
I could see it in his eyes, in his demeanor, and in the manner in
which he prepared for our second attempt. "If Roskelley isn't up
for the climb physically," he thought, "I can do it alone."

Mountaineering is as much flexing the muscle between the ears as pumping up biceps, deltoids, and quadriceps. As I scrambled up the steep yak trail toward advanced base, my mind raced through a myriad of climbing scenarios. How would I feel watching Jeff continue on alone? What if one of us were hit by falling debris high on the wall and unable to function? How does one cut the rope on a partner? What were our chances of retreat during a major storm or if we encountered route problems? I went through each one and more, from Scene 1 to "The End," playing out the action in chesslike moves until I was satisfied with each MGM lion-roaring ending. We never lost. By the time I got to advanced base, I would have soloed the wall.

Jeff waited in Pheriche for friend and former climbing partner David Braeshears, who with Mike Weiss was guiding rock star David Lee Roth on a trekking peak called Lobuje three miles up the valley from Tawoche. There was a slim chance that Braeshears had news from our wives since he had recently left the States.

Their trek was a zoo. Roth attracted an entourage of groupies and hangers-on that followed him from the States and along the trek. Unlike our "Tawoche Twosome," which traveled through the Khumbu incognito, at overnight stops the Roth "expedition" resembled a blowout at Wembley Stadium. Even in remote villages such as Dingboche and Pheriche the Sherpas knew someone important was coming, and with importance came electronic gadgets and sometimes gifts. They would take time from their winter chores to see who this Roth was.

I personally didn't care. "Isn't that the guy who eats the heads off live chickens onstage?" I asked Jeff one evening.

"Naw, that's someone else," Jeff replied. "Jesus, Roskelley, where've you been all these years?"

"I don't listen to that shit."

Jeff's liberal ear tuned into rock, Bach, and antiestablishment sound. A Sony was glued on his ears whether at the Houstons' or on the trek. Luckily, Jeff is a silent listener who mouths a few bars, then stops. Some Sonymaniacs like my nine-year-old son, Jess, noise along without knowing they're squealing the same tune as fully set air brakes on a semi.

I didn't bring a tape deck to Tawoche. It's the hunter in me. I use my sense of hearing as much as my vision. The music of the earth sets my mood. Animals and insects, the wind through the trees, water over a falls, and just plain quiet all provide me with beats of their own. The only time I listen to music is when I'm trapped in my truck. Then I tune in to sounds of the sixties, seventies, and eighties, switching channels like lanes on the freeway. Hard "Roth-type" rock is out.

"Was it worth the wait?" I asked Jeff as he arrived at advanced base.

"There was no news from home," he replied, "and we're lucky we're not baby-sitting that group. You didn't miss much."

I knew that already. The last thing I wanted to do was talk climbing when I was about to try one of the hardest unclimbed walls left in the world and had already once been stricken with cerebral edema. My chances of pulling this off didn't look good, and explaining potential failure was a prelude to disaster. I wanted to be left alone. Until I was counted out for good or finished the climb I was a social misfit, especially to a herd of punk rockers.

We reached our original bivouac site from the previous attempt by midday. The wall was quiet, almost ethereal. The game of hauling from this point was out. I had brought with me from Pheriche a larger, "expedition-sized" pack to accommodate all my gear, and Jeff had done the same. We spent several hours repacking our equipment from the haul bags into the smaller packs.

Something had to give. We had space for gear for a two-day winter climb, but needed enough for eight days. Once the essentials such as sleeping bag, mat, cookpot and stove, additional clothing and survival equipment were stuffed in the pack, the remaining paraphernalia was hefted for weight, judged on necessity, and discarded if possible.

Spare ice tools, three of our six ropes, a rack of hardware, some very frozen dinners — extras of any kind — were jettisoned to the foot of the wall. One small climbing pack served as a catchall for surplus hardware, day food, water bottle, and camera gear. The second man would carry this pack as he cleaned the pitch.

There were three to four hours of daylight in which to move up the wall when we finished. I led the first pitch off our ledge, a mixture of ice runnels along flakes and slabs. Snaking from ice to rock back to ice, I avoided several blank areas of rock. Jeff removed my protection on the pitch, quickly jumaring the eighty-degree slope with ease.

"Go for the next one, Jeff," I said. "Looks like a good bivy straight up to that icefield."

Jeff ran the rope out using the short, inch-wide cracks along a flake, then front-pointed smooth, sixty-degree ice. At the top of the small icefield, he slammed in a series of solid pitons, slotted a few nuts, and yelled, "Off belay!"

Once untangled from the belay and attached to my jumars, I shouldered the small, twenty-five-pound pack and cleaned the few pieces of protection Jeff had placed along his route. Then it was down the fixed rope to our two loads. They were murderous. I faced the wall, took a good shoulder-width stance on my ice ledge, grabbed the shoulder straps, and jerked the load to my knee while bracing it up against the rock. Then I slid it up the wall, squatted underneath, and put on the straps while turning. There would be no tossing this cement sack onto my back. I then put my hands to my knees and pushed myself up into a standing position. Insane? The thought all but short-circuited my mind. But it beat the hell out of hauling.

Three hundred feet above our high point was as far as we managed with the fading light. The slope was lower-angled than below. Within an hour, Jeff and I hacked two decent ledges out of the ice and were well protected from falling debris by a rock bulge above our bivouac. By dark we were thawing the microwave dinners. They tested better than freeze-dried—if we ever got to eat them. Packed in their own juice, they were frozen so solid we could use them for snow anchors up high. It was going to be a long climb.

I was gopher-deep in my down bag and reluctant to move at dawn. A quarter inch of ice coated my bivy sack, and any movement of my head and arms brought a dose of it onto my partially exposed face. It was an eye-opener.

The night was a good one: no wind, a pleasant ten to fifteen degrees. The wall stayed deathly still except for an occasional lone rock whistling toward the glacier from somewhere in the center of The Face. My initial fear of getting hit was fast disappearing with time spent on the wall. The old saying "familiarity breeds contempt" came to mind.

"How's the eyes?" Jeff yelled from his tent.

I was watching the sun's morning light spread its life over the frozen peaks when it dawned on me my eyes were fine. To be sure, I tested each eye as if putting my mouth to a cup of hot coffee. Easily at first, searching for even the slightest blur. Nothing. A hawk couldn't see better. "No problem. Looks like we're in business."

The cerebral edema would linger in the back of my mind like a slinking cat, but my initial apprehension was gone.

After pouring the remains of my water bottle into the small pot, I lit the gas burner on the stove hanging slightly behind my head, burrowed back into my bag, and waited for the sun to hit our ledge and warm the air. It didn't take long.

Rockfall announced the sun's initial arrival on The Face. Our bivouac was a whisper-length left of the center of falling-debris activity, which was heating up rapidly. The right side of the concave wall faced slightly more to the east than our side and began talking in exploding ice and an occasional rock as fast as a fruit vendor on a busy street.

I opened two packages of peaches-and-cream oatmeal, emptied them into my cup, added hot-tub warm water, and ate. All my desire for Western food was swallowed whole in one bite. I washed the dry oatmeal down with several cups of hot cocoa. Breakfast was over. It wasn't much, but having grown accustomed to Tenzing's cooking, I was not quite used to partially hydrated food.

While I melted enough ice for my day's quart supply of water, I shook the hoarfrost off my bivy sack and sleeping bag, stuffed them into my pack, and strapped, buckled, and slung climbing gear over myself feeling more like a marine about to attack a beachhead than a world-class climber. With everything packed, I was ready to lead the next pitch.

Jeff and I ran out two easy 150-foot pitches of mixed ice and rock to a bulkhead. Looking at Tawoche's face from Pheriche, it was hard to imagine that an easy, laid-back section was possible. The Face seemed as steep as the trunk of a tree. But scoops existed in the otherwise vertical wall, and there we could make up for lost time.

"Looks pretty dry," Jeff announced as he helped me attach my pack to an anchor. "I'm going to switch to my rock shoes after your pitch."

Not only was the ramp dry, but the wall where we would end up was, too. I hand-searched the top portion of my pack and came out with a pair of Nike running shoes.

"Can't climb slabby stuff like that in boots," I announced.

I loathed removing my crampons and boots while I stood stork-legged, balanced on a slim edge of ice smeared thinly against the rock. I have about the same flexibility to touch my toes that a board has to touch both ends together. When I bend at the waist to perform such acrobatics, my balance is thrown off, which leads to mistakes. With the thought of watching a crampon or boot plunge down the wall, I grasped each with an iron hand.

I secured my crampons to my pack with a carabiner before releasing the step-in binding, then I clipped and strapped them to the side of my pack. My boots were next. Microclouds of steam from sweat-soaked socks rose then vanished in the crisp air as I changed footwear. Again, I clipped a carabiner and runner to the laces before pulling off the boots and slipping on my running shoes. I tied my boots securely to strap inside my pack, then stuffed them under the lid like so much extra meat in a taco. The less I had to do this changeover, the better.

The midmorning air this low on The Face bit at my exposed skin, but frostbite from wearing tennis shoes was far from my thoughts. Climbing the next pitch would be much easier in a flexible shoe. If my feet started to freeze, I would rappel back to the loads and put on my boots.

Laden with a rack of thirty pins and assorted nuts, I crab-legged right trying to avoid the snow and ice that coated ledges and bumps along the ramp. The ramp system was layered and down-sloping like a shingled roof. As I ran out of holds on one level, I moved up and onto the next. Seventy-five feet from Jeff I crossed the center gully, *The* gully, the direct line to the upper two-thirds of The Face. I scuttled across to the shelter of small two- and three-foot roofs on the ramp. With a final difficult pull-up over a block, I anchored the belay as best I could without good cracks. Sitting beneath a small roof, I was protected, at least in my mind, from falling debris.

Jeff didn't raise an eyebrow at the problem of cleaning the slightly rising traverse. As I waited, impatiently switching my feet from narrow ledges to small holds trying to get into a comfortable position, Jeff, using jumars as a self-belay, climbed the pitch to the gully, then put his feet in étriers to scale the small roofs to where I stood. I stared hard at my anchor pins with all the faith I could muster as Jeff put his weight plus that of our hardware and an extra rope onto the one small, thin scrap of iron to which I had attached him. I expected the pin to pop with Jeff's every jerk and pull as he climbed to the belay. It didn't and I still don't know why. It wasn't until he was above me with a bomber piton welded into a crack—and I remained hanging on the wall in one piece—that I could take a full breath and work some spit back into my mouth.

Jeff lucked onto a pretty pitch all clear of rubble and split by several jam cracks. He turned steep blocks and pillars by free-climbing their openings and found himself 150 feet out before the hour hand had turned a half circle. It was lucky for me, too. My belay stance was not a stance at all, but a dance from comfort to discomfort and back. While I didn't mind, my feet did, and move-ment up the rope to Jeff was the only way feeling would return.

Leaving a rope to our loads below, I cleaned the cracks of Jeff's few pieces of protection while trying to warm my tingling, but still alive and wiggling, toes.

"Which way?" I asked. Our ramp highway ended thirty feet above on a concave, crackless wall.

"I'd try that smooth rib to the right," Jeff replied while putting on his coat. "But it looks tough."

He handed me the rack. I removed a selection of hardware that didn't look usable on the blank rock, slung four webbing runners over my neck, and began climbing on pencil-thin wrinkles plastered on a slope as steep as an old church belfry.

I tried climbing to the right as Jeff suggested. The slab arched to vertical, where I "putsed"—put something here, put something there. Nothing worked. I didn't have the edge control in my Nikes to climb the small, onion-peel-like wrinkles that plastered the wall.

Backing down carefully, I inched over to the left of the concavity and climbed toward an area with multiple horizontal cracks and a small ledge. I got higher than before, but then backed off carefully, as if I had just encountered a grizzly bear. "There's loose rock and it's a hand traverse into thin air," I complained to Jeff. There was no pity or remorse in his silent gaze, only a shrug as if to say, "That's what it's all about, Roskelley."

The rest of the pitch was going to take John Wayne courage, which this pilgrim knew was lurking deep within but not eager to surface. "I'll give her another try."

Once rested and psyched, I reclimbed the rock to my last pin and tried the traverse. It ended rather abruptly in the smooth wall. I reluctantly descended back to my resting ledge.

"John, let me give the right side a try in rock shoes," Jeff yelled to me.

I could keep throwing myself at the left side, but sooner or later I was in for a flight without wings. "Okay," I agreed. "Lower me down to the belay."

Jeff was anxious to give it a go. Sitting at the belay watching me climb everywhere but up was harder on him than leading the pitch. He was up to my high point on the right side of the concave wall within ten minutes. Jeff balanced on two small holds, reached until I thought I could hear his shoulder socket snap, and then inched upward. Jeff was making the moves look smooth, too smooth for my ego, but I was watching an alpine master at work and this stretch of rock was his element. With a quick lift of his right leg and a grunt, Jeff shifted his weight and stood up on easier ground. He continued out of sight to the next belay.

With Jeff's yell of "Off belay!" I rappeled the two rope lengths to our loads, leaving Jeff to clean his own protection. My toes tingled inside my Nikes, an indication that they were still on the thawed side rather than frozen, but I needed to put on my boots to warm them. Jeff reached my side as I was ready to go.

"Well? How hard was it?" I asked.

"That move on the slab was a hard 5.10, maybe 5.11," Jeff guessed. "You would have had trouble in running shoes."

I would have had trouble in rock shoes, but I let him placate my bruised ego, shouldered my pack, and began jumaring the first rope. My pack hadn't lost pounds sitting on the ledge. Every few feet I stopped and rested, tightened my waist belt, adjusted the shoulder straps, anything to eliminate the strain and pull on my muscles beneath the pack.

It was late afternoon when I reached the top of the three ropes. Jeff was jumaring below, picking up anchors and two of our three fixed ropes as he reached the next line. It seemed I was always jumaring first, leaving him with the pickup of gear. It occurred to me to leave my load on the ledge, rappel down, and relieve him of the hardware and extra rope, but instead I waited at the belay.

Jeff reached me in the same mood Mike Tyson works himself into before entering the ring. "Why didn't you come down and take some of this gear?" he reprimanded. "I've been doing all the cleanup on the pitches since we started. Get with it."

I was guilty as charged. Not from being lazy or ignorant of the extra mile he was going, but because I was deferring to his talent. This was Jeff Lowe. Anyone else and I would have taken charge. But Lowe's talent intimidated me. My reaction was to stand back and pay attention, at least for a few days, then dive in. Jeff's easy chastisement under exhaustion signaled a green light for me to use my initiative. Nothing more, nothing less.

Our lodestone for the night was the top of a forty-foot-long eyebrow of sixty-degree ice just above our belay. I fought the idea of putting on crampons for such a short section. It was just a few feet—maybe I could make it. Nope. I pictured myself dangling free from the overhanging lip below our belay, with Jeff holding a knife to the taut and saying, "We won't have any more stupidity on this climb," and cutting the rope. I removed my crampons from my pack and finished the short pitch to the icefield's top edge safely in minutes.

As Jeff arrived at the bivy site, I dropped the forty feet for my load and ferried it to the anchors, then descended once more for hardware and ropes left at the belay. Evening alpenglow lit the tips of Everest and Makalu with an ember orange as Jeff and I finished hacking out our sleeping platforms and began the long process of melting ice and cooking.

I jerked on the anchors, checked the knots, even doubled the carabiners connecting me to the wall. Despite my housekeeping, I wasn't going to feel at home here. The only solid was at my back. Everything else was air—above, to my sides, toward the valley. Underneath was a thin field of ice that offered no obvious means of support. The only solution was to bury my head in my bag and think about home.

A wall the size of Tawoche's is not silent. Even during the coldest nights there are the sounds of moving ice, rockfall, sliding snow, Jeff turning over, glacial groans from below. And they're amplified. I slept, but with the instinctive ear of an animal of prey. The wall was my only protection. At any sound I was awake and into the wall, searching space around me through hearing to identify, locate, and determine the danger. I could do it, too, if my heart wasn't beating so damn loud.

"Jeff, you awake?"

"Yeah. That was a close one."

I'm aware, not scared, like a gazelle that is aware of the predator and knows an attack will come. Rockfall was imminent. A matter of time. With my senses on full alert I might beat the attack.

8

---

gul·ly \ ˈgəl-ē \ *n* The last place on a big mountain you want to be.
(*Roskelley's First Climber's Dictionary*, 1991)

JEFF LED A doozy at first light. It was a short, Z-shaped pitch that demanded balletlike moves over a slight bulge to our left, then stemmed back right between the mother wall and a separated child, a six-by-twenty-foot flake that wanted to fly with the first good thaw. He ended the top traverse of the Z in his rock shoes, hand traversing an overhanging concave wall to an exposed pedestal. Damn, I hate cleaning traverses almost as much as leading them.

My pitch had looked icy from below, so I was wearing boots when I arrived at Jeff's belay, an aerie just short of the rockfall zone. I fought my way around him using his harness as my first hold, then traversed a foot-wide ledge to the dead center of the gully. Above me was four thousand feet of potential rock and ice sewage ready to flush, and I was standing in the opening to the septic tank below. It was a nasty thought.

After a short, easy aid section I reached the ice. Did I have enough rope to reach the protection of the overhangs on the right side, or should I climb straight up to a small roof? I went right and paid the Man. I was short. Jeff was out of sight below humming a

Tracy Chapman tune, something about "Baby, can I hold you to-night?" when I yelled down to him the bad news, "Off belay!" I was ten feet short of the ultimate belay, a stance *and* a roof. Like a quail out of cover, I hunkered on the gully's debris cone, which was prone to ricocheting pieces, but not direct bombs. It was the best I could do short of rope.

We dropped to our bivouac. I removed my protection from the top pitch while on rappel. Cleaned of fixed points, we jumared from our bivouac to the debris cone without having to occupy the gully zone for more than a few minutes. Maybe ferrying the loads on our backs was safer, but jumaring over Jeff's rock bulge didn't make it any easier.

February 7 was made for the beach, not Tawoche. The belay was an outdoor suntan booth. Although I huddled deep into my Marmot Gopher down bag at night, by 9:00 A.M. the temperature was a balmy twenty degrees. Almost too warm.

Above my belay, the center gully, our intended route since the conception of the climb, narrowed to a six-foot-wide slot, an open mouth that led to its long, deep throat. It was Jeff's pitch, a Rocky Mountain winter frozen waterfall, the kind of ice I would give a weekend in Banff to climb.

One look at Jeff and there was no question which side of the sport influenced him most: sport climbing. Dressed in a purple helmet, kelly green pile jacket, grape pile pants, bright blue gaiters, and black boots, with neon pink runners over his shoulder, he looked more like a snowboarder or a windsurfer than a mountain-eer. The sport was changing, and I had the feeling I was traveling the road of the brontosaurus in my black and red.

Playtime. Steep, vertical water ice with a rock move or two mixed in is the ultimate alpine statement. We were in it. Why did I want to climb Tawoche? Because this one expedition would justify the years of hard work, dedication, practice, and self-sacrifice. Finally a bit of sense from a senseless activity.

The rope continued to inch out through my hands as, high in the gully, Jeff was swallowed and eaten whole. I knew when he moved by the occasional rock or chunk of ice that was disgorged from the mouth and flew into space. To hide from the ricochets, I climbed waist high on the anchors and leaned toward the right wall. The bigger the missile, the louder Jeff yelled "ROOOCK!" or "IIIICE!" If I heard "SHIIIIT!" I got ready to dive anywhere.

Then it was my turn. As my full weight plus small pack, extra hardware, and two spare ropes elasticized the nine-millimeter string I was on, I inched sideways into the gully on front points. There was no way out. Anything down that gully and Roskelley would be past tense, raven fodder at the bottom of the wall. I wondered fleetingly if I had mentioned to Joyce to have Bob Christianson write my obituary. Something humorous, light-hearted, with a poke or two at alpine club members.

I was owl-eyed halfway to Jeff when I spotted the rope stretching over a knife-edged rock, sawing itself cleanly in two and leaving flecks of blue perlon sheath like powder burns with my every move. Jeff made a good lead, I had to hand it to him. I could at least dodge anything coming down the chimney by swinging on the rope. He had been locked onto his ice tools and crampons while leading, a similar feeling to being tied to a railroad track and not knowing when the train was coming. I removed the few rock pins and Friends he had used for protection and jumared as quickly as possible to his belay, a cubbyhole partially protected by a chock-stone blocking the gully.

We switched hardware racks carefully at the belay.

"We can't bivy in the gully," I said. "I'll check out the snowfield off to the left. It doesn't look too bad."

It was a loser. As soon as I fought my way over the chockstone and studied the seventy-five-degree, pancake-thin icefield, I had the feeling it would be named the "Death Bivouac" within an hour of our camping there.

Out of the gully on a rock rib high above to my right, I spotted a potential bivy spot on fifty-degree snow and ice. Using my hands and feet on opposite walls, I chimneyed a vertical, sluice-shaped furrow until I was able to exit the gully by climbing the steep side wall via small ledges and ice runnels in the smooth rock.

"Ten feet!" Jeff yelled.

I was close to a good stance, but ten feet was a short shank. "Give me all the slack you've got!" I pictured Jeff removing the belay and adjusting his anchors. Nobody could squeeze extra rope from nothing like Jeff could.

It was enough. Once I reached the icefield, I lassoed two runners over a rock obelisk, placed a tubular ice screw in concrete-hard gray ice, and caught my breath. It would take hours of hacking with ice hammers to put in two bivy ledges, but the site seemed safe from falling debris.

Jeff dropped from his belay to our loads at the base of the gully, while I cleaned the pitch of protection on rappel. He was loaded and ready to jumar the two lines to the icefield when I joined him at the anchors.

The nine-millimeter rope finally stopped stretching under Jeff and his hundred pounds of gear. He inched over the initial ice bulge and out of sight, puffing like an old steam engine. In my impatience to get moving, I clipped my jumar to the line and removed the anchors before he yelled, "I'm off!"

Despite my waistbelt digging a permanent tattoo on my hips and the shoulder straps trying to dislocate my arms, the jumar to the first anchor was easy in the vertical gully. Not so the chock-stone. I grappled and fought my way over and around the big rock, finally winning, but at a cost of total exhaustion. A half hour later I reached Jeff on the ice field.

We yo-yoed up and down the icefield seeking a spot to hack out a platform. Jeff settled for a hanging bivy from the rock wall and a small ice platform for his gear. I was in a bind. After an hour of chopping, my platform was the size of the seat of my pants, and by the looks of the rock that was showing, it wasn't in danger of getting bigger. Self-belayed, I climbed to the crest of the rib sixty feet from Jeff, dropped over, and found a thicker layer of ice. Out of sight of Jeff, but not out of mind, I sculpted a suite of a platform to get the night's sleep I hadn't gotten below.

At 18,500 feet the clear winter night's temperature plunged, causing the ice around me to pop and snap. Not a sound cut the still air except for the ice talking and the rustle of my frozen nylon.

Sleep took the form of fragments determined by aches and thirst and sometimes thought. I sat up at 3:30 A.M., leaned against the ice wall, and stared out at the starlit Himalayas. Odd—one of the stars blinked, and it was below the summit of a peak. Another. Headlamps? Sure, it was Braeshears, Weiss, and Roth on Lobuje. Two climbing teams in the entire Khumbu Himalaya, and I spot the other. The odds against this happening were the same as having my wife along on this climb: nil. But there they were. And going down so early in the morning. Pulmonary edema? Cerebral? We would find out when we got down. [Author's note: Roth had no desire to continue, so they were descending.]

The three lights stuttered slowly down the dark side of the East Ridge, disappearing when the owners turned their heads away from Tawoche. I lost sight of them as they angled south. The thought of signaling Braeshears occurred to me, but I didn't want him to mistake my headlamp for a rescue signal.

At 7:30 A.M., Jeff, fully loaded with gear and hardware, rappeled into the gully, fighting to stay as high as possible by penduluming back and forth. Belayed by the rappel rope, he climbed to a stance beneath a small roof after having lost only one hundred feet from our bivouac. I followed the same track, retrieving the rappel ropes and jumaring to his belay.

There are pitches in climbing I never forget. Like the pitch leading out of the Black Cave on the North American Wall on El Capitan or the Exit Pitch at the top of the Ramp, Eiger North Wall. Their severity or esoteric nature leave them dangling out of place in an otherwise neatly filed memory. The one rising above me was a dangler.

I was at the top of my form. Granted, it took three days of climbing to get the "Old Roskelley" back, but I was there, pulling my weight and mentally fixed on the climb and not on skull-whackers, storms, or broken bones. Just on climbing to the sky. Jeff said the word and I led off oblivious of anything but the next move.

It was vintage Tawoche, a thin, two-foot-wide wash of water ice cascading through a narrow vertical chimney, steep as a mule's face. I front-pointed with one crampon in the center ice, used the rock on the corner for my right foot, an ice tool up high, the other fist in an inlaid crack. The next move was a mirror image. And the next. It was hard, but I turned and flowed with the ice and rock like Baryshnikov in *Swan Lake*.

"You've got thirty feet!" Jeff yelled. Two minutes later, "You've got ten feet!"

I pulled and inched my way over an ice bulge into a cavity. This was not a good place to belay. But off to my right were three one-foot-wide ledges, each slightly higher than the other. The three-tiered stance looked exposed to missiles from above, but more comfortable than standing in étriers squashed into a two-foot-high cave.

I placed a pin in the ice, grabbed the rope, and stretched horizontally for the ledge. The rope stopped me. It wouldn't budge. I yelled for more rope.

"You're out!"

"You gotta get me two feet!"

Silence. Then, "Try that!"

This time I reached the ledge with my extended arm, straddled the gap with one leg for balance, then slotted a small nut in a vertical crack. It wasn't much, but it held long enough for me to pull myself over to the ledge.

My belay was a cobweb of anchors, small stuff capable of holding their own weight plus a few pounds. Not much more. I stepped on the key player, a baby angle piton holding Jeff while he jumared. My action was self-motivated. I didn't like watching the pin move in the crack as he bounced about below cleaning the pitch.

"Nice lead, John," Jeff said.

Jeff doesn't hand that stuff out. I knew he meant it. With those words I could whittle two or three Tawoches down to size.

Jeff led forty feet of loose building-block stuff without knocking the route down onto me, then vanished inside the gully. After forty more feet, the rope went dead in my hands. A minute later, three feet slithered snakelike back into my belay. I adjusted my feet on the ledges, zipped my coat, pulled down my hat, and blew warm air into my gloves. Freon-cold air crawled down the gully to filter through the openings of my sweat-soaked clothes. I knew that whatever Jeff faced up there must be a humdinger to stop him dead.

The rope rose from my belay at the speed of a growing weed for thirty feet before accelerating to Jeff's speed limit. The rope was history in my hands when he yelled "Off belay!"

I started up the rope like the Tin Man but warmed quickly to the work. Eighty feet up I butted heads with Jeff's problem, a manta-ray-shaped, thirty-foot-square ice flake overlying the gully. The rope went into the ray's mouth and ended above it, where Jeff was sitting.

"How did you get over this?" I asked.

"It didn't seem safe to climb on," he admitted, "so I chimneyed underneath. It's a tight squeeze."

Twenty-four years in the mountains and I had never seen a formation of ice like this. It was originally an icefield, which had aged into a water ice plug that stoppered the upper gully. Melt during the warmer months had eroded the bottom so that there was only a saucer-shaped remnant tilted on its edge at eighty degrees. I was stuck. The rope went underneath, and to clean Jeff's protection, I had to follow.

I jumared into the lower open cave. It narrowed to chest width. How Jeff led the slot was secreted within him. Poised within earshot above me, he tested the validity of his masterpiece by my groans and moans. It was priceless. If it had been rock, my chest would never have fit through. Ice allowed me to slither upward. The narrowest section filled me with fearful memories.

In 1983 I climbed the Steck-Salathe route on Sentinel Rock in Yosemite Valley with Kim Momb. We reached a chimney section called the Narrows. It was Kim's lead, and looking up into that miniscule hole I jumped up and down inside for having the luck of the Irish-English mongrel I am.

Kim took one look at it, shook his head, and asked forgiveness. "I can't lead that, John."

"Not even a little try?" I begged. But I felt guilty. Kim had climbed for only a year. As callous as some climbers think I am, I wouldn't pressure him to lead that slot. I knew it was mine by the "rule of experience."

I slithered my head, shoulders, and upper torso into the crack, leaving my legs chimneyed against an outside wall. With nothing short of levitation, I fought my whole body into the chimney and quarter-inched up and sideways for an hour before breaking into daylight and life again.

The ice shelf reminded me of those Narrows on the Steck-Salathe. I swore I would never do the Narrows again, and once to Jeff, swore I wouldn't trap myself beneath that ice on Tawoche either.

We rappeled three hundred feet into the depths of the gully for our packs, using our haul line on the outside of the ice sheet and the fixed line on the first lead. Jumaring from the innermost depth of the gully was like climbing out of a tomb. Jeff had placed his anchors at the end of his lead below a sixty-foot rising roof at the foot of a permanent icefield, the catch basin for debris from the upper gully. We were safe at his anchors.

Three long, steep ice leads from Jeff's belay ended abruptly at an overhanging rock band to the right of the main gully. At the gumline between sixty-degree ice and ninety-degree rock, we excavated two small "plats" without the "-form." The latter would have taken the energy we had already fed to the gully earlier that morning. I fell into an exhausted sleep after drinking some tea and putting a hot water bottle inside my bag to toast tingling toes. To hell with dinner. This was our hardest day yet.

9

rock·fall \ˈräk-fȯl\ *n*   High-velocity, gravity-fueled missile(s) found in mountainous regions, capable of disrupting your day.
(*Roskelley's First Climber's Dictionary*, 1991)

OUR WORLD CAME apart in seconds. From thousands of feet above, a car-sized rock broke loose with the morning sun. It may have hit once, maybe twice, then bounced away from the wall in a cannon-shot leap for space.

Exhausted from our efforts of the previous day, Jeff and I woke with the 6:30 A.M. sun peeking over the summit of Makalu. The air was deathly still. Without speaking, we lay in our bags taking in the beauty of the early morning Himalayas. Human voice would taint such a sight. My mind wandered from the climb to my family, to the feeling of being so alive.

The rock entered our hearing space nearing the speed of sound, punching a hole through the air like a meteorite. Instantaneously it exploded into the ice fifteen feet below Jeff, shattering the icefield and creating a cavity that would take a backhoe an hour to dig. As it came, so it departed. A monstrous apparition that hurtled in and out of our lives in a blink, leaving our hearts beating at the speed of a hummingbird's wings and us melted into the rock wall as far as we could squeeze.

Like lampreys attached to a great white shark, small debris followed the monster, striking the rock and ice around us. As each piece hit, I cringed and compressed, trying to hide my head and as much of my body as possible beneath a foot-wide roof next to my ledge. Jeff had nothing, his hanging tent exposed to the sloping wall above him. The rockfall ended with a bit of sand and ice floating down the wall above us and onto our ledges.

"Jeff, you okay?"

Slowly Jeff peeked from his hanging tent at the sky, then down at the destruction below him. His breath pumped bitty clouds into the cold. Regaining composure, he said, "Yeah, I think so."

He dug around inside of his tent and pulled something out. It was a rock the size of a racquetball. "This one tore through my tent and punctured a hole in my sleeping bag." He tossed it down the slope.

The sound. I have been around a lot of rockfall. In fact I was almost killed by rocks in a gully during the trek to Nanda Devi in India in 1976. While filling my water bottle in a small creek drainage, four car-sized boulders careened through the gully. I dived for an overhanging boulder as they exploded around me. Silence proved I was still alive. Falling rocks sound pretty much the same as they hit walls and roll through. But it was the sound of this gigantic rock cutting through air without warning that I will never forget. "Time to die" was my only thought.

I've heard the sound before. Not in the mountains. Not anywhere in reality. It was in *Star Wars*. Only George Lucas could create a noise so sinister, so diabolical to human ears that it is capable of producing instant, startling terror. Little did he know the sound of his Empire space station punching outer space would come to life for me on Tawoche.

I figured we were out of real danger once we'd left Tawoche's shooting gallery, the lower gully. Our bivy was off to one side on a rib directly beneath a vertical rock band. Rockfall until now had been scarce, almost rare. But this wasn't just a rock. It was a meteor, the single largest gravity-fueled mass I had ever seen so near.

Truth was, the climb was just starting to heat up. We were on the upper two-thirds of the face. "Retreat" we defined as an extra candy bar. Neither of us would descend that Face short of death.

That left up. Barring a major storm, high-altitude disease, injury through falls or hits, equipment loss, or some unforeseen disaster, we figured four days to the top. That was a lot of "ifs."

"If" number one showed itself immediately. The "meteorite" had eaten one of our three ropes. Our arrival at the bivouac the day before preceded nightfall by an hour. We hacked out two platforms by dark and spent several hours cooking and housekeeping. We pulled two ropes up to the bivy and coiled them. The third lay on the ice. It was shredded by the rockfall.

The first pitch that morning was mine. I angled down ten feet to a rock corner split up the center by a one-inch crack. The slope below our bivouac was steep, but it at least gave the impression that I had something underneath me to stop a free-fall. My new vantage point opened up another perspective — depth. The Face dropped away beneath me for three thousand feet.

I aided the crack thirty feet to a diagonally right-sloping ramp that sliced the two-hundred-foot rock band defending the upper face. The ramp was slabby but protected. I ended the pitch in a small alcove and called for Jeff. For the first time that morning I felt secure, well covered by a six-foot rock roof over my head.

Jeff's pitch was a mirror image of mine, reasonable free-climbing along a fifty-degree slab under a continuous roof, with a hard move or two to keep things interesting. He was through leading the pitch by noon. We retreated to our bivouac site.

As much as I needed rest, I didn't need the anxiety aroused at that bivouac site. I felt violated, exposed by the morning events. Sitting on my ledge brewing tea calmed me. We had the afternoon to organize our gear, hydrate, and get ready for the final push up the headwall. I was ready to get off this face.

The temperature dropped overnight and high mares' tails floated overhead. It was the first "weather" we had seen since our arrival in the Khumbu. It didn't look serious, but any change of weather in the mountains leads to speculation, and Jeff and I can do that as well as anyone. A storm was brewing and our final decision was to keep climbing right on through. The Face was too steep to hold snow, and we didn't have enough food or gas cartouches to sit out a major storm.

Jeff was off his ledge and jumaring the ropes with his full load before the sun hit the top of Tawoche. We were not about to have another episode of *Star Wars*. I followed slowly, the load much lighter without the past days' food and camp gas. In addition, I jettisoned a three-hundred dollar Gore-Tex bib suit, my Nikes, and a few other nonessentials. Because of dropping temperatures, I decided to climb in my down jumpsuit.

Once at the top of the ropes, I led along the ramp for fifty feet before breaking onto a fifty-degree icefield, which I followed diagonally until out of rope. I chopped two good steps for my feet, screwed in several long ice screws, and waited for Jeff.

Thick clouds broken by sunlight in the valley indicated a storm was on its way. I started to examine every potential ledge or bivy spot I could find. Nothing. The icefield was too steep and solid for us to hack two platforms. Jeff might find something up higher.

On his pitch he front-pointed to the right off my belay on steepening water ice to avoid vertical rock slabs, then climbed straight up for eighty feet. Above him the ice ended in a crackless, four-foot rock roof that had a cap of thick ice over its edge. Using his ice tools over the lip, he pulled up with his arms while sucking his lower body under the roof, then moved his tools higher one at a time. As smooth as the ice that held him, he went up and over like a lizard scrambling under a ceiling.

Jeff's pitch ate up the clock. "There's nowhere to bivouac up here," he yelled down to me, then descended to my belay.

We still had several hours of daylight, but the chances of finding a decent place to spend the night looked grim.

"Let's get the loads up to here," I recommended. "If need be I'll just sit on the packs for the night."

Jeff didn't want that to happen. "We can squeeze into my tent if it comes down to that," he offered. As much as I appreciated his thoughtfulness, I knew it was impossible.

We searched for a bump, a potential rock ledge beneath the ice, a rib, anything that looked like it would work while jumaring the loads to my upper belay. We knew it was useless to seek a site along Jeff's pitch above.

With daylight a fleeting ghost, I tied into our free rope and went left along the band of ice and beneath another vertical band of rock. One hundred feet from the belay, almost another pitch, I spotted a potential cave. Either this worked or I was looking at a cold night sitting on a loaded pack. Yes! It *was* a cave. I excavated the snow around the entrance and found a hole in the rock wall big enough for two to lie down, with a ceiling high enough for us to sit up. The floor was almost level ice and gravel. It was perfect.

I fixed the rope to the cave roof, and Jeff, fully loaded, hand-lined over. I retrieved my pack as clouds smothered the wall like a wool glove.

Jeff chose to live in his hanging tent on the lip of the cave, while I chopped ice and moved gravel around inside to level a place to sleep. It was the first time during the climb we were close enough to hand things to each other. Our gear fitted nicely along the lip and at my feet. Out of despair came overwhelming relief. It was the finest bivouac on the route, fully protected from above and Snoopy-blanket secure.

"If" number two descended on Jeff. He was nauseated. This was not life-threatening—yet. But he couldn't seem to hold any fluids or eat without wanting to vomit. That in itself was trouble. He had to hydrate and store energy. We had two, three, maybe four days before summiting. At altitudes, dehydration quickly leads to cerebral or pulmonary edema. Jeff's history, a series of bouts with cerebral edema, indicated a potential threat. All the joy was gone in Cavesville that night. If Jeff worsened during the night or had obvious signs of high-altitude disease, we would have no choice but to descend. To continue up meant certain death for anyone with edema. It was the longest night of the climb.

Jeff still couldn't eat the next morning, but managed to choke down a cup of hot cocoa. Unburdened of the fear of flying death from above, I hibernated most of the night inside the cave getting my best night's sleep on the wall. It was a relief not to have that constant threat hanging over me.

The storm started during the night. "If" number three was fully upon us by daybreak. Light snowfall, the kind you'd think about listening to mood music like "Sounds of Silence" to, fell quietly, while massive cumulonimbus clouds bullied their way into the valleys, ramming the peaks under full steam. The temperature plunged from an already arctic low. Even so, it wasn't a real smoker, the kind of storm I've been in on Everest or Makalu where staying alive was in question. This storm came in quietly like a kitten walking on a rug and never grew to lion proportions.

"Can you move, Jeff?" I asked. "Or do you want to stay put and see how it goes?"

"I don't think it's edema. We've got to keep moving," he replied. "If I get worse, then we can talk about turning back or going on."

We finished boiling water, packed up our gear, and started for the top of Jeff's last lead. Jeff was slow, dehydrated, and hungry, but his engine kept on chugging along and he soon joined me at the belay. It was my lead.

Tawoche unmasked a different face. We were on the far right of the mountain's side visible from Pheriche. Tawoche's west wall was now partially revealed, and it didn't look any easier on that side. The immense rock headwall above us stretched from the center gully around to the west and out of sight. Our choice was simple. We had to take a diagonal back to the center route to break through the upper face.

I front-pointed horizontally left from Jeff's icefield belay, working my way in and out of steep-sided ice troughs. The icefield continued to steepen left, so I climbed up to a rock band hoping for relief for my burning calves. I was out of sight of Jeff, traversing my way toward the gully, when I felt the tug at my waist. I was out of rope.

I like to end a lead and let my partner have his turn as much as the next guy, but this wasn't the place. The solid ice of the field below had turned into bottomless crap the consistency of moss. I had to move on if the belay were to be any good. I yelled for Jeff to tie the second rope onto the end of the first. I needed fifty more feet to get to a reasonable stance and good anchors.

Once the belay was in, I returned to Jeff for my load. With both ropes used on the pitch, we had to move up with the loads first before leading another. I went first, thinking Jeff would lower out from his belay when he came across the jumar to each point of protection. He thought I was going to belay him from above. I should learn communication skills or mind reading, but not both. For lack of the first and a poor attempt at the second, I put Jeff's life on the line as he had to self-belay along the troughs to the first anchor. Jeff's skill got him out of this bind, but he was so hot under his helmet he could have risen to the summit. I moved in a blink to set up a belay for him once he arrived at the fixed anchor.

Jeff's illness had turned the corner. He began eating and drinking without the nausea. He took the next lead, a short, steep ice traverse to an ice rib just shy of the center gully. Not wanting to get caught short of rope, Jeff climbed to the top of the rib where it butted into a rock wall and anchored the lead. I left the rope tied to my anchors and jumared with my load to his belay. Ironically, after all the problems from my previous lead, Jeff was stuck retrieving his load and reclimbing his pitch again. The traverse pitches are always more difficult for the second climber.

The possibility of finding a bivouac site beyond the rib where we stood seemed as remote as reaching the summit that night. But that didn't stop us from fixing a lead to the center gully.

I dropped thirty feet vertically into a trough, then climbed the same distance up the other side. The ice formation I reached was as unusual as the manta-ray-shaped block far below. The upper gully regularly sloughed gigantic cornices, which hung over the face. Ice and rock avalanches had scoured out two separate funnels, one on each side of the rib I was on, because of a rock formation above. Consequently, an immense, phallic-shaped ice pinnacle rose from the rib behind me. It faced northeast toward the valley and the highest peak on earth as if to say, "Up yours, Everest."

The cold welded itself to the rib and spent the night cowering around my down bag. The numbing air sensed exposed skin and sneakily attempted a bite or two. My jealousy of Jeff's fully enclosed tent hit the ten mark on a scale of ten. I knew how warm an enclosure could be: the dead airspace holds heat from one's breath and body. I used a Gore-Tex bivy sack on part of the wall but finally jettisoned it. Every morning there was more hoarfrost build up between my sack and sleeping bag than if I used nothing at all. For its treachery, it won a free flight to the glacier.

By morning the storm was well on its way to the Karakoram. Sun warmed our small ledges at first light. I waited and watched as its heat took the frost from the surface of my bag as a prisoner of war and put it to the torch. The moisture then melted into the seams of my sleeping bag.

My food reserve verged on a critical shortage. I didn't waste what could be eaten, but some of the fresh microwave dinners were so frozen and the air temperature so cold at night, I wasted valuable gas needed for hydrating trying to melt them. Both Jeff and I gave up and tossed the last few to the goraks. Drinks were far more important at this stage of the climb. Jeff had an extra day's rations from his day of illness, but his also bordered on empty. We were both going to lose weight on this climb.

Once at the "phallic" pinnacle, Jeff jumped on his étriers to bypass the vertical rock buttress above. Summit exit gullies appeared to the right of the main center gully, visibly more protected from falling debris. Jeff angled right into the first good one, free-climbing over several chockstones and large blocks. When his gully started to look blocked by ice above, he traversed along a horizontal crack system back into the center gully. The summit cornices were finally visible several pitches up the gully.

We retrieved our loads at the bivouac and were ready to gain new ground by 11 A.M. I led steep slabs up the tongue of the center gully. It wasn't difficult climbing, yet every move was potential disaster for Jeff. The entire upper gully was shattered and broken, a scree slope glued in place at sixty degrees. Jeff was off to one side of the shooting gallery, but anything I cut loose was a potential bullet meant for him. My every move was delicate and catlike.

I was out of rope again stuck in the upper gully with nowhere to put good anchors. Our ropes were 165 feet, but I needed 200 feet. Of course, if I had a 200-footer, I'd need a 250-foot rope. It's Murphy's law of the mountains.

Jeff tied our other rope to my lead line. "You've got about seventy feet before the knot hits your first pin!" he yelled.

That should do it. I moved delicately into the center of the gully, a mess of rubble and blocks on slabby bands. Carefully I climbed my way from band to band to a potential belay. Good— there were solid cracks. Within minutes the belay was bombproof and I descended for my gear.

The gully swept into a vertical ice wall abruptly one hundred feet above crowned by house-sized overhanging cornices. It was easy to see why the center gully was so pronounced. One or two of those cornices sweeping the face each year had enough power to wipe out a small town. I wanted out of that gully.

Jeff traversed back across to the left side one more time seeking an easier exit from the face. He leap-frogged from solid rock to ice to unconsolidated windpacked snow, finally reaching a lip of ice below an eighty-degree slope. It was most likely a glacial bergschrund, but it served our purpose. By the time we had both loads to the belay, there was enough daylight for me to lead one more fast pitch up a snow and ice gully.

Just to have sky over my head instead of ice and rock would release a reservoir of tension and stress that had built up inside me over the past eight days. I fell short by one hundred feet.

We knew we were close, but we couldn't take the chance of finding hard ridge ice and nowhere to bivy. High up on a snow slope below an obvious ridge, we bivouacked one last time on the wall. I dug into the slope, building a comfortable snow cave big enough to sit up in if I bent at the neck. It was completely enclosed except for the crawl-in door. Jeff hacked out yet another ledge sixty feet above me and slept against the ridge. We were within two hundred feet of being off The Face. Alive and uninjured. That was all that mattered.

10

sum·mit \ 'səm-ət \ *n*   The end to a means.
(Roskelley's First Climber's Dictionary, 1991)

DAWN UNVEILED A new morning, timelessly, like the creation of frost on a leaf. By the looks of the horizon beyond my cave door, the Weatherman had gone to a great deal of trouble to pull up a day so fine just for Jeff and me. There was a whisper of a breeze, just enough to wake the skin, and one Pooh cloud hiding north of Everest. All around us was unending peace in the Himalayas. It was February 13.

I was awake but reluctant to begin another day. As I lay wolf-curled in my bag, capturing a BTU or two of body heat with only my nose exposed to the chill, I dreamed the pleasures of early morning dreams. Dreams of life and love. Not the worry ones brought on by the edge of night, which have no hope or another sunrise.

The sun peeked over Makalu then jumped into the morning sky. As its warmth melted the hoarfrost off the foot of my sleeping bag, I filled my cookpot with ice shards, started the stove, and sat back to watch the Himalayas unfold for the ninth morning, their beauty no longer scarred by the fear I had felt below.

Occasionally I centered myself in the cave opening and

glanced toward Jeff's ledge sixty feet above. Distance prevented communication, so when the tent bulged and swelled I assumed he was dressing. When I heard the pots clanging I knew he was cooking. By the time I saw him on the ledge packing, I was ready to leave the cave and jumar to his position. Not a word passed between us.

We were no longer lost in a sea of rock and ice. Thirty feet above Jeff's bivouac was a snippet of Tawoche's East Ridge, heavily corniced and not very inviting. Beyond was more open sky than we'd seen in days, and it looked close enough to touch. Jeff, fully loaded, traversed the forty-degree snow slope underneath the cornice searching for an opening through which to climb upward. He ran out of rope twenty feet short of an exit slope.

I grabbed the next lead and followed the easiest path angling up and right. The slope soon fell on its nose, and after one hundred feet I crested onto a flat shoulder, the top of Tawoche's wall. We were off The Face.

I'm not much for summits. I've been to plenty of them and there's not much there — a bit of joy, a little self-gratification, and a whole lot of apprehension concerning the descent. But there's a bit of an ache in my chest that eats away at me when I don't finish something, and I guess that's why I struggle off a face like Tawoche's and still want the top. But I try hard to put my summits in perspective. The route is more important to me than any summit. Besides, Tawoche's wall just about depleted all the cockiness I'd been saving up in twenty-four years of climbing. Lying flat out on that shoulder, not caring whether I took a leak in or out of my climbing suit, I knew exactly where I stood in the scheme of things: I was one puny human in a world of hurt. Where we rested, it would have been easy to pack up and start rappeling down. And that crossed my mind. If Jeff's eye had twitched to the down side and he had started a sentence with "Well . . . ," I'd have broken in quickly and finished his thought my own way — "You're right, let's head down" — and hooked up my figure eight and launched myself down the ridge. We'd be drinking a Star beer and eating popcorn in

Pheriche that night. But that smidgen of a twitch didn't show. Instead, he stripped himself of all his useless paraphernalia, squinted at the summit pyramid as if there might be a hidden tram to the top, and launched himself upward at the rate granite decomposes. Still attached to the rope, I followed.

Summits

A PR man hired by Du Pont to promote my image and Du Pont's product asked me prior to my departure for the North Face of Everest in 1984 if I intended to use bottled oxygen. "No," I said. "Why go to the Himalayas to climb but eliminate their main challenge, the altitude?"

He didn't understand. "Get to the top by any means," he said, "or you won't last with Du Pont." It was not a threat, just a fact of marketing.

I reached 28,000 feet without bottled oxygen. With no feeling in my hands or feet and no food, I chose to descend, knowing that to go farther risked my life and my partner's and the expedition's success. My partner, Phil Ershler, used bottled oxygen, which fed his blood and warmed him comfortably, and he climbed to the summit.

It hurt, I won't deny that. But I felt comfortable with my decision. I set my goals years before challenging Everest and decided that *how* I get to a summit is far more important than just getting there. The climbing game can be as easy as I want it, or I can challenge the peak on its own terms. Why, then, should I not raise myself up to the challenge rather than drag the peak down to a lower level? The summit is the end to the means, not a goal in itself.

We put too much emphasis on winning and not enough on how we win. Fame and fortune are powerful rewards. If those who summit at any price, regardless of ethics or self-control, knew how much "fame and fortune" I've gained in two decades of Himalayan climbing, they'd take up tennis.

I actively promote (and have for years) raising the standards of Himalayan climbing. There's no secret to it, you just have to believe in yourself and your abilities. Climb with small alpine-style teams instead of large expeditions; use porters and Sherpas only to base camp; consider oxygen a drug, and as the saying goes, "Don't do drugs."

My Himalayan ethics weren't as defined in 1973 as they are now. I'm guilty. I summited Dhaulagiri using Sherpa support. As with all large Sherpa-supported expeditions, our Sherpas carried most of the loads, cooked the meals, set up tents, dug out snow-bound tents, broke trail, and basically put us on top. I still ask myself repeatedly, "Why did we allow them to risk their lives for our glory?" The expedition was inappropriately named the 1973 "American" Dhaulagiri Expedition. I now call it the "Sherpa" Dhaulagiri Expedition with American Support. And there isn't an American expedition that has used Sherpas in the same way whose title couldn't also be changed.

I didn't use bottled oxygen in 1973 and never have on any Himalayan expedition. Messner and Habeler's ascent of Everest without supplemental oxygen on May 8, 1978, eliminated any reason for me or, for that matter, anyone else to use supplemental oxygen. Unless, of course, a summit by any means is all that matters.

Someone once wrote "When the risk is little, the reward is little." Three hundred yards to the south and two hundred feet higher was a reward of a lifetime — Tawoche's summit. Tawoche was one of the finest climbs I have ever completed. Not because we risked it all and survived or because of the technical difficulties or because it was a winter ascent alpine-style. No, I considered Tawoche a human achievement. Jeff and I had started as friends and would finish as friends. No other measurement or statistic was important.

The climbing wasn't over. Jeff and I leap-frogged leads while traversing upward along a steep slope until we reached the crest of the summit ridge. We pushed our physical limit. As easy as the summit pyramid was, I was having trouble just lifting my legs and placing my tools. Fatigue settled in and I realized Jeff and I were holding on to a very thin line between control and error.

True "Pigs," mountains that challenge the inner soul, have at least one false summit, a place to dash your hopes. Super "Pigs" have many. Luckily, Tawoche was only a "Pig," but it was damn near enough to turn us around. Jeff's shoulders slumped so far when we crested on the false summit that I thought they were a second set of hips. But Tawoche strung us along with hopes that the next bump several hundred feet away was its top.

I dropped fifty feet to a col then, angling off to one side of a massive cornice, post-holed through foot-deep wind crust toward a high, indistinguishable knob. I stopped on the knob's crest, checked thoroughly for hidden cornices, then turned and began pulling in the rope.

"What do you see?" Jeff asked, as he approached my position.

"Nothing. Absolutely nothing," I said. We were there.

Okay, I had a tear in my eye. It just kind of welled up and spilled out when Jeff and I clasped arms and said nothing except a volume or two with our eyes. I'd have bet my ice axe and an ice screw right there that we were in the center of the Himalayas, perhaps even the whole universe. One look around and I con-firmed it. This was the center—until maybe the next summit.

I wish I had a buck for every time someone asked me how long I stayed on the summit. If the event had been on a time exposure we'd be a blur. Jeff and I snapped a few photos, pointed out a few notable peaks and villages, and most important, got a bearing on our descent route. Then we started down. The elation of success disappeared with the prospect of traversing a route we knew nothing about except that a Japanese climber had died some-where along it during a previous attempt. A comforting thought.

The southeastern flank of Tawoche is a jumbled mass of ice-falls and hanging glaciers separated from the northeast escarpment of rock and ice walls by a broad, low-angled snow ridge. We spent a few minutes repacking our fifty-pound loads and trying to mus-ter some energy to get moving. My body was running on empty and I don't know what Jeff's was running on, but it wasn't food. Six 150-foot, fifty-degree rappels down the northeast glacier put us on the main east ridge. Setting the six rappels and mistakenly hanging up several ropes on ice horns took hours to accomplish safely, using a strength that was coming from our hearts because our bodies were finished. It was a two-man effort just to lift our loads to our shoulders, let alone coil a rope and throw it.

Once onto the flat broad humps of the ridge, the descent turned into a stumble. Few sections required a belay. The ridge finally narrowed before us. With daylight all but gone, we found a wind depression behind a snow dune and leveled two ledges in the ice. We would spend another night on Tawoche.

It seems that no matter where I am on this earth, whether on a porch, in my car, out walking at night, or on Tawoche, when I first glance at the evening sky I look straight at the Big Dipper. Try it. You'd think there were no other stars in the sky. Peeking out of my sleeping bag, the Dipper was there. And again and again. Every time I awoke, curled in a ball, so cold I didn't think I would wake in the morning, it was there urging me to hang on for the morning sun.

Early, around three o'clock, my body's pilot light was all but out and I just knew I wasn't going to make it down. I wouldn't die from a fall or a rock or a cornice. I was freezing to death. Hypothermia. My core temperature was lower than a Popsicle's and my mind was on holiday to conserve heat and energy for the vital organs. I had no more calories to burn, and with just a two-ounce box of raisins left between Jeff and me, it didn't look good.

"I'm really cold, Jeff," I said.

"Me too."

"If the sun doesn't come up in the morning I'm going to have trouble getting up," I admitted as if to ease my own mind.

"Me too."

It was years since I was this exhausted, this close to calling it quits. On Makalu's West Ridge in 1980, I reached the summit alone after climbing eleven hours with my two partners and two by myself. During my solo descent I sat down and decided to bivouac in the open three different times. Each time, I fell asleep for a few minutes only to wake freezing in my own sweat with the realization I would die if I didn't keep moving. I reached Camp V and my teammates late that night. A blizzard, the worst we experienced in forty-five days of climbing, hit Makalu after midnight. If I had bivouacked, I would have died.

Jeff and I lay still in our bags until the sun's warmth spread over the ridge. We crawled out from them only when the sun hit a slope nearby. We hunkered like two batteries on trickle charge, feeling each ray give life back to our bodies. It worked. Motivation returned.

Comically, Jeff split the box of raisins between us: "One for you, one for me, one for . . ." It wasn't much, but I felt every one of those raisins burst inside me with a little energy.

Our descent gully dropped off the ridge less than one hundred feet from our bivouac. The tonguelike ice gully had been climbed by some previous expedition. Successful or not, we didn't know, but their passage was evident. Held in a viselike grip by the ice, short sections of fixed line were still in place, strung taut like guy wires from the pull of the gravity-fueled moving ice.

Jeff and I hugged the east wall of the gully using the rock for our anchors, which we placed two at a time. Jeff set up the first four rappels and I set up the next four, rotating our positions as our strength ebbed. The gully was low-angle, forty-five-degree rock and ice and easy to rappel, but retrieving the ropes deadened already fatigued muscles. Early morning rockfall was our only concern beyond making a mistake in anchor placement. Several hours after leaving the ridge, out of carabiners and rock hardware, we reached the end of the consecutive rappels.

Tawoche wasn't about to let us go easily. Extreme nieves penitentes, jagged two-foot-high ice pinnacles formed by intense radiation and atmospheric conditions, pocketed the snowfield we descended. I remembered this slope from 1984 when Sakishita, Bridwell, and I had reached this altitude. It was one of the reasons I gave up. The needlelike ice pillars grabbed at our crampons and stabbed at our legs. Annoying buggers, but at least the slope was safe. In fact, after ten days of wearing a harness and rope when climbing, sleeping, and even relieving ourselves, we removed them to descend the snowfield. An hour later we down-climbed the last of the difficulties. Jeff and I were safely off Tawoche.

There's really no end to a climb like Tawoche. The more emotional the experience, the more indelibly it is etched upon the
mind. Seldom in my twenty-four years of climbing has a mountain
experience moved me to so many emotional ends.

I ask myself repeatedly, "What got us up Tawoche?" Was it
skill? Determination? Experience? Maybe a lot of things. But I
believe our success began and ended with Jeff and me. It is only
when a team becomes one that success has a chance. Jeff and I
joined together in mind and spirit at the right time in our lives.
Kind of like a full eclipse, the combination seldom happens. But
when it does, walls like Tawoche's come tumbling down.

EAST PEAK
MENLUNGTSE
23,560

West Pk

III

II

I

Advance
Base Camp

East Peak,
showing highest
point reached

West Pk

East Pk
23,560

Approach route is
up Menlung valley
hidden behind ridge

MENLUNGTSE

From southeast,
rising high beyond
foreground peaks

11

re·spon·si·bil·i·ty \ ri-spän(t)-sə-ʹbil-ət-ē \
n   An emotional anchor that increasingly weighs
one down the older one gets.
(Roskelley's First Climber's Dictionary, 1991)

MY PERSONAL BATTLE to climb Tawoche took four short years. A single breath of time. I was lucky. Menlungtse, a 7,000-meter peak on the Tibetan border, had intrigued me for eleven years before the door opened and I was able to come to grips with its difficulties. I knew it was there all along, locked behind China's bamboo curtain, beckoning me to return.

Summit Day, Gauri Shankar West Face; May 8, 1979

Dorje froze into a crouched position at my anchors and gripped one of the knots tightly.

"Dorje," I said, "do you know how to belay?"

No answer. His eyes were riveted on the smooth, glassy, fifty-degree ice slope above us. There was no longer any fixed rope. Three hundred feet up, the ice ended abruptly at an overhanging rock band. "The sahib is crazy," he must have thought. "There is no way to the summit from here."

I finished uncoiling the 165-foot climbing rope, tied into one end, knotted the other end, and slipped it into a carabiner at the anchor. To hell with a belay.

"All right," I said, more to myself than to Dorje, who spoke Pidgin English at best. "Don't let the rope catch on something." I pantomimed the rope becoming hung up on a rock, then flipped it as an example of how to see it free. "Understand?" He nodded.

The instant I caught his gaze, Dorje's eyes confirmed everything I already knew. Dorje expected to die. He had the look of a deer I had mortally wounded years before. Fear. When I approached the downed animal, it knew I had inflicted the pain and suffering. But what disturbed me most was the questioning look in the animal's eyes as if the deer were asking, "Why me?"

I had a difficult time killing deer after that incident. True to form, I was reluctant to ask Dorje in his state of fear to continue following me. He was a young and upcoming Sherpa "tiger," but his experience was limited to Everest's easy slopes, and not formidable ice and rock walls such as Gauri Shankar's.

The Roskelley demeanor surfaced. Sure we were in a tight spot—unclimbed face, rockfall, Dorje with no technical experience, a virtual dead end above us—but we could do it. I had to exhibit absolute confidence or Dorje would refuse to continue.

Our expedition team to Gauri Shankar consisted of five Americans and five Nepalis. Under Nepali government regulations, to climb this holiest of holy peaks, the team had to include both nationalities. Under the same regulations, I couldn't summit without a Nepali team member. Dorje was my last hope.

I arced my ice hammer through the air, splintering the concrete-hard ice, and set the pick an inch deep. "I'm off. When I wave like this, attach your jumars and come up."

He seemed to get the picture, so I turned, swung my other axe, planted it, kicked in a crampon, moved up, and climbed quickly, repetitiously, toward the rock band.

I agonized and sweated for Dorje at each of his moves when it was his turn to follow. Even though he was only jumaring—climbing the rope using mechanical ascenders—he accomplished the task with little training or sophistication. Did he trust the rope and jumars? Not likely. Did he trust me? Slim chance. Was this an auspicious day to enter the abode of the Goddess Gauri Shankar? It must have been. Dorje kept coming.

After two 150-foot pitches up the steepening ice face, I reached the overhanging rock that hung out over the valley like the eyebrow of a giant. I was outnumbered ten to one: ten massive tiered overhangs and just me to fight them. But off to my left appeared to be a natural break in the rock, a slightly rising ledge system.

Dorje's face now showed a new emotion, one I've seen on many a partner's face: doubt. He knew this was the end. We would retreat. No one, not even this crazy American, could go over the protruding rock sheltering our position. All around us, except for the icefield below, seemed blank, sometimes bulging at the seams. The Goddess Gauri Shankar, the Hindu goddess of love, would remain virgin.

Soloing the steep ice below without a belay was not difficult for me, no more than for a mountain goat feeding along a cliff. But the obvious difficulty of the rock traverse and the potential disaster to both of us if I should fall forced me to give Dorje a crash course in belaying.

I put the coil of rope around his waist, through the carabiner at the backup anchor pin, and said, "Hold this end. Yes?" He grabbed it so hard I thought he would break his hand.

Dorje stared at the wall above, then shook his head. "No, sahib. This no good. We go down."

I placed a solid hand on his shoulder. "Just follow the rope, Dorje." There is more power in a single touch than in all the words in the English language.

The traverse ledge, a shattered dike of crystalline granite indented into the wall, was riddled with holds and foot placements; I only had to solve their puzzle. A mistake would cost me a short flight and Dorje's commitment. Sucking my rear into the wall, I grasped the lip of the dike jutting out over my head and inched sideways using the front points of my crampons on small ledges below. As usual, the climbing was easier than it looked, but that wouldn't help Dorje's peace of mind.

The crux came at the end as if the script had already been written. After sixty-six pitches on the wall, one of the most difficult climbs I had ever been on, the last move over a rounded bulge proved the worst. I tried stemming to the side. That didn't work. I found an off-width crack and tried jamming that. No good. Finally, I hugged it like I would a fat lady's bottom and shinnied up it. The face was climbed.

Following a traversing pitch is often worse than leading one. Knowing Dorje's skill was limited, I placed pitons every ten feet so that if he took a swing, it would at least be short. A determined Dorje set the teeth of his jumars on the rope and detached himself from the solid anchors. Finally, there was confidence in his demeanor, a cockiness the young Sherpa had displayed throughout the expedition until his arrival the day before at Camp III, a bivouac camp with no visible means of support underneath a partially pitched tent. Once at Camp III, he knew that the climb was beyond his abilities, but somehow he kept trying like the little engine who could. Now he knew we were going to summit.

I stretched the rope out 150 feet along the twenty-degree summit snowfield. Gaping ice crevasses in the summit snowcap revealed that the snowpack was more than a hundred feet deep; while along the East Face, great, wavelike ice cornices formed by the wind leaned into Tibet. The Goddess was intent on protecting her summit. We left the sunless West Face and burst into the warmth of day. It was an easy walk to the top.

I belayed Dorje the last thirty feet. He unwrapped a Nepali flag from his pack and, with his ice axe, carefully poked for hidden breaks in the cornice as he cautiously moved upward then stopped. Silhouetted against the blue sky, he turned with a smile so big it was like another sunrise and raised his flag. Gauri Shankar was ours. We were the first non–deities to reach its 23,405-foot summit.

The Himalayas soared around us: Everest, Cho Oyo, and Makalu to the east; Annapurna, Dhaulagiri, and Shisha Pangma to the west. Lesser peaks within Tibet and Nepal stood as footmen to these 8,000-meter giants. As spectacular a sight as this was, one peak, a long spit across the border into Tibet, kept drawing my eye. A peak so close that if I leaned and stretched, I could almost touch its summit. Menlungtse.

Hidden from view for two months while we climbed the West

Face of Gauri Shankar, Menlungtse chose only now, as we stood on the summit of its sister, to display its beauty as if this view were our just reward. I studied the massive orange granite of its West Face, the intricacies of its icy north side and pinnacled south ridges. But one route grabbed my attention and held it firm. A ridge, long and exposed, straight as the shaft of an arrow. The Southeast Ridge.

"Dorje, I'm going to climb that ridge one day," I avowed, and pointed directly at Menlungtse's Southeast Ridge.

He understood. The sahib wanted that peak. "Yes, sahib," he replied, and there was no doubt in his mind after what he had seen today that Menlungtse would be mine.

Spokane International Airport; March 26, 1990

"John, I know this peak is important to you," Joyce said, "but please be extra careful. We need you back."

Yes. Menlungtse was important to me. It fascinated me more than any other peak in the Himalayas. Menlungtse isn't a spectacular-looking peak like Nanda Devi or five and a half miles high like Everest. It doesn't even have an appealing name like Makalu or Jannu, which conjure images of infamous routes, climbing heroes, and summit struggles.

But like the opening of an Egyptian tomb or the discovery of a gold-filled Spanish galleon, Menlungtse has mystique, an aura of forbidden fruit. It enticed me far more than peaks that have been climbed time and again.

"Don't worry, I'll be back," I said. "I've got to save Tyler."

Joyce viewed Tyler, my registered Appaloosa mule, as meat on the hoof and money better spent on new furniture and clothes for the kids — anything but a useful animal. It was a standing joke between Joyce and me that if I were ever killed, Tyler would end up as tough-as-leather steaks in a Japanese restaurant.

Since 1973, when I first went to the Himalayas, my life had taken a slow but serious turn from "I'm going climbing" to almost, but not quite, that of a "nine to fiver." Back then, at age twenty-four and married only a year, I wasn't concerned about living or dying. That was part of the game. Race car drivers, professional soldiers, risk takers of any kind learn to live with death and its permanency. I was young and life was only as important to me as my next meal.

That philosophy, or perhaps ignorance, changed with the birth of my son, Jess, in 1982 and a continually developing sense of self-destiny. With Jess I acquired another purpose in life beyond climbing. That purpose needed to have his pants changed, to be fed, and to be helped to achieve a positive self-image. And for some unknown reason, that purpose seemed far more important than reaching the summit of the next peak.

I knew having the responsibility for Jess would change my hard-driving, noncaring, get-the-summit-or-else attitude. I still gave my climbs 100 percent, but when it came to decisions concerning life or death, frostbite or fingers, I reined in and turned around.

The 1984 expedition to the North Ridge of Everest was a classic example. I had driven myself hard to reach camp VI at 26,500 feet. My feet were swollen and painful from frost nip and past frostbite damage. I took a Tylenol that night to relieve the pain, then, in a hypoxic daze, forgot and took another. The next morning, as Jim Wickwire, Phil Ershler, and I climbed up the gully for the summit, I began falling asleep. We thought it was high-altitude sickness and descended back to Camp VI. The expedition was finished, unsuccessful, homeward bound, or so the team thought.

Sitting in the tent at Camp VI, I remembered taking the two Tylenols and knew then that the pills had affected my metabolism.

"I'm going back up in the morning," I said, "with or without you."

Wickwire decided for personal reasons not to go for the summit and promptly offered the only bottle of oxygen to Phil, who was dead set against another try. He finally acquiesced. Phil and I would go for the summit the next morning.

As I noted earlier, I reached 28,000 feet and, with no feeling in my hands and feet, made the decision to descend, while Phil, climbing with bottled oxygen, went to the summit. What I didn't mention was that Jess was with me at 28,000 feet. He wasn't there, but his smile, his future, his life were before me. Did I have the right as his father to go beyond acceptable risk? I answered myself and descended.

Joyce and I have said our last good-byes in airports eighteen times. We don't just kiss and think we'll see each other later. That's too matter-of-fact. Too simple. Himalayan climbing has more potential for finality than leaving on a business trip. The risks are magnified by higher atltitude, more personnel, difficult approaches to the peak, extensive icefalls, extreme avalanche danger, and the amount of time spent around these situations.

Our "good-bye" is final. If I survive and come back home, we pick up our lives again from that day forward. Until then, Joyce makes her plans knowing she and the children are on their own.

Invariably someone will say to me, "It's a good thing Joyce knew you were like this when you got married." Well, she didn't. I quit climbing in 1972, the year we were married, and went to work for the U.S. Bureau of Mines. I grew up believing the husband was the breadwinner and never intended the situation to be different. But in January 1973, I was asked to replace a climber who dropped out of the Dhaulagiri Expedition. I went to the Himalayas and have been doing so ever since.

Climbing in the Himalayas is hell on a marriage. Let's face it, life's tough enough without having your partner leave you alone to raise the children, go to work, feed the animals, take care of the house, pay the bills, and so on. Most women will not put up with it and haven't. The divorce rate among Himalayan climbers is staggering. I was fortunate to have married an understanding woman who has been strong enough to carry the load when I leave for up to four months at a time. But it hasn't been easy.

Joyce and I were married nineteen years ago with our eyes wide open. She thought she was in "love" with me and I figured "love" was a much too overused word. We soon found out that "love" meant accepting each other's many faults and playing the game to the end, and we're still doing both. But the faults aren't that big anymore and the game has less rules and pitfalls.

I'm comfortable around Joyce. She makes me feel important for no particular reason, and her energy makes me humble. She creates every emotion within me, good and bad: joy, sadness, impatience, anger, jealousy, and so on. Marriage is an emotional roller coaster that dives into depression a hell of a lot faster than it climbs out. Negatives and positives notwithstanding, I know I couldn't find a better woman, then or now.

Most important, she has given me one of the greatest gifts in life — children. And for that alone I owe her my respect and allegiance for the rest of my life. Those of you who have sweated alongside your wives watching their pain and strength during the delivery of your children know what I'm saying.

We were on our way home from Tawoche in February 1989, relaxing in our hotel room in Bangkok, when Jeff, after talking with his wife, announced, "Janie said you'd better call Joyce. Something's up."

He sounded different. "Yeah? What?" I asked.

"Hey, I don't know," he replied, feigning ignorance. "Maybe your pipes froze like mine. Janie said it's been one of the coldest winters in Colorado history."

The pipes hadn't frozen. In fact, my pipe was working just fine. Joyce was pregnant. And this after she had been told her chances of having another child after two miscarriages were as good as my having two wives. Nil. It's these damn departures and bedroom good-byes that keep fouling up my dedication to the sport.

So the Roskelley good-bye for Menlungtse wasn't quite as "dead" serious at they were ten years before. I knew I would return as I gathered my brood in for one last hug and tear: Joyce, who needed the break again; seven-year-old Jess, who would be lost without me as his primary playmate; and six-month-old Jordan, who would no longer have Daddy as the baby-sitter. The final boarding call blared over the intercom system as I walked to the gate and stared once more at my family before plunging down the jetway to the waiting plane.

"No," I thought, "it's not dying that bothers me. That's part of the game. It's letting my kids down. I brought them into this world and I should be around to set them on the right track."

And I will be.

12

Men·lung·tse \ Men-'lùn-tse(ē) \ *n* An erro-
neous name given to the unclimbed Tibetan peak
Jobo Garu by a foreigner who didn't have the
right. (See Sagarmatha-Everest, Denali-Mount
McKinley.)

(Roskelley's First Climber's Dictionary, 1991)

TEN MONTHS BEFORE our departure for Tibet, the Chinese wired
Jim Wickwire as to the status of our application.

"Menlungtse's ours for the spring of 1990," Wickwire said.
"But we have to approach the peak through Nepal because of
martial law in Lhasa."

Wickwire and I had been scheduled to attempt the peak in
1989, but the Chinese revoked our permit because of an open
rebellion by nationalistic Tibetans in Lhasa. God knows they
should revolt, but not quite so soon after the Chinese relaxed their
rule. It doesn't matter now. The Chinese quickly and ruthlessly
crushed the rebellion, killing a score of rioters. Lhasa and the
surrounding area were put under strict martial law until further
notice. Foreign visitors, including the press, where persona non
grata.

I preferred the alternate route by vehicle through Nepal, across
the Friendship Bridge into Tibet, and along the Chinese-built
road to Tingri. I had taken the seven-day, dusty, tiring Beijing-
Chengdu-Lhasa-Tingri route four times and had no desire to repeat the journey.

Besides, it's expensive. Group travel, such as an expedition or tour, gives the Chinese an excuse to tack on additional costs. American businessmen move over — the Communist Chinese have replaced us as world capitalists. For example, the 1983 American West Ridge of Everest Expedition paid one hundred dollars per person per night in Chengdu because it was a registered "group." One team member's girlfriend, traveling alone through China, stayed in the same hotel in a room similar to ours for twenty dollars per night. The extra eighty dollars we paid was filtered into the Chinese Mountaineering Association coffers as "organizational expenses."

"The trek from Tingri to Menlungtse will be the same," he continued. "Bonington sent me a letter describing the approach and some superb photos of the peak. I'll get a few shots enlarged and off to you by the end of the week."

Our 1990 attempt on Menlungtse would be the third official attempt on the peak. "Official" in that who knows how many "free spirits" have entered Tibet from Nepal illegally via the lower Rong Shar Chu gorge (*chu* means river), sneaked up the Menlung Chu, and made a stab at reaching Menlungtse's summit. Stories are rampant in climbing circles of such antics. In fact, the initial exploration of the peak was done illegally.

In November 1951 two British mountaineers, Eric Shipton and Michael Ward, and a young Sherpa, Sen Tensing, crossed from Nepal over a 20,000-foot snow saddle they later named the Menlung La and descended into a great glacial basin. Centered within the basin was a magnificent double-summit peak isolated within a ring of smaller mountains very similar to that of Nanda Devi's twin summits. In Shipton's words, "On every side its colossal granite walls were pale and smooth as polished marble." He later named the peak Menlungtse. It was clearly beyond 1950s technology and techniques to climb.

Shipton was at a loss as to their location. He knew they were on the central spine of the Himalayas, but where? Standing on a rock pinnacle gazing down the only drainage gorge out of the basin, Shipton realized he was at the headwaters of the Menlung Chu, a river whose mouth had been reached by the first Everest Reconnaissance Expedition in 1921. The magnificent peak to their south was Gauri Shankar. They were in Tibet illegally.

Their only recourse was clear: retrace their steps over the Menlung La. If they didn't, there was a good chance of capture and the possibility of being accused as spies by the Chinese. But great explorers are born with a heart for madness, a flippant attitude toward regulations. To explore is to chance.

Every mountaineer has a little exploration in him. On the retreat from Gauri Shankar in 1979, Kim Schmitz and I broke away from the main expedition for a day and skirted Gauri Shankar's West Ridge by running up the Rong Shar Chu trail. Unlike Shipton, our goal was to intentionally enter Tibet illegally and hassle the Chinese border guards if there were any. All this just to say, "I was in Tibet." To our surprise, the border was unmanned. Only a cement marker with red Chinese writing inscribed on its four sides indicated we had fulfilled our goal.

Shipton wrote, "Even in the old days, to be caught in Tibet without a special permit was a serious matter; now, with the country in control of the Chinese, there was no knowing what our fate might be."

The party was joined by Bill Murray, Tom Bourdillon, and their Sherpas, who had followed over the Menlung La several days later. Shipton decided to attempt an escape down the Menlung Chu and the Rong Shar Chu to Nepal despite the risk of discovery at the Chuwar Monastery at the rivers' confluence, or at a Tibetan fort, or dzong, on the Rong Shar Chu that was manned by fierce soldiers.

The expedition surprised two yak herders walking up the Menlung Chu and, some time later, women from the monastery gathering fuel. The women seemed unconcerned and went about their chores. Late that night the expedition sneaked through the village and past the fort without being detected despite the inevitable barking that precedes visitors into every Tibetan village. But they left bootprints in the trail below the dzong.

Early the next morning as they hiked along the river's shore, sure that Nepal and safety were within reach, the trail behind them exploded with noise.

"Suddenly there was an uproar behind us and we turned to see seven Tibetans charging down upon us, brandishing swords and uttering wild cries, their pigtails flying out behind them," Shipton later wrote. "It was a bizarre sight, but no less terrifying for that. I was relieved to see that the Sherpas stood their ground with apparent nonchalance, which suggested that they, at least, did not expect to be cut to pieces."

The women above the monastery had reported them to the dzongpen, the local military ruler, who didn't believe the story until bootprints were found on the trail. He dispatched his soldiers immediately to apprehend and return with the foreigners. Rather than be hauled back to the dzongpen, then perhaps to the Chinese in Tingri, the Sherpas bartered with the soldiers for their freedom. Bribery worked. It cost Shipton seven rupees, one rupee for each member of his team, to buy them off. The equivalent of seventy cents. The long fingers of Chinese rule had yet to reach this far into Tibet.

Officially, Menlungtse had been attempted twice. Both attempts were led by the indomitable Briton Chris Bonington, who has racked up more first ascents in the Himalayas than have Hindu and Buddhist deities. Certainly more than mortals such as I have.

The first attempt in the spring of 1987 ended three thousand feet short of the summit. Bonington, along with fellow Briton Jim Fotheringham and four Norwegians, Odd Eliassen, Bjorn Myhrer-Lund, Torgeir Fosse, and Helge Ringdal, attempted the central buttress of the South Face, one of four very difficult and exposed south ridges. Their first attempt almost ended in tragedy at 20,000 feet.

Bonington later wrote of the incident: "Jim and I were digging into the crest of the steep, narrow snow ridge (to bivouac) when I was aware of a high-pitched buzz. Jim collapsed onto his knees. 'I've been struck,' he muttered. It was lightning."

The storm intensified during the night, tearing the Norwegian tent to shreds. They had to descend the next morning in a raging storm from nine rope lengths above their fixed lines. Again, tragedy almost struck. Bonington, perhaps disoriented by the wind and snow, clipped badly into the rappel rope and fell, grabbing the rope at the last second before plunging off the buttress.

On April 16, they made another attempt on the buttress, only to be pushed back to base by another storm. The weather cleared the next morning and they resumed their attack, reaching their original high point on April 22. That afternoon a third storm ravaged Menlungtse, shutting the door on further progress up the buttress and putting an end to the expedition.

Bonington wouldn't be Bonington if he had fled Menlungtse for good. No. There is a good reason why "Onward Christian Bonington" is sung throughout climbers' pubs in Britain. Bonington gets his mountain the same way a bounty hunter gets his man — through perseverance. He reapplied and was granted permission to attempt the peak in the spring of 1988.

Bonington pulled my runner-up all-time-favorite scam for raising money for his second Menlungtse attempt. And, believe me, there have been some brilliant sting operations in mountaineering in the quest for supporting dollars. Medical research, "Put a Woman on Top," "Cowboys on Everest," even climbs funded on "Peace," just to name a few. Marketing people for big companies actually fall for these proposals.

Before explaining Bonington's runner-up, I have to describe my all-time-favorite funding scam. It was the 1986 Post-monsoon American-Canadian-British-Men-and-Women-in-Search-of-Fifty-Year-Old-Dead-British-Climbers Expedition. The British Broadcasting Corporation was actually persuaded to financially support and film the team searching for Britain's Mallory and Irvine who had died on Everest in 1924. God, I wish I'd thought of that one.

They didn't just stop there. These guys were professionals. They added the one thing marketing people can't possibly turn down: women. Three pretty ladies were asked to join the team. ABC's "Spirit of Adventure" program bought the rights to film the first ascent of Everest by an American woman. The expedition failed to reach the summit, but it was properly financed to the point that even the climbers received a salary. Well done, men.

But Bonington is still a summit or two above these other fund-raisers. At least the two missing climbers Mallory and Irvine actually existed. Bonington sold the BBC on filming a search for the yeti in the Menlung Valley. That's right, an entire expedition of writers, cameramen, and climbers poking around every bush and rock searching for a mythical man-ape beast. My hat is off and my head is bowed to Chris Bonington. That took balls.

The 1988 expedition climbers, Britons Bonington and Andy Fanshawe and Americans David Breashears and Steve Shea, made their first attempt on Menlungtse's West Face May 7 through 11. They reached their high point of approximately 22,000 feet, below the massive headwall, on May 10 after climbing some technically difficult hard, green ice. Faced with the headwall, short of rations, and laden with film gear, the team retreated to base to reorganize for another push.

On May 19 Andy Fanshawe and Alan Hinkes, a Briton originally hired to deliver mail and film safely to Kathmandu for the expedition, made the final attempt on the peak. Their climb to the top of Menlungtse's West Summit reads like a nightmare. Avalanches, thunderstorms, difficult climbing, and total fatigue hampered their progress. But finally on May 23 they overcame the last obstacle, a "frighteningly loose over-hanging chimney" at the top of the headwall and reached Menlungtse's lower western subpeak at 10:30 P.M., Beijing time. Menlungtse's main summit was a mile across a snow saddle and too far to go without bivouac gear and provisions. They descended back to their high camp in the dark and to base the following morning.

Menlungtse remained unclimbed. No matter how an expedition slices the pie, a mountain only has one summit. Not two or three. Just one. Any other point reached is a subpeak or false summit regardless if it's later named Nanda Devi East, Guari Shankar South, or Menlungtse West. In the Himalayas, as in all mountain ranges, the summit has been reached when and only when there is nothing above you but sky. I've never had a problem determining where this occurs.

Wickwire and I organized and financed the American Menlungtse Expedition based on the premise that the peak was unclimbed. Rather than follow in Bonington's footsteps, we chose to center our efforts on the Southeast Ridge, the sweeping narrow line I had seen from Gauri Shankar's summit eleven years before. Finally my dream would be fulfilled.

13

team \ 'tēm \ *n*   Two or more units of measure
that, when mixed carefully, lead to success.
(Roskelley's First Climber's Dictionary, 1991)

CLIMBING IN THE Himalayas is the easy part. Fund-raising, sponsor
follow-up, and general preparation are the real work. We began
getting ready for the Menlungtse expedition two years before our
departure for Tibet. In some ways, the expectation of what will
come is far more exciting than reality. Hopes and dreams, even
despair and disappointment, surface month after month as plans
fall into place or prospective sponsors respectfully decline our
entreaties.

Unexpectedly, selecting a team turned into a six-month nightmare. Fifteen years of Himalayan expeditions has taught me that
cohesive teams are winners whether they summit or not. Unfortu-
nately, climbers are basically social misfits who, when given a
choice, would rather be in their own pastures than with the herd.
I've found most people can't get along with their wives, whom
they supposedly chose for life, let alone survive one to three
months with people they hate for major personality quirks like
parting the hair on the wrong side, belching at dinner, licking the
peanut butter spoon, or throwing gum wrappers at the foot of
their tent.

There are several mannerisms in partners I can't tolerate. Snoring is a minor one; "putsing" (the inability to sit still) a major one; a hacking cough, especially in a two-man tent, intolerable. I'll drive a cougher into the snow before being subjected to an annoying, random bark, and yet at high altitude coughs are common.

Body odor can be particularly enriched after two or three months on an expedition. Most climbers wash their hands and faces, sometimes their feet when they can, but if they're camped high without base camp fuel, personal hygiene is difficult. On K2 in 1978 I went sixty-eight days without removing my one-piece long underwear or shorts. I had to pluck the wool and angora fibers out of my skin, which was inflamed with pimples, after peeling my underwear off. I didn't think I stunk, although our porters, Balti tribesmen, moved upwind of me when I first arrived at base.

Then again, there are those who take cleanliness too seriously. Every day Caroline Gunn, our attractive base camp manager during the 1984 North Ridge Everest Expedition, took a "bath" in a side creek so cold it would have frozen the nuts off a seal. It was hard—on us. Then she'd serve dinner in the mess tent and leave a wake of Dial and womanly fragrance that left our eight tongues on the tent floor. That was a tough trip.

In my early expedition years I was as self-righteous as they came. I had a reputation to uphold. "Roskelley's a hothead," or "That guy creates more shit than a grizzly bear at a barbecue." I have my reasons. There are two things that still make my caldron boil. Number one: I'm not going to sit on my thumbs and let a less-experienced "professional" make a decision that's going to kill me or my partners. And number two: I have a personal stake in the outcome of the expedition, as it's time away from my family and my livelihood. Most, if not all, the others on the team climb for other reasons, then return to established jobs. I can't afford to fail because of someone else's lack of commitment.

On Nanda Devi in 1976 I pushed the ascent to success, fighting not only the mountain's many difficulties, but also the reluctance and outright mutiny of some of my teammates. Right or wrong, the expedition succeeded.

On the other hand, in 1981 I pulled out of the American Everest East Face Expedition. As much as I wanted that face and Everest, I realized my teammates were taking excessive chances with avalanches and making what I considered absurd mountain decisions based on emotion rather than fact. At that point, they were on their own. Rather than remain at base and disrupt their attempt, I left.

Wickwire and I were selective at first, almost cocky, about who should be invited. We chuckled to each other over the phone about having the most sought-after permit in Tibet.

"Let's just kind of let the word out we're selecting a team, Jim," I suggested. "We'll take the top two out of the hundreds that apply."

The phone never rang.

"Maybe we'd better loosen up and ask a few guys," Jim said eight months before departure.

I felt like a door-to-door vacuum-cleaner salesman. The more climbers I asked, the more doors were slammed in my face. Jeff Lowe, that lucky devil, was off to the Karakoram to do the first free ascent of Nameless Tower. Mike Kennedy's wife was expecting their first child. Others were expeditioning here or working there. America's alpinists were taking the year off.

Depressed, I realized I was fighting respectability and maturity. "John," I said to myself, "after this trip you're going to have to get a real job like everyone else." I went into a bottomless depression.

Six months before the trip, not one climber even indicated interest. Those we asked couldn't even spell the mountain's name, let alone wanted to climb it. Four months before departure I didn't think there was an alpinist left in America willing to climb.

What I considered an opportunity of a lifetime — an unclimbed 7,000-meter peak, one of the last great virgin summits in the Himalayas — was harder to sell to America's great alpinists than a free pass to the next Everest slide show. Finally we were only three months from departure. Wickwire and I needed a team of four; the two of us were not strong enough to tackle the Southeast Ridge alone.

Sure, I had climbed Tawoche. That put the "go" back in ego. I even led twenty-one of the twenty-seven most technical pitches on the North Face of Kangchenjunga that same spring after joining up with Lou Whittaker's team of young Rainier guides. That was a boost. But still, I'm eroding as fast as an old mountain. To stand up straight in the morning I need two cups of coffee, three aspirin, and a hot shower. Worse, that "eye of the tiger" attitude that drove me for years developed a mental cataract.

I was amazed that Wickwire, who has eight years on me, still had that drive to climb the big ones. If I've noticed my own demise since thirty, what's it like to close in on fifty and still want to go to the Himalayas?

An old friend of mine, Joe Collins, who turned sixty-five this year, once said, "Roskelley, that climbing of yours is like sex; you're never going to lose the desire, just the tools to work with." Hopefully, Wickwire still had his tools.

I can't remember precisely when I first heard of Jim Wickwire, or "Wick" if you're a close friend. But I do know it had something to do with Mount Rainier's Willis Wall. Wickwire's early reputation was built on ballsy alpine ascents of this ugly rock-and-avalanche-strewn face on Rainier's north side.

I do recall Wickwire's first K2 attempt in 1975. Stories circulated wildly about the expedition, which consisted of Wickwire, Lou and Jim Whittaker, Leif Patterson, Galen Rowell, and a host of Northwest hotshots. Here is a classic example of a group that never became a "team." The Northwest Ridge route they attempted was later abandoned for this and other reasons.

Rowell's book *In the Throne Room of the Mountain Gods* painted a dismal expedition and shed light on the main problems. Wickwire, though, emerges unscathed by Rowell's pen. Obviously, Rowell had a great deal of respect for Wickwire's ability and strengths.

There is one photo taken by Rowell that tells me more about Wick than numerous pages of descriptive prose. Wickwire will never be beaten. Slowed up maybe, but not in his lifetime defeated. In the photo he and Lou Whittaker during their retreat to Rawalpindi are seen with Reinhold Messner. Wickwire, all five foot eight inches of him, is burdened under a monstrous load as though he had never heard of porters. Seldom, if ever, does any climber I know carry a respectable load unless on the mountain. Yet Wickwire, obviously exhausted after months of effort, treated his retreat as an exercise to strengthen himself. "Here," I thought, "is a winner."

Prior to the 1978 K2 expedition, and for several years afterward, Wickwire took some outside heat from the climbing community and the press. The focal point was Ol' Man Death: Wick was with four partners killed in the mountains in four years.

In 1984 Wick and I planned to be partners on Everest's North Ridge. "You're not climbing with Wickwire?" a climbing friend of mine exclaimed. "He's a jinx. Everyone who gets near him dies."

His reputation spread as fast as oil on water with the gruesome deaths of Chris Kerrebrock on Mount Denali and Marty Hoey on Everest. Enough so that Morley Safer of "60 Minutes" did a segment on Wick and his karma.

I ignored the innuendos and theories and stuck to the facts. They were accidents. Human error caused by fatigue, stress, and altitude. Only Kerrebrock's death could possibly have been prevented.

"We were traveling too close together," Wickwire told me. "His plunge into the crevasse pulled me right in on top of him."

I climbed with Wickwire on Everest and consider him one of the safest, most experienced mountaineers I have had the privilege of roping up with.

Wickwire and I tested each other's skills and strengths, cautiously at first, then all out during the successful 1978 American K2 Expedition, led by Jim Whittaker. I wouldn't have been invited on that expedition if it hadn't been for Wick. For once, though, my reputation was an asset.

"We want the best on K2 this time, Whittaker," Wick said. "Give Roskelley a try."

Whittaker acquiesced. If Wick wanted Roskelley, so be it. Wickwire could have the devil if he wanted him.

Wick and I became friends right out of Skardu, Pakistan. Not in the States, not in Rawalpindi. I look hard for a bit of cowboy in my partners; a little spot of hell, you might say. I found it in Wick in Skardu. Not a big spot, but enough to know he was one of the guys.

Six of the team, including Wick and I, piled into a beat-up jeep at the guesthouse early on the morning we were to leave Skardu for the roadhead. Whittaker and the other members of the team were nowhere to be seen. Rather than wait and eat Whittaker's jeep dust, as the group had been ordered to do upon our arrival in Skardu, I suggested we depart early.

As the jeep approached the equipment godown in Skardu, we spied Whittaker inspecting some boxes with our Pakistani liaison officer and several Skardu officials. This was our chance to jump ahead.

"Go! Go! Go!" I yelled at the Balti jeep driver.

My exuberance cut loose a Balti A. J. Foyt. Obviously this guy had waited his entire jeep-driving life for this moment. Pedal to the floor, he shot down the dirt road raising a roostertail of dust that all but buried the godown. If I'd heard all the yahooing and hollering from a distance like Whittaker did, I'd have figured the six of us had robbed the expedition booze supply. But it wasn't booze. And it certainly wasn't disrespect. We were just slicing and cutting and releasing the stress that expeditions bring on. "Eat my dust, Whittaker!" I heard from behind me as we sped out of sight and into the dust and heat of the Indus River valley. Funny? Whittaker didn't look amused.

The jeep broke down halfway to Shigar, our destination. I expected Whittaker, all six foot five of him, to roar by in his jeep any minute like Field Marshall Rommel, give us the one-fingered salute, and laugh all the way to Shigar. Our jeep driver was too good a mechanic, though, and Whittaker never caught us.

Wickwire, after the initial fun, had turned deathly quiet. We soon found out why. "I know Whittaker. There's going to be trouble over this," he said.

"Forget it, Jim," I suggested. "Whittaker knows we were just kidding. Besides you're with us and he'd never jump on you."

I was wrong. Wickwire did know Whittaker better than we

did. Whittaker called a team meeting that afternoon that almost ended the expedition. The six of us left a pound of nose flesh on the floor apologizing, but it had little effect on Whittaker. We were on notice.

The incident left a bad taste in my mouth. Everybody's mouths for that matter. But I didn't worry. I'd found out what I wanted to know about Wickwire. He was part cowboy.

The "Wick" in Wickwire came within a stiff breeze of burning too short on K2. He and Lou Reichardt summited together late on September 6, 1978. After Wick snapped a few photos of him, Reichardt started down. Wickwire had waited all his life for this moment and wanted a few more minutes to realize his dream.

"Go ahead," Wick said, "I'll be right with you."

But a few minutes turned into five; five into forty. He started down only to realize it was too late. Darkness overtook him 400 feet from the summit. He had to either bivouac or take the chance of plunging down the South Face in the night.

Perched on a snow ledge at nearly 28,000 feet, Wick crawled into his bivouac sack, burned his Bluet stove until it ran out of fuel, and shivered through the night, wiggling his toes and fingers trying to stay awake and reduce the frostbite he knew was inevitable. To sleep was to chance never seeing another sunrise. As if it sensed its first victim, the wind howled its pleasure and scoured the summit block. But Wick survived.

Rick Ridgeway and I, on a Wickwire body hunt the following morning, met him on the traverse above the upper icefall. At first I thought he was dead, frozen in a standing position against the slope. Then he turned his head. He still looked dead.

"How ya doing?" I said when I reached him.

"We made the summit," Wick replied. "Did Lou get down?"

"Yeah. Can we help you down?"

"No," he said, "I can make it."

I was hesitant to let him descend alone, but without a rope, Ridgeway and I could be of little use to him. We let him pass and continued to the summit. I'll never forget Wick's ghostly apparition robotically climbing toward me that morning with his bulldog-determined gaze.

Even after twelve years, I knew Wick was still part bulldog. Enough to climb Menlungtse, but not with just the two of us.

"I'd rather go to Menlungtse," Jeff Duenwald said between bench-press sets. "The Jannu expedition has collapsed."

Duenwald had been scheduled to attempt the French route on Jannu in northeast Nepal during the same months as Menlungtse, but the effort had fallen apart.

"Great! You're on our team," I replied.

Duenwald was an old climbing partner of mine since Dhaulagiri days. As Wick had insisted on my going to K2, Duenwald had pushed for my acceptance on the 1973 Dhaulagiri Expedition one month before the team left for Nepal. He was the only climber on the team who knew me, even if by reputation alone.

Dhaulagiri tested Duenwald's "Himalayan Fat Theory"—leave the States twenty pounds or more overweight because you're going to lose it on the mountain. I have a photo of Duenwald in the courtyard of the Kathmandu Guest House looking like a Buddha protégé: the fat stage of the fat theory. Jeff didn't make the summit, but I don't think it had anything to do with his theory. He was strong as hell.

Jeff moved off his farm near Davenport, Washington, in the mid-1970s to take a job as an emergency room veterinarian in Spokane. He worked nights and weekends, but during the mornings he worked out with weights and sports and turned into an animal. The "fat theory" is now the "muscle theory."

Duenwald is a mountain climber's mountaineer. Not one who tackles great technical problems like Tawoche or Uli Biaho, but the kind of alpinist who logs miles, ferries loads through bush-choked valleys, and climbs aesthetic routes no one knows exist. His sport is one of adventure, of exploration, of sweat and chance. Duenwald's been at it for thirty years and will be still at it when I'm flat on my ass watching the Seattle Seahawks blow another close one.

I was glad Jeff wanted to go with us. He's a tough character who'll break a knee-deep trail all day just to show that age has no bearing on strength. Jeff's an inch or two shorter than I, but with the same wiry build. When he and I play racquetball or compete in any way, it's never a relaxing game; it's for blood. I've never seen him without his brindle-colored beard. What he doesn't have up top—and I could shave using the shine on his pate—he makes up for on his face.

Besides his years of expedition climbing, Duenwald is a veterinarian. He's the kind of doc I'd want laying me out cold and opening me up if I were a car-hit Lab or a Doberman-chewed cat. He would serve our expedition as both climber and bone-setter.

I could spout off tales of danger and derring-do that Jeff and I have been through on nasty frozen Canadian waterfalls, Alaskan peaks, or Himalayan giants, but as I look back on all our trips, the last one to Liberty Bell in the North Cascades is my favorite. It was late August, clear sky, air so still the earth might have stopped spinning. Jeff and I were after Beckey's North Face route, one of those nebulous lines described in the guidebook as "from the large platform at the N.W. corner of the summit structure." Try finding that. Then Beckey proceeds to zero in on more detail, such as "prominent ledge system" and "prominent couloir." Everything looks prominent standing underneath that face.

"Throw that son of a bitch in the car," I instructed Duenwald. "Guidebooks do nothing but put other climbers' fears in those who read that garbage. We'll find the route ourselves."

And we did. Warm, crystalline granite; cathedral roofs jutting out over our heads; an easy line rising diagonally into the eastern skyline. It was one of the finest days I've had climbing since my early years in Yosemite's Tuolumne Meadows.

Relaxing on the summit with Jeff, I realized we had achieved what mountaineering is all about: good friends exploring a fun line on a beautiful day in the mountains. I'd forgotten this lesson through all my years of new routes and difficult ascents. Mountaineering was again something to look forward to in the years ahead. And despite being eight years my senior, Jeff would be there with me.

"Seems like she was hard as wood," Greg Child, our fourth member, said. He broke off a piece of stale toast, spread it with strawberry jam, and took a bite. "The Japanese wrapped her in a bivy sack and lowered her down the mountain, but she broke up into pieces."

"What pieces?" I asked.

"Er hade," he garbled through a mouth full of toast and egg.

I wasn't sure whether it was Greg's Australian brogue or the food, but I didn't understand.

"Her head," Wickwire clarified.

Bite swallowed, Greg continued. "Toward the bottom, her head fell out of the sack and rolled off to one side and onto a glacier. Turns out this Japanese lad climbed over to it, picked it up, put it under his arm, and began traversing back to the others."

"With the head?!" Wick asked.

"Sure," Greg continued. "This never came out in the press, ya know."

I was sure of that.

"What did they do with her then?" Duenwald asked.

"Anyway, this Japanese fellow got so upset and nervous, he hacked out a little spot in the snow, put her head there, covered it, and left. The body they buried with rock at the bottom."

"Good God, how did you learn this?" I asked.

"I spoke with the little buggers at K2 base camp during our attempt on the West Face," he replied.

The Japanese must have been little. Greg's only five foot eight and built like a willow, except for his Popeye forearms. Sitting with Greg in the morning for breakfast was the same as reading "Accidents in American Mountaineering" for entertainment. At thirty-two, Greg's experience in the Himalayas was loaded. Yet I was uneasy. In nineteen years of climbing in Australia and throughout the world, he'd seen or been part of more accidents than I have in twenty-five years of climbing.

For instance, an English climber had died of cerebral edema with him on Broad Peak several years before. We heard that account on the flight to Tokyo. Greg had taken a serious fall in Australia in his youth and broke his arm. We heard that one from Tokyo to Bangkok. A detailed account of the woman's tragic death on K2 because of hypothermia was our breakfast conversation in

Kathmandu. I started to worry that next year's tale would involve Roskelley's demise on Menlungtse. It would be another emotionless, slightly humorous account of folly and human weaknesses.

Greg's macabre humor is classic down under, *Crocodile Dundee* stuff. He could just as well have been talking about the morning sunrise rather than a rolling head. But it made for an interesting breakfast.

Child is known for his Australian wit and, probably more so, for his risky climbs and escapes. Many of his climbs exhibit what I term "creative risk": if the route isn't dangerous enough, create one that is. I displayed creative risk on one or two routes when I was Greg's age, but not much anymore. I leave that to the Aussies and Japanese who are brilliant at this little-known side of the sport.

"Greg's in Australia climbing rock," Wickwire informed me over the phone, "but his wife, Sally, assured me he would go."

"She must want him out of the house in bad way," I replied. "Isn't he supposed to go to K2 in June with Steve Swenson and Greg Mortimer?"

"Yea, but Sally's not putting up with another four-month trip. Two months on Menlungtse is enough. She said he has to make up his mind, her or K2."

Oh, well, he can't stay married forever. Nobody else does.

Greg has been married to Sally for ten years and is an old hand at convincing her that the next trip will make some money. I've been giving that line to Joyce for almost nineteen years and it's still working, although, I'm beginning to think, for Joyce more than me.

Wickwire outlined our intentions to Greg when he arrived back in the States: "Alpine-style ascent up the Southeast Ridge. Bonington's teams thought it was too corniced, but it's the finest line anywhere in the Himalayas."

"How are we funded?" Greg asked.

"Roskelley's just about got the budget raised through corporate contacts. You won't have to pay a thing."

"Ya got yourself an Aussie."

[Author's note: Greg and three other climbers went to K2 several months after Menlungtse and summited via the North Ridge without bottled oxygen. More importantly, he and Sally are still happily married.]

I would have to have had a lobotomy not to know something of Greg's climbing career. I have an aversion to reading mountaineering magazines that report monthly to those who give a shit on anything climbed and named over twenty feet high. But at the same time, every once in a while, like when Halley's comet comes around, I hear of a route climbed where I take notice. Greg's ascent of Gasherbrum IV with American Tom Hargis and fellow Aussie Tim McCartney-Snape was one. I read his account thoroughly and recognized the boldness of the ascent despite Greg's careful wording, masking risks and dangers so as not to brag. Typical Australian.

His prose didn't throw me. I felt the exhaustion, heard Tom's cough, chilled in their sweat, and saw death on the ridge where Tim slipped. Well done, lads.

Greg deserved Gasherbrum IV. Other summits, such as Broad Peak, Nameless Tower, Lobsang Peak, and K2 avoided his footsteps. Not because of his determination. Good peaks, true "Pigs," deserve more time, more effort than we're willing to give at times in our lives. We are forced to return, over and over, until the mountain takes pity and gives us its summit.

With the addition of Greg, the Menlungtse team had the ability and experience to climb most anything. I saw in Greg the strength and vitality of youth, a rope mate capable of sharing the responsibility of "first on the rope." Wickwire and Duenwald I knew were solid climbers and complemented each other, and Greg's strengths complemented mine. The route's difficulties would have to defeat a well-balanced team. I was completely confident Menlungtse would be ours.

14

no·mad \ˈnō-ˌmad\ *n*   1. A member of a people free of stress and madness created by house
payments, car expenses, charge cards, and civilized life. 2. What I should have been.
(*Roskelley's First Climber's Dictionary*, 1991)

"I AM LI WENLIANG, your English interpreter. You can call me William."

Li Wenliang didn't look old enough to be out of short pants.
He was obviously still a student. How he had managed to capture
a cushy job as a Chinese Mountaineering Association interpreter
after the student uprising in Tiananmen Square is anybody's guess.
I have to admit William didn't look like riot material. With his easy
demeanor, I couldn't imagine him fighting for a place in line, let
alone stopping a tank.

"William it is," I obliged. "This is Dr. Jeff Duenwald and I'm
John Roskelley. Mr. Wickwire and Mr. Child are coming by truck
from the Friendship Bridge, and judging from the condition of our
truck, we've got a bit of a wait on our hands."

"Oh," William sighed, "Mr. Chen and I have been waiting for
you here in Zhangmu for two days."

Having passed through Zhangmu in 1986, I sympathized with
William's impatience to leave. "Well, get ahold of yourself, William, Zhangmu isn't the worst dive we'll be staying in," I replied.

Granted our expedition was a day late, but to have traveled

halfway around the world, relying on telegram time schedules and escaping through Nepal, with only a day's loss was something of a miracle. Wickwire had hired a trekking agency in Kathmandu to eliminate unnecessary problems, but still it had taken us half a day to extricate our previously shipped equipment from the customs godown and two days to purchase food and base-camp equipment. William didn't know how lucky he was to see us so soon. One look at the bus we had used as transport from Kathmandu to Kodari and he would have been impressed we were even there.

Our trekking agency in Kathmandu hired what seemed like a pre-World War II, thirty-foot Tata bus to transport us and our gear to the border. Tata is to trucking and transport in Asia what GMC is in America, except bigger. I suppose there are new Tata trucks out there on some Asian road, but I'll be damned if I've ever seen one.

Trucking and transport is the largest single industry in Asia. What's more important, each truck or bus supports at least three people: a driver, a mechanic, and a young boy, a trainee, who performs the grunt work such as pumping gas, checking tires, and washing windows. He also sleeps with the vehicle. Asians work their way up through each job from youth. Transport positions pay well in Nepal, and those involved stick with it.

I've been impressed with the professionalism, ability, and camaraderie among transport people in Nepal. Drivers can jockey a vehicle through the gleam of a raindrop and sometimes have to on the narrow, winding mountain roads. To the drivers' credit, I've never been involved in an accident in Nepal during thousands of miles of travel. India and Pakistan, yes, but not Nepal.

As good as the drivers are, the mechanics must be better. Training is on the job. When an ancient Tata truck or bus mangles a transmission, eats a differential, or blows a tire, the mechanic takes it apart alongside the road and fixes it on the spot, even if it takes days. Parts are built from scrap iron, wire, anything available. Eventually the vehicle moves. It has to — I've never seen a tow truck in Nepal.

Much to my surprise, our Tata bus survived the difficult trip through Nepal's northern foothills, and we arrived a few minutes past 6 P.M. in the Nepalese border town of Kodari. Customs had closed at five o'clock sharp. Zhangmu, one of the few Tibetan towns with electric lights, sparkled four miles up the gorge and three thousand five hundred feet higher, so close I could almost smell the oily wok cooking and taste a Tsing Tao beer. But we had no choice but to spend the night in Kodari in a smoke-filled, crowded guesthouse awakened on the half hour by tubercularlike coughs and crying children. And William thought he'd had it bad.

A quick glance at William's soft, white hands told me that a pen was the heaviest tool he had ever used. "Ever been in Tibet before, William?" I asked. "Or even camped outdoors?"

"No, this is my first time."

Jeff and I exchanged "I knew it" glances. The Chinese are tough, though, and there was no doubt in my mind William would make it to base camp. He might not stay, but he would die trying to get there.

William wasn't one of the thin, long-fingered Chinese I was so familiar with. In fact, for a Chinese, he was large. Not fat exactly, but soft like the Pillsbury doughboy. I liked him immediately, which is unusual for me. Many of the Chinese I have dealt with in the past have been overbearing. William was fresh at the job. He had no idea what he had gotten himself into. That would soon change.

Out of the customs building strode a muscular, block-shaped Chinese with a 1950s flattop haircut, squinting from the cigarette smoke drifting into his eyes. One look at Mr. Chen Jianjun, our liaison officer, or L.O., and I knew why our American forces had been stalemated in Korea. This guy could make first-string defensive linebacker on any number of NFL teams. Despite his sumo-wrestler build, Mr. Chen's movements were economical and fluid as if it cost him yuan, the Chinese currency, to step too far or reach out unnecessarily.

"Aaahh, Mr. Chen," William said. "They have arrived."

We shook hands all around, then William and Mr. Chen conversed in Mandarin. I had the feeling our late arrival had put us on the wrong side of that flattop. William confirmed my suspicion. "Mr. Chen says you are late."

"Tell Mr. Chen I'm not getting paid enough for this shit. Have him take it up with Mr. Wickwire."

"I don't understand 'shit,' " he said.

"It's American for anything that's a problem, like that," I answered, pointing at a pile of cow dung on the road.

"Oh, I see." The puzzled look was quickly replaced with a smile. "Yes, yes. I know what you mean. Good word, 'shit.' "

The truck ferrying our gear the four miles from the Friendship Bridge on the border to Chinese customs at Zhangmu broke down incessantly. It took hours for Wickwire, Child, and our Sherpas to reach customs and our impatient hosts. They weren't alone. In addition to our team and gear, the truck was carrying more than a dozen Nepalis and Tibetans who had hopped aboard with heavy loads. That didn't help the sputtering diesel lorry creep up the steep, rutted road.

Parked at customs were the team's vehicles, a two-ton lorry and a Toyota Land Cruiser hired to transport us through Tibet.

"William, ask Mr. Chen if he can send the Chinese vehicles to get Mr. Wickwire," I said. "It would save a lot of time."

"They cannot go beyond here," he replied. "They do not have the proper documents."

You don't bend regulations in China's Tibet. Either you have permission or you don't. Marco Polo ignored them; Sir Francis Younghusband used military might in 1904 when he took Lhasa; we relied on American dollars.

We made another round of introductions when Wickwire, Child, and the Sherpas arrived sitting atop our loads in the two-ton lorry that was belching black diesel smoke and coughing like a three-pack-a-day Camel smoker and just as close to death. Mr. Chen asked the inevitable "late" question, then had us fill out forms in quadruplicate to explain ourselves: forms for the gear, forms for money, forms for the two Sherpas, and forms for anything that recorded, clicked, or talked back.

The Chinese insist on a completed expense budget and written protocol detailing the trip six months prior to arrival in Tibet or

China. Expenses for vehicles, food, L.O., translator, hotels, yaks, and yak drivers, among others, had to be precisely calculated and paid for in American dollars before our arrival in Tibet. The L.O. was then responsible for paying all bills incurred by the expedition with the estimated funds. No matter how careful the planning, though, unexpected costs that are not mentioned in the protocol crop up like weeds. These expenses are a problem and must be dealt with and agreed upon by the L.O. and expedition leader before purchase.

For instance, after our four-mile walk from the Friendship Bridge, Duenwald and I requested a bottle of Tsing Tao beer while we waited for the expedition to arrive. Minutes of discussion in Mandarin between the Chinese ensued, then William asked, "How is this to be paid?"

"Tell Mr. Chen to put it on the bill," I said. "For God sakes, William, you've got twenty-eight thousand dollars of ours. Surely we can afford a beer?"

We got the beer, but it took Wickwire and Mr. Chen a half hour to work out the billing. The beer wasn't worth it.

Zhangmu teems with a melting pot of occupying Han Chinese, nomadic Tibetans, and highland Nepalis who exist precariously thousands of feet above the Bhoti Kosi gorge. The one-lane gravel-and-mud road, built by the Chinese People's Liberation Army in 1958, is an engineering nightmare that twists, tunnels, and winds its way from Kodari to Zhangmu to Nyalam twenty miles under sheer cliffs and across landslide-prone slopes. Rock-slides, washouts, and even complete eliminations of sections are common throughout the year and expected during the monsoon.

We spent the night in Zhangmu's "modern" three-year-old Chinese-built hotel. What we take for granted at the worst fifteen-dollar-a-night motel in the sleaziest part of San Francisco are luxuries in a Tibetan hotel. Toilets don't flush, bathtubs have no water, wiring is exposed and threadbare, and lights seldom work. Don't even think about telephones or TVs.

Meals favor the scientific. Every bite is an experiment, although a tasty one. The Chinese eat five to seven courses at each meal, including several boiled or wok-cooked vegetables, such as bamboo shoots, cabbage, or potato; mixed meat-and-vegetable dishes using yak, seafood, or fowl (there's no way of telling which); a bowl of rice; thick, steamed rolls; watery soup (or leftover vegetables); and tea or coffee.

"What's this?" I asked, holding aloft a piece of meat resembling a roadkill.

"Why, it's a chicken head, I think," Child replied. "There's the beak, even the cock's comb."

"If it's recognizable, it's from the outside of the animal," Duenwald added in his authoritative veterinarian voice. "If it's not, don't eat it."

It was good advice. The food was tasty, no question about that. I just never could figure out what it was I was eating.

Zhangmu is a blend of Chinese steel and concrete box-shaped buildings, Tibetan corrugated shacks, and Nepali bamboo hovels, all of which cling like parasites to the muddy, single-lane road slicing back and forth up the steepening gorge. To me, the town is in a struggle between ancient and modern cultures. And there's no winner.

Zhangmu is a border town heavily populated by transient people and, as such, lacks the identity that village tradition provides. It is a blend, a gray sky of cultures, that shouldn't be there—perched at the butt end of the gorge, sitting atop a slope ready to slide.

The Menlungtse Expedition—four Americans, two Sherpas, two Chinese, and two Tibetan drivers—drove through Zhangmu late the next morning. Seven of us crowded into the Land Cruiser with our day packs and camera gear, while Mr. Chen, burdened by a habit he knew was unacceptable to us, chain-smoked in the truck with the driver and our Sherpa cookboy.

"I wonder if we can get the backseats lowered to make more room," I asked.

"I'm sure we could," Child replied, "if we filled out another form."

Street vendors and side shops were open and displayed everything from Chinese coats and thermoses to yak meat and rice. The merchants' customers were nomadic Tibetans, low-land Nepalis, and curious Chinese. Young children barely old enough to walk played in the filth and sewage along the road. Slinking in deep doorways and narrow side alleys, emaciated curs, some with sarcoptic mange eating the flesh from their bony bodies, sought meager scraps and shelter from rock-throwing Tibetans. Zhangmu isn't the last place on earth I would want to live, but it's damn close. Twenty miles up the awesome Bhote Kosi gorge is Nyalam. I would rather live in hell than Nyalam.

To acclimatize properly and prevent our coming down with a high-altitude disease, we chose to spend an extra night in Nyalam at 12,300 feet below the edge of the Tibetan Plateau. Our Chinese hosts were disappointed in our decision. The protocol we had signed did not call for an overnight stay in that village. Again, Wickwire spent hours negotiating the finances to make the change.

Whereas Zhangmu has immense waterfalls, bamboo forests, langur monkeys, and highland rain, Nyalam, less than fifteen miles up the gorge but on the crest of the Himalayan chain, resembles an atomic-bomb test site, especially in late March. Only low-cut thorny brush and winter-shriveled bunch grass survive the steady bone-chilling wind. Not a tree breaks the mountainous horizon. Even the adobe-walled, whitewashed buildings with corrugated roofs that line the mud highway remind me of photos of ground zero prior to the first test blast in Nevada in 1944.

But there are similarities between Zhangmu and Nyalam. Garbage is moved only as far away as one can throw or drop it. It's everywhere and consists of crawler tracks, truck bodies, fifty-five-gallon drums, cardboard, tires, paper, glass, and anything else that has no use or can no longer be repaired. Tibet doesn't have a landfill. It *is* a landfill.

As much as the garbage assaults the vision, it is nothing compared with the human waste that burns the nose. Feces piles litter the ground around every building and along walls. The single outhouse across the road from the truckers' guesthouse where we spent the night was flushed by the creek running through town and into the gorge. But with the many dogs lying in wait for dinner, seldom did any of it reach the river. In fact, the Tibetan mongrels that prowl every village are in actuality roving sewage-treatment plants.

Nyalam is a raven's idea of a resort town. The inhabitants are mostly threadbare Tibetan road-maintenance people working for the Chinese. They live in squalor along the road in constant threat of being hit by one of the thundering transport trucks driven by road jockeys desperate to reach the night life of Zhangmu before dark. Wailing Chinese radio music drifts through the wind, highlighted at intervals by the howl and cry of rock- or truck-hit dogs, a sound as common as a car horn is in downtown New York.

Hygiene is an alien concept in a Tibetan village. It is easy to pick up a stomach illness despite a rigorous prevention program. I take all the precautions. I drink bottled or treated water, eat only canned or cooked foods, and stay away from enclosed public buildings. Despite all this, I invariably get something over the course of a trip. Throughout my years of Himalayan mountaineering, I've had eight cases of giardiasis and one case each of whipworm, bacillary dysentery, amoebic dysentery, spinal meningitis, malaria, and an assortment of gut busters physicians can't even diagnose. So it was no surprise when Child announced his insides were about to become outsides. He fell victim to Buddha's revenge, which revenge nobody knew.

As if the victim will cure the vomiting and stomach cramps by detective work, hours are spent trying to remember what was eaten that could have created such gastrointestinal havoc.

"I ate what you guys did except the milk in my coffee," Greg said.

"That's always pasteurized," Duenwald explained.

"Oh? Well, maybe it was the Spam. It had a funny flavor."

"It was canned," I said.

"Oh."

The stomach has a mind of its own when it wants to get rid of lunch. Invariably it's at bedtime, just after you zip up your sleeping bag and feel your body heat warm the inside. About then, you get a gaseous roll in your lower intestines, then stomach acid rises into your throat. Quickly, you gulp and swallow, but you know what's coming up, and soon.

"Oh, God," I heard Child say, then the pull tab on his sleeping bag ripped quickly along four hundred nylon teeth. I watched Child's silhouetted form scramble for the doorway, dash down the deck, and disappear.

Wickwire's headlamp went on. "Did he make it?" he asked.

We listened. Greg had made it to the far end of the guesthouse balcony before heave and wretch joined in tune, quickly followed by the distinct splash of thick fluid hitting the frozen ground ten feet below. Growling, whimpering, and an occasional cry of pain drifted up to our ears from the dogs below feeding voraciously on Greg's "cookies."

"Barely," I whispered.

Nyalam is the gateway to Tibet's high plateau. Picture yourself on the moon, but with a fine, flourlike airborne dust that penetrates vehicles, cameras, even sinuses. The skin, flesh, and organs of this land have been eaten away by centuries of wind. Only its rock skeleton is exposed and visible. Ribs of sedimentary rock colored in the hues of a Navajo blanket lie tilted, layered, and abandoned to the elements.

Tibet has a beauty all its own. It isn't found in a single rock or within a village or even along a meandering creek, no more than a single brush stroke in a Renoir captures the mood of the painting. No. Tibet's beauty, its inner soul, is in the depth and breadth of a distant horizon, the magnificence of time and space, of peaks and valleys and plains that never seem to end. When I look out upon Tibet's endless views, I dream of riding a horse into the distant hills forever and never coming back.

Tingri

In the decades since the Chinese Cultural Revolution ravaged the country, Tibet has changed very little. There's an occasional tractor belonging to a particularly wealthy commune, even an hour or two of electric lights in the larger towns like Lhasa. But in general, the land has stayed the same and the people and their lifestyle have not changed. They still dress in black wool homespun; wear yak-leather-soled boots; eat tsampa; drink rancid butter and salt tea; and rely on the yak for their food, clothing, shelter, fuel, and transport.

The land has won. Not the village Tibetans, who perish soon enough from dysentery and other illnesses, or the Chinese, who have ruled precariously on and off for centuries, but the land and its challenges to life under such extreme conditions. Only the no-mad, who moves with time, is in harmony with the land in Tibet.

We entered Tingri late in the afternoon after traveling one hundred miles from Nyalam, over the 17,000-foot Sepo La and through the Phung Chu basin in less than four hours. I'm sure our Land Cruiser used to be as tight as Lycra undies, but after cruising forty-six thousand miles at highway speeds on gravelly, wash-boarded Tibetan roads, there was more dust inside our vehicle than out.

Dust is the traveler's curse in Tibet. I relied on a wet bandito scarf over my nose and mouth to breathe, while the others did everything from holding their noses to Wickwire's donning a pro-fessional, rubber breathing apparatus. Nothing helped the eyes.

Tingri is hidden on the east side of a three-hundred-foot-high rock dome. It gets the warmth of the morning sun but is to the lee side of the everpresent wind. On the cold, windy plateau of Tibet almost all villagers are situated away from the wind. Nomads and travelers follow a similar procedure in setting up temporary camps. In Tibet it is the wind that kills.

Tingri was once a thriving trade village with a magnificent dzong. But now it is poor and populated by no more than five hundred extended families. Yak caravans that once crossed the 19,000-foot Nangpa La into Nepal with salt, butter, and tsampa to trade for wood, potatoes, and Indian-made goods no longer make the six-day trip to Namche Bazaar. The seasonal pass is now used only occasionally for Sherpas and Tibetans visiting relatives across the border.

I've traveled thousands of miles through Tibet, explored miles of country, photographed its monasteries, and spoken with its people, young and old, through interpreters. I cannot remember a single Tibetan I didn't like, or laugh with, or consider a friend. But tragically, I feel an overwhelming despair for the land and its people when I realize to what extent the Chinese Red Guard and their Tibetan sympathizers went in an effort to destroy Buddhism and, in many respects, Tibetan culture.

Kim Momb and I, while exploring the "inaccessible" alleys and streets of Lhasa in 1983, stumbled onto an old monastery not far from the Potola Palace and in the center of the Tibetan quarter. The Red Guard had done its work. Brightly colored wall frescoes, lifesize clay Buddhas, parts of books, anything not of value, were strewn about, burned, or destroyed. Along an interior wall, human violence was evident. Bulletholes pitted the clay veneer over adobe bricks at chest level. Unmistakably, reddish rust auereoles of dried, splattered blood surrounded the holes. This monastery hadn't quite made the Chinese govenor's clean-up campaign—yet.

The dzong in Tingri, once a towering walled fortress high above the village, was falling into ruin from Nepali invasions as far back as the eighteenth century. But dynamite and howitzers completed its destruction during the 1950s' and 1960s' People's Liberation Army campaign. It is only one of thousands that lined the main trade routes, now leveled to the ground as though their destruction would translate into the genocide of Tibet's people.

It didn't work. The Dalai Lama and Buddhism are too important to a people that has nothing except its belief in its gods. The Chinese destroyed the monasteries and the physical remnants of a culture, but not the Tibetans. Thirty years later the Tibetans are as strong in their beliefs as ever, and it's the Chinese who have changed.

Our accommodations for two nights in Tingri were in a former military installation renamed the Mount Everest Hotel. It hadn't taken long for Tibet to reclaim itself even within the compound. The ten-foot-high walls surrounding the barracks were mostly intact, but the iron gates at the entrance were either tilted

on their hinges or on the ground. I knew the iron gates would turn
to dust before they would again provide a semblance of security.

There were five one-hundred-foot-long, twenty-foot-wide
buildings in various state of disrepair against the back of the compound. We were given rooms in the one nearest the gate. Each
room had three steel cots with thin mattresses and typical heavy,
thick quilts for bedding. I used my sleeping bag. Lice and other
vermin love Tibetan guesthouses and especially quilts.

Hot water was provided in thermoses for washing and tea.
A young Tibetan girl dressed in Chinese blues, her long braids
wrapped around her head, kept the thermos full and hot. The floor
was cement. Cold penetrated right to the soles of my feet. In the
center of our ten-by-eighteen-foot room hung a single light bulb
that flickered annoyingly with power surges from the large,
gasoline-powered generator. I pitied the Chinese soldiers who had
lived there. The Tibetans lived in better homes.

Duenwald and I grabbed our cameras early the next morning
and walked toward the adjacent village. The contingent of army
personnel that had once occupied Tingri must have totaled hundreds. In the center of the compound were the remains of a dairy-
barn-sized greenhouse for raising vegetables. In fact the Chinese
had gone to great lengths to use solar power, not only for growing
food, but also for heating water. Lying about the yard were white,
concave solar heaters similar to satellite dishes. Solar power helped
reduce gasoline consumption, a costly commodity in Tibet that
was transported from long distances.

There must have been a battalion of dogs in Tingri to handle
the compound's sixteen-slit latrine. What they didn't eat, herds of
swine that populated the village would. Final garbage disposal,
usually that of dead and dying life, was left to the Himalayan
gorak, an over-sized crow that can sense a dead breakfast on
Mount Everest twenty miles to the southeast and be back in Tingri
for lunch. This trio is perhaps the most efficient waste-disposal
unit in the world.

If I were in charge of locating Chinese army installations via
satellite for the CIA, I would search for basketball courts. That's
right — the Chinese army may be able to hide tanks, missiles, even

troops, but not China's national pastime. Throughout Tibet, in the most remote villages where Chinese soldiers are stationed, are clay courts and dilapidated hoops, some with rotting netting, most without. But the hoops and courts are always there. At the end of our compound were the remains of the troop's movable unit, hoop up and backboard in the dirt as if Darryl Dawkins had slam-dunked a stick of dynamite. With it lay Tingri's vestige of Chinese occupation. Once again, Tingri had returned to the Tibetans.

The village is centuries-old Tibetan. It is a labyrinth of narrow alleys channeled between eight-foot-high, whitewashed adobe walls that surround each extended family home. Within four of these walls, each topped with cut juniper for fuel, is the family dwelling, a two-story adobe-and-mud home. On the other side of the walls live neighbors, but there is no entrance to a family compound except from the alleys. Tibetans know that strong walls make good neighbors. And vicious dogs make honest ones: Inside the compound, usually on a stout, rusty chain, is at least one large mongrel made mean by rock-throwing children and family members. The lower floor houses domestic animals such as chickens, cows, and horses, while the second floor is the living quarters. Each home has an accessible flat roof used not only for sun-drying foodstuffs, but also as a private sundeck for the women. A sturdy wooden door with a medieval-looking lock secures family possessions from wandering nomads, village thieves, and, perhaps, curious trekkers.

I took a wrong turn while following the maze of alleys and was pleasantly but firmly warned by an old lady with a shake of her finger not to go any further. The same woman pointed me in the right direction. Standing outside the walls, I sensed security for those within. From wind, cold, dust, even each other.

One Tibetan in Tingri had a good sense of humor or a not-so-unique sense of marketing: Outside the walls of the village and along the dirt road leading toward Everest and the Nangpa La was a tiny adobe shop that sold Tibetan foodstuffs, buttons, cloth, soap, and Chinese odds and ends. Above the door a sign read "Last Shop before Everest." There was no doubt in my mind it was.

15

yak \ ˈyak \ *n* A Tibetan way of life on the hoof.

(Roskelley's First Climber's Dictionary, 1991)

BREAKFAST ON THE morning we left Tingri removed any thought of satisfying my hunger. I picked away at the deep-fat-fried peanuts, but left the cold cabbage slices and rice gruel for the goraks. The gruel, a liquidy substance with a small portion of rice, was the consistency of seawater. "Even Ivan Denisovich," I thought, "would leave this for the Gulag's dogs."

Tibet's expanse spread beyond Tingri and toward our goal, the Phusi La. Everest and Cho Oyo were capped with heavy cloud, but like a cheap dance-hall whore, Cho Oyo kept showing us glimpses of a sunlit ridge that tantalized our climbing hormones. Our little Toyota raced across the empty plains along a ghostly track, tossing us to and fro, up into the roof and down onto the seat. It was urged impatiently to greater speed by our driver, who wanted to be rid of us and off to Lhasa, the sooner the better.

Small, whitewashed Tibetan villages hugged gully washes and small canyons far in the distance against mountains of scree. Sharp, reptilian, scalelike sedimentary outcrops topped each hill, and from a distance they appeared as roundbodied stegosauruses lying in wait to devour yak herder and yak.

Two Himalayan bharal, or blue sheep, small, delicate animals, scampered off to the side of our vehicle looking similar to the fat Tibetan hares that dashed through the scrub brush and rock ahead of us. A large hawk left its adobe wall perch, set its wings, and waited for our driver to flush another meal.

Our tan Toyota, bald tires, rattles, and all, climbed the pass toward the Nangpa La, the old trade route leading to Namche Bazaar and Nepal. Locked in four-wheel drive, it negotiated two- and three-foot-high snowdrifts easily. Larger drifts took a battering ram approach to break through or serious off-road pathfinding through rocky terrain to avoid.

The Sherpas, Ang Nima and Chering, acclimatized to Namche's 11,000-foot elevation, dug the vehicles out of any drifts that trapped them. Finally our drivers joined in open rebellion at our insistence upon continuing, sat down, and smoked another cigarette, one in a continuous cycle of endless smoke.

"We must camp here," Mr. Chen advised.

"No," Jim replied firmly. "They can make it. Have them walk down and look."

Drivers don't walk anywhere, but with persistence, we got both of them to do so. Their answer was the same: the drifts were too deep.

Behind us was a large international expedition intent on climbing Cho Oyo. They had stayed in Tingri at the same compound and had indicated that their drivers were eager to please. Sure enough, the driver of their lead vehicle skirted around us, sped up, and drove through the frame-deep, one-hundred-yard-long drift easily. Their heavily laden trucks followed suit.

Embarrassed at having lost face, our drivers continued to sit and smoke, complaining about "Not enough gas" and "Too rough on vehicles." But eventually, after much "face-saving," our Land Cruiser's driver rose, slowly stretched, ambled to his vehicle, then drove the gauntlet of easy, now rutted, drifts.

A mile farther, after skirting several more snowdrifts, we climbing over a morainal ridge and dropped into a snow-packed creekbed. It was impossible to negotiate. The expedition would now continue via the only reliable system of transportation known to man—on foot.

The Cho Oyo team had sent ahead an advance party to set up a communications camp. They did so along the creek. With the arrival of the climbers and the rest of the expedition, the camp became a small city of barrels, boxes, and tents. They even pitched an "outhouse" tent.

Our expedition was one-tenth the size of theirs. We unloaded our truck in ten minutes, thanked our drivers for their "cooperation," and began setting up our own camp on the flats above the creek. We were organized; within an hour of arrival, three sleeping tents and a cook tent were pitched and Ang Nima, with Chering in tow carrying cups and cookies, served our first hot Sherpa tea.

Toward nightfall, herds of yaks and naks, the female yak, and their Tibetan owners arrived as scheduled by the Chinese. They were splendid, large beasts that were well behaved and would come like dogs when called for their share of tsampa. Most of them were jet black, some were a deep gray, and a few were brown or spotted black and white. They were decorated with intricately patterned, handwoven collars that each held a bronze or brass bell. The patterns indicated the yak's owner. Several of the lead animals wore red-dyed, yak-hair ear tags and headpieces similar to toupees. Having owned horses, I knew by looking at these yaks that they were well taken care of and were the pride and joy of their owners. For that, I had great respect for the herders.

Yaks are the lifeblood of a Tibetan. Naks' milk, richer in fat than cows' milk, gives a Tibetan butter for his tea and cheese for the trail. The yak's meat is dried and smoked, and the animal's blood is used in sausage. The Tibetan uses the long, tough wool of the yak for carpets, ropes, and clothes, its tail for a broom or fly whisk. Yak dung is used for fuel. A big yak supplies all this to its owner and can also transport up to 250 pounds of cargo long distances if necessary. Our yaks would be required to carry only 130 pounds each for a very short distance.

Yaks are high-mountain cattle. They live and function best above 11,500 feet. A more versatile animal for villages located

near Nepal at lower elevations is the zopkio, a cross between
yak and cattle. Zopkios are male and are infertile like mules.
Zhums are female crossbreeds and are bred with the yak. I noticed
most Tibetans raise some of each, depending on their needs and
lifestyles.

An overnight snowstorm left an inch of powder by morning.
At 15,500 feet, the temperature was a chilly fifteen degrees Fahren-
heit. The yaks were happy. We weren't.

"I believe last night we were at the bottom end of the Volcano's temperature range," Jim said. "I damn near froze to death."

The Volcano, a narrow-cut, synthetic-filled sleeping bag
given to us by one of our sponsors, was not quite warm enough for
fifteen degrees. The bag had become a source of humor during the
trip because of a peculiar design quirk. Near the neck of the bag
were two large, square baffles that were supposed to go around the
neck but didn't. They did flop about the face. They would have
made superb breast warmers for shapely women. The bag became
known by us simply as the Volcana, the feminine gender of the
Volcano.

Tibetans move when the urge strikes them, usually late in the
day. Ours were in no hurry. It was noon before the herders began
loading our gear onto the beasts and breaking down their tent,
large canvas sheets the color of coal and ash pitched with two to
four poles like an extended oval pup tent. Their tent was floorless
except for their sheepskin coats and blankets. It was ventilated by
an adjustable flap opening at the peak and along the bottom edge.
The tent's edge was pulled onto the ground and heavy bundles of
grass hay and rocks were used to hold it in place. The same yak-
hair ropes used to tie loads to the animals were fastened to the
sides of the tent and to the ground as guy lines. Once inside, the
Tibetans started a yak manure fire to cook their rice and tsampa
and boil water for tea. Our Tibetan herdsmen were expert campers
and would often have their tent pitched and fire started before we
could find our tents among the loads.

Two hours after leaving camp, Jim and I arrived at our next

one at the foot of the terminal moraine from the large glacier descending the Nangpa La. I get bored to death in Nepal during treks because the porters are so slow and cover such short distances. But Tibetans are worse. Seldom did we have to walk more than three hours to reach the next camp. The herders would take six hours or longer to cover the same distance after breaking camp at close to noon.

That night I learned one camping tip to be taken seriously in Tibet: camp as far upwind of the yak herders as possible. The rancid, acrid aroma given off by a yak-dung fire permeates everything and is nauseous to the uninitiated. Despite the cold and problems of finding another campsite on the rocky moraine in the dark, Jim and I moved.

The Phusl La

I didn't have an exceptional night. We retired early, and by 1 A.M. I was awake entertaining a recurrent but mild altitude-related headache. By morning my head hurt, I was puffy around the eyes, and my hands and feet were obviously swollen. All the symptoms of retaining fluid and the makings of cerebral or pulmonary edema. It didn't matter which; one was as bad as the other.

I tried eking out a spark of sympathy from Wickwire, but his back was out and he was barely moving. None there. I went to Jeff and Greg with my problems. Nothing doing there either.

"Take it elsewhere, Roskelley," Greg said. "You're stronger than any of us."

Greg was the only energetic one of the four of us. The previous afternoon, while Jeff, Jim, and I acted as tent weights, Greg hiked a mile over the glacial moraine to a monastery destroyed during the Cultural Revolution. The People's Liberation Army must have destroyed their own culture as well, unless they thought eating warm, fried, and salted peanuts three times a day constituted culture.

As usual, the yak herders were waiting for Christmas before moving. Besides, their yaks had sought greener pastures. I spotted them on a hillside an hour's walk from camp. It was a chilly ten degrees below before the sun crawled over the Himalayas and filtered into camp. By ten o'clock we were feasting on fried eggs, pancakes, and mush. By eleven I had the first cups of French-roast coffee poured. Finally at noon the Tibetans began taking down their tent and drinking the last of their tea.

It was one o'clock by the time the yaks were fed, loaded, and herded toward the 17,750-foot Phusi La. Jim and I hiked away from camp an hour early, followed the wrong route, and reached the Phusi La minutes before the yak herders, who took a more direct, or rather correct, route. Jeff and Greg, the mellower twosome of the team, were content to accompany the yaks and enjoy the leisurely pace.

The sun's rays danced upon the shoulders and ridges of the surrounding peaks with just enough visibility through the cumulus clouds to create an air of suspense. What unclimbed peaks could these giants be? A stiff wind cut through my wool shirt as we descended sharply over snow-covered meadows and frozen creeks to our night's camp at 15,800 feet, a sloping yak pasture alongside a small ice-capped lake. It was an idyllic campsite until the yaks smelled fresh creek water and plunged into the bubbling spring. Ever try to move an eight-hundred-pound bull yak from water? We boiled it.

April 6 was a day to remember, an extraordinary day for a mountaineer. Our trek was all downhill. The yak herders were on the road by 12:30. Yes, a road. The Chinese had built a one-track, seasonal truck road to Changbujian, the largest village in the Rong Shar Chu gorge. According to Alan Hinkes, one of the British climbers who had reached Menlungtse's western subpeak on Bonington's 1988 expedition and member of the international team attempting Cho Oyo, it was built to log the Menlung Valley.

"Clear cuttin' the blooming 'ills," he told us in Tingri. "The road was built to help destroy the area quicker so it will look more like Tibet!"

In 1979 the Gauri Shankar Expedition had followed the Rong Shar Chu to the Tibetan border, then veered off into another gorge to reach Gauri Shankar's West Face. In 1980 we were at the opposite end.

Jim, Greg, and I descended one thousand feet from camp that morning and reached the Rong Shar Chu headwaters, a small creek at the confluence below our valley and another drainage system dropping off the Tibetan Plateau. It seemed impossible that the water in this small creek at the edge of the Tibetan plateau would eventually become part of the Ganges, India's largest river, and end its long journey in the Bay of Bengal.

We descended through an ever-narrowing gorge of soaring granite walls. Each bend in the Rong Shar Chu looked like a dead end for us, but always the path continued snaking its way over or around seemingly impassable obstacles. Wicked-looking ridges and summits peeked through side gorges at our progress. The hillsides were noticeably barren of vegetation this close to Tibet. A low scrub juniper was the only green in sight this time of year. While we hurried through the gorge seeking more spectacular views, Jeff, Mr. Chen, and the Sherpas stayed with our yak herders, not to push them to greater speed, which was impossible, but to offer moral support.

Early that afternoon we entered Dazhang, a large, adobe-stone village of perhaps two hundred people nestled under one-thousand-foot-high cliffs and located at the mouth of a clear creek entering the Rong Shar Chu. Small, fallow potato fields lay between glacial rock outcrops below the village and along the river, terraced on top of the adjacent field as close to the cliffs as the sun could reach.

Children spotted us immediately. Telepathically, thirty of them, ranging in age from two to fifteen, assembled at our rest spot. As Greg so aptly put it, "A delegation of snot-nosed children was sent to greet the expedition."

The adults were curious but reserved and not prone to running after us like the children. The easiest method to rid our rest spot of their curiosity was to point our cameras toward them. Instantly they turned their heads, covered their faces, or ran for the villages. It was good sport, but both teams, climbers and children, soon tired of the game. By the time the yaks arrived amid a snow-storm, only a few children still stood in front of us obsessed with our inaction. We were reading books.

We camped along the Rong Shar Chu an hour's walk below the village. Life on the trail was becoming routine. Ang Nima had the kitchen in order and meals were no longer a Chinese experiment. Mr. Chen, an old mountaineer himself who had reached 27,000 feet on Everest in 1962, was turning into "one of the guys" and helped pitch the Chinese tent, unload yaks, and, in general, save the expedition money—at least on paper.

The team had also sorted itself out nicely. Jim and I had been on three previous expeditions together. We enjoyed each other's company and both of us knew that quiet is sometimes the most enlightening conversation. Besides, we were both avid readers. Life on an expedition is just one *New York Times* best-seller after another.

Jim has one habit that needles my curiosity: He is obsessed with writing in his diary. I can handle snoring, even a partner's occasional attack of freeze-dried-food-induced flatulence, but Jim's diary writing drives me nuts. The writing in itself is not annoying. I write in mine. But Jim often writes for an hour or more, quietly glancing in my direction every so often. Then suddenly out of the clear blue, he'll ask me a question like "What part of England did your mother come from?" I'd give anything to read his diary. Boredom creates scenarios within my mind that even Stephen King could use for fodder.

Jeff and Greg had formed a strong bond in Kathmandu and it had grown stronger during the trip through Tibet. Jeff preferred to travel with the yak herders, which was fine with me. Someone had to do it and I was glad it wasn't me. Their slow pace with long midday stops is not my style. I like to move quickly, get where I'm going, photograph along the route, and read when I get there. Jeff liked the camaraderie of the yak herders, the interaction with another down-to-earth people. Jeff had grown up on a large wheat farm in eastern Washington, and his roots were with people who live and work off the land. He was intent on learning about the herders and the yak. By traveling with them, Jeff was accomplishing his goal.

Greg moved between the groups as his mood suited him. One day he would travel with Jeff, the next with us. He enjoyed a more leisurely approach to the trek to photograph and absorb the experience. He didn't have Jim's and my urge to see around the next bend. I envied him.

Changbujian

The gorge dropped slowly the next morning, although the walls above us rose dramatically thousands of feet, as if we were entering a well. Himalayan granite turned to metamorphic gneiss as we descended. Cracks that ran so straight and parallel in the granite walls now discontinued or bottomed out. Massive, orange-colored walls shot through with bands of black diorite exhibited nature's strength and intensity. The Himalayas are a young mountain range and display an awesome array of needle-sharp peaks and vertical depth rarely seen around the world. Guari Shankar, its massive head towering above the gorge for several bends in the river, reminded me of Dorje and my summit day eleven years before. How time eats away at strength and ambition.

Within three hours Jim and I arrived in Changbujian, the largest Tibetan village in the Rong Shar Chu gorge. From the description I had read of the size of the village, I expected it to be in a large floodplain with room for potato fields. I was surprised to find it nestled up against towering walls, perched on a three-hundred-yard-wide glacial moraine one hundred feet above the river. The fallow fields were small and spread along the river where yak-drawn, single-shear plows could bite into the thin but rich black soil.

Changbujian, at close to 12,000 feet, is in the rhododendron, juniper, and pine forest zone. Unlike higher Tibetan villages, Changbujian's homes are made of river rock and wood, abundant resources along the river and up the canyons nearby. I noticed a stronger cultural tie to the Sherpas in Nepal than to their Tibetan cousins. Their dress was more Sherpa and the interiors of their homes were distinctly arranged like those of Sherpa homes. Their food—meat, vegetables, and boiled potatoes—was similar to that of lowland tribes. The Tibet-Nepal border should have been drawn closer to Dazhang, culturally very much Tibetan.

The Chinese flag, brilliant red with yellow stars, flew high above the government compound as we approached the village. There were no Chinese. The compound was now used as housing for Tibetan government workers and their families. The compound, located above the main village, was near a clear creek and had a small generator to provide electric lighting. Buildings, court-yard, wiring—everything was in total disrepair.

It wasn't long before the villagers learned of our arrival and began gathering at an unplanted potato field where we intended to camp. Older children accompanied by siblings arrived from the village. Individually they were shy and concerned, but in numbers they turned into a pack. Soon we found ourselves being tagged, gestured at, and the brunt of jokes that only they were privy to. By midafternoon I was hoping the Pied Piper would just happen to walk through and take a few of the wilder kids with him. I'm sure none of the team would have paid the ransom.

Our yaks and herders arrived late in the afternoon. Instant chaos resulted as hot, ornery, heavily laden yaks were corralled into the small, rock-walled potato field with fifty curious villagers, most of whom were children of all ages in a carnival frenzy. No-body had to wonder where we were; they just had to look for the dust storm rising above the village.

I was not excited about camping within walking distance of the village, let alone within it; we would never have a minute's peace from kids. But convincing the yak herders to travel another half hour beyond Changbujian proved impossible. The expedition would make a yak change here from the Tingri yaks to those owned by Changbujian herders. The following day would be a rest day as the local yaks were located and brought down from the high pastures. Our herders would return to Tingri loaded with local goods such as wood planking and potatoes. They were an honest, hardworking group of Tibetans, and we would miss their company.

Bonington had suggested in a letter to Wickwire that we hire a Changbujian villager named Kusang. "He speaks passable English," Bonington had written, "from working in his uncle's curio shop in Darjeeling. He was a great help to us in 1988." We located Kusang that afternoon and hired him immediately.

The team rested April 9, washed clothes, and photographed the village and its people. The dust around camp would just start to settle when another herd of children would arrive from doing their chores. Afternoon tea served by the Sherpas outside the cook tent brought the little beggars to a halt. Fifteen kids watched intently as I spread a thick layer of peanut butter over a cracker and took a bite.

"That probably looks like we're spreading shit on crackers," Greg said.

He was right. No wonder they were in awe.

I must have lost my mind to think we would leave Changbujian prior to midday the following morning. The team was up early, dropped the tents, packed, ate, and was ready to depart by ten o'clock. The yaks didn't show. We had lunch; then a snack. What the hell, I dropped to a grassy meadow along the creek and bathed.

Spring had arrived in Changbujian and with it the butterflies, insects, and heat. I lay out in my shorts soaking up the sun's warmth and wondered how the villagers could be dressed in two or three layers of wool clothing and sometimes a heavy sheepskin jacket-pant suit. Sweat dripped from their brows, yet they refused to remove a layer of clothing. It stands to reason: The yak wears its hair all year around, why not they? It must be pleasant not to have to worry whether clothes wick moisture or are waterproof but breathable or are so-much percentage warmer when wet than goose down. How did man make it through the ages without modern technology to burden his thought?

Our yaks arrived late in the afternoon. Jeff described the scene as chaotic. "The more people that arrived, the more yelling that took place. Roskelley, you would have gone berserk."

He was right; I can lose it easily. When dealing with porters, yak herders, or villagers I'm at my best walking down the trail away from the conflict. The porters, Sherpas, and L.O. always work it out, so rather than steam for days, I leave.

"The yak drivers say we will camp at the Chuwar Monastery," Mr. Chen informed us through William. "It is only a half hour away but will give the yaks more time to make the next day's camp up the gorge."

No legitimate explanation, just another day's pay for the herders, who received six of the thirty-six dollars paid to the Chinese Mountaineering Association for a herder and three yaks. They alluded to a long trek the following day, but that again turned into another easy day. There was no room for barter. We either played their game or the herders would take their yaks home.

In the gorge below Changbujian, glaciers had ground and cut their way through metamorphic gneiss. Water completed a masterful job of finish work. The trail descended six hundred feet within two miles to the ruins of the Chuwar Monastery, our camp for the night. Miles beyond, silhouetted on the horizon and thousands of feet above the Rong Shar Chu, was the old dzong Shipton had walked silently beneath on his way to Nepal. We were at the mouth of the Menlung Valley and only days away from our goal: Menlungtse.

The Northeast Face of
Tawoche towers above
Pheriche, Solo Khumbu,
Nepal.

Himalayan tahr billy
near Tengboche
Monastery,
Sagarmatha National Park.

Sherpa children in Namche Bazaar.

Jeff Lowe below Ama Dablam, a short day's walk from Pheriche.

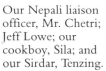

Our Nepali liaison officer, Mr. Chetri; Jeff Lowe; our cookboy, Sila; and our Sirdar, Tenzing.

Packing in Pheriche — an adult version of eeny-meeny-miney-moe.

The Tibetan lama who blessed our adventure in Pheriche.

Ama Dablam seen
from Tawoche as
young Sherpa girls
ferry our loads
toward advanced
base camp.

Lowe leads the first steep pitch off the glacier on Tawoche's Northeast Face.

Lowe doing what he does best: leading difficult alpine terrain four days into the climb.

Approaching the center gully. Ama Dablam is in the background.

Early morning light on our fifth bivouac. Lowe inspects the day from his chrysalis before rockfall craters the icefield.

Lowe follows the long ice traverse back to the center gully on the eighth day.

We're off the face. Lowe's bivouac tent the morning of our summit day.

A bluebird day in the Himalaya as Lowe climbs toward the summit ridge.

Nothing on the summit —
except another dream fulfilled.

Exhausted and spent,
Lowe fights his way
through nieves
penitentes near the
base of our descent.

The beauty of the Tibetan plateau is in its depth and distance.

The Tibetan border town of Zhangmu clings precariously to the Himalayan foothills.

Our first yak camp on the Tibetan plateau below the Phusi La.

Changbujian village children watch fascinated as Jim Wickwire writes in this daily journal.

Ang Nima (left) helps a Tibetan yak herder wrangle a load onto a large beast.

Bullet tracks of a Chinese machine gun wreaked havoc on this Buddha image.

The Menlungtse team (left to right): Greg Child, John Roskelley, Jim Wickwire, and Jeff Duenwald.

Duenwald (left) and Child pitch their tent below Menlungtse's West Summit one day from base camp.

The West Summit of Menlungtse seen above base camp.

Child (foreground), Duenwald, and
Wickwire pick their way across "Ugly" Glacier.

Duenwald climbing
on the lower buttress
of the Southeast
Ridge.

GREG CHILD

Duenwald belays Roskelley below Camp I.

Child and Duenwald begin the
traverse below the icefall blocking
the route above Camp I.

Child prepares
breakfast at Camp II
on Menlungtse's
Southeast Ridge.

Roskelley leading out of Camp II.

GREG CHILD

Child prepares to bivouac in the ice cave, Camp III.

16

ye·ti \ 'yet-ē \ *n* (Tibetan; 1951) **1:** A source
of funds for another free trip. **2:** A Tibetan bogey-
man.

(*Roskelley's First Climber's Dictionary*, 1991)

THE CHUWAR MONASTERY, one of four Buddhist monasteries in Tibet of strategic significance, was destroyed by the People's Liberation Army (PLA) in the mid–1960s. Unlike other monasteries,
which are located on the Plateau within reach of tourist eyes and
cameras, the Chuwar had not been restored. Isolated by political
borders and geological upheaval, the monastery's death was openly
displayed.

The Chinese built a long, narrow rock–and–adobe compound
and a soccer–field–sized parade ground directly above the monastery. The base acted as a military cork in a bottleneck. So narrow
and vertical were the rock walls rising above the compound, that
anyone or anything traveling up the Rong Shar Chu would have to
pass by under close scrutiny.

The monastery was built on glacial debris hundreds of feet
thick, eaten away by the Menlung Chu on the southeast and the
Rong Shar Chu descending from the northeast. In its full glory
many years before, the Chuwar Monastery could have been mis-
taken for James Hilton's *Shangri-la,* the mythical religious center in
the Himalayas. But not anymore.

I explored the monastery while waiting for our yaks to arrive. The main entrance, two six-inch-thick, eight-foot-high, wooden swinging doors, was intact despite the destruction around it. A pair of half-ton snow leopards, intricately carved of rock, had at one time sat faithfully by the doors protecting the deities within. Now only one was left, tilted and off to one side of the entrance as though in disgrace for the destruction. Its twin was partially buried in rubble nearby.

Most of the twenty-foot-high courtyard walls were still standing, but the second-story walkways had caved in or were hanging in space ready to do so. Enormous beams hand cut from giant timbers, some twenty-five feet long and twelve inches thick, were holding aloft portions of the walkways around the courtyard as though in defiance of the destruction around them. Like Buddhism, the beams portrayed a strength unending through time and man's continual inconsideration to man.

I found a side door that was slightly ajar and squeezed into the courtyard. Rubble of old wood and stone covered the clay floor. I was afraid to touch a standing beam or a leaning timber for fear of being buried alive under tons of debris still hanging in space. Carefully I scrambled through the stalagmites and stalactites of wooden pieces to the monastery's main hall entrance.

Anarchy. The PLA had gone mad inside the hall as if Tibetan Buddhism were a disease capable of destroying the thoughts of Mao. Perhaps angered by the benevolent faces before them, PLA soldiers had used hammers, explosives, axes, even machine guns to desecrate the ten lifesize Buddhas sitting along the walls and the once-towering central Buddha that should have sat before me, now only massive folded legs and shattered debris. Man-sized clay arms, legs, feet, and other Buddha body parts were scattered around the room. The bodies of the deities could have been torn open in a violent search for precious jewels or gold, but I suspected hate was the primary motive. Machine-gun bulletholes ripped across one Buddha's intricately painted gold face. Despite the desecration, the deity remained visibly passionate as if to say, "It is no matter how far into dust I go, I will still 'be.' "

Thousands of handwritten pages from Tibetan books were strewn across the room, their wooden covers stacked in a disorderly pile off to one side. Amid the chaos, someone had swept the entrance floor clean to the base of the central Buddha, a work of art reduced to plaster, wire, and papier-mâché. There at the deity's folded legs was a recently placed one-hundred-pound mani stone, its Tibetan message painstakingly and brightly painted. A pure-white silk kata lay draped carefully over the stone.

This simple gesture by a monk in the face of total destruction epitomized the Tibetans' faith. The "all-knowing" would know that its faithful don't need icons or symbols to keep their faith. Buddha is in their hearts and mind, not in gaudy forms of clay and paper. A Buddhist's goal of inner ascent is to awaken to the empty nature of reality embodied within the spirit of Buddha. A believer has to awaken quickly at the Chuwar Monastery.

The destruction touched us all in some form. Greg and I tried to capture the violence on film, while Jim filled page after page in his diary. Ang Nima, who chants mantras morning and night and has never failed to ask for my deliverance from a mountain, entered the Buddha's Hall at dusk and poignantly said it all: "My God!" he cried, and slowly bowed his head.

The Menlung Valley

Jim, Greg, and I hiked up the Menlung Chu away from the Chuwar Monastery at 10 A.M., climbing steadily through almost impenetrable bamboo thickets, old-growth pine, and canopied rhododendron forests. The trail was well used by yak herders who pastured their animals underneath Menlungtse and by woodcutters logging on the forty-five-degree slopes above the Menlung Chu. I exaggerate in calling their operation "logging." One logger in Idaho cuts more trees in a day than all the Tibetans from Changbujian in a year.

The entire operation was done by hand. Two-man groups of woodcutters busily chopped and sawed trees, dragging them to camps or the trail and making finished lumber before transporting the product by yak to Changbujian. Poles, planks, short four-by-six beams, and more-massive lumber of various lengths were stacked or left on the trail for their owners' yaks. A one-by-two-inch plank five feet in length, which took hours to cut and trim, was worth one yuan (about fifty cents) to the woodcutter. A large beam was worth ten yuan. Not much for the sweat of cutting, trimming, and hauling needed to deliver the product to Chang-bujian.

Hinkes had been paranoid over the "extensive logging" taking place in the Menlung area. By his description, I thought the slopes had been clear-cut. I forgot his heritage. Coming from Britain, where "logging" more often describes the act of writing in a journal, Hinkes would obviously think a few trees down meant total destruction. From my perspective, the woodcutters were just thinning the forest. It would take the Tibetans two hundred years to log the Menlung Valley with axe and handsaw and transport the lumber to Tibet. Even if the Chinese did supply the Tibetans with chainsaws, which is as likely as their giving Tibet back to the Dalai Lama, I wouldn't worry. Nothing in Tibet that runs by engine continues to do so very long.

My first view of Menlungtse burned an indelible imprint on my mind. The West Ridge rose from the valley floor at forty-five degrees to an immense icefield. The ridge's pink granite steepened like the bridge of my nose as it reached out for the sky, only to end abruptly on the West Summit. Menlungtse's fortresslike northwest flank dropped vertically from the twin summits guarded at every turn by immense fields of hanging ice. We were soon to learn that ice avalanches swept the flank hour by hour.

Compared with Menlungtse's western flank, which looked formidable, perhaps suicidal for a climbing team, Gauri Shankar's Northwest Ridge across the valley seemed to invite an attempt. One thing was apparent: there was still plenty of snow in the Himalayas to keep us at base for a few weeks.

We camped at Shapche, a woodcutter's camp, on a steep hillside underneath overhanging cliffs. Jim and I searched higher for a flat spot closer to water but could not convince the yak herders to move another inch upward. We were only two hours' walk from the monastery.

The yak herders wanted to leave early the following morning. Something about a long day, which I assumed meant four hours rather than two. The usually relaxed morning affair turned into a semiriot as herders requested our tents and packed loads before breakfast. By 9:30, the yaks were loaded and bemoaning their fate in loud grunts and groans as they were reluctantly herded onto the trail. A rough one it was, too.

The trail descended two hundred feet into' the river bottom, then disappeared into a landslide. The yak herders had rebuilt the trail with sod and poles the night before, and it now continued steeply upward into a forest of pine trees and groves of rhododendrons not yet in bloom. An hour up the trail, Jim and I caught up with the trail crew of Greg, Ang Nima, Kusang, and William, who had started off before we did. A small landslide had removed seventy feet of the trail the season before. Heavy rains had continued the destruction, eliminating past improvements. With any tool available, our crew was digging and chipping a new trail.

"Grab a ski pole, Jim," Greg yelled, "and start digging over on the right."

We pitched in, hacking and stabbing at the loose sand and rock with ski poles, kukris, a pickaxe, and a walking stick. Yaks are mulelike in their movement and habits, taking small, careful steps and placing their large noses to the ground to identify and smell their way along the trail. A yak might be misplaced by the herder at one time or another, but the animal itself always knows where it is. Would they cross our makeshift track so heavily laden with gear? Our sirdar, Ang Nima, a yak herder from the Khumbu, worked the thin spots to his meticulous standards. If one yak tumbled into the river five hundred feet below and died, a three- to four-hundred-dollar loss, the herders would refuse to continue. The large beasts approached the fresh trail, hesitated long enough to recognise the crossing, then negotiated the thin, collapsing track.

The valley widened and exposed immense, open slopes of rhododendron, waist-high juniper, and scrub brush, which ended thousands of feet above us in vertical walls cut with deep, ragged gorges drooling with waterfalls and creeks. Menlungtse presented a hologram image in the midday sun of white glaciers and a sea of pink gneiss against a flawless blue sky. I could feel the earth coming to life beneath my feet. It was wild country.

Despite being an eternal pragmatist, I found myself wondering if the yeti, or abominable snowman, actually existed at one time. Naaaawww. But the Menlung Valley is so remote, so untouched by man, it's easy to imagine a beast that's part man, part ape living undetected along the subalpine zone where even the yak herders seldom venture. Virtually unexplored, home to hundreds of species of wildlife and vegetation, with an unending area of habitat, the Menlung Valley would open anyone's mind as to the existence of the yeti. Even a mind as closed as mine.

Yeti'nother Sighting

I'm not a believer in the abominable snowman, but after a careful study of "yeti encounters," I have drawn some conclusions as to their "habits."

Yetis love to run across snow slopes and leave lots of tracks, but they're careful to leave them in snow where melt can distort their footprints. By all accounts, yetis are omnivorous, living on a diet of fruits, berries, and well-fed yaks, which they skin carefully. Their spoor, or "yeti shiti," when discovered, almost always includes hair and bone.

They're obviously nocturnal, too, although once in a great while an insomniac yeti is spotted in daylight. These sightings frequently occur late in a festival as if all the music, laughter, and drinking arouse the yetis' curiosity. But at the sound of a monastic horn, they quickly depart. And last, the yeti lives below the snow line but sometimes has to cross expanses of snow, and this is when it is spotted or its footprints identified. So the question of what a yeti can be doing on a glacier is superfluous. As a British mountaineer put it: "The yeti will probably ask us the same question."

The abominable snowman goes by many names in the Himalayas. The word "yeti" is a compound of "*ye*," meaning rock, and "*teh*," meaning animal. Natives also use other terms, depending on the size of the animal and the nature of the local dialect: *mi-teh* (an animal that looks like a man, or an anthropoid ape), *kang-mi* (snowman), and *dzu-teh* (cattle animal, as the yeti is said to have a predilection for yak). The Plateau Tibetans call the creature *me-tohkangmi* or "the wild man of the snows."

It seems that just about every prominent mountaineer who ever left a boot track in Himalayan soil and wrote about it has some tale to tell of the yeti. Most of these writers are careful, though, only to speculate and not insist on its existence. The fact is, there's a lot of pressure from their publishers to "spice up" a travel book.

"Don't be so stuffy, Shipton, ol' boy," his editor probably said. "Your book, *That Untraveled World,* needs the yeti to pick up sales. And while you're at it, stick in some, you know, sex."

Lieutenant Colonel C. K. Howard-Bury, D.S.O., wrote in *Mount Everest: The Reconnaissance, 1921* about his team's encountering tracks near the Lakpa La in Tibet (close to Menlungtse). "We were able to pick out tracks of hares and foxes, but one that at first looked like a human foot puzzled us considerably. Our coolies [Author's note: Howard-Bury must have been an Indian transplant to call them "coolies"] at once jumped to the conclusion that this must be 'The Wild Man of the Snows.' These tracks were probably caused by a large 'loping' grey wolf, which in the soft snow formed double tracks rather like those of a barefooted man." Good explanation, Howard-Bury.

Tenzing Norgay, who made the first ascent of Everest along with Sir Edmund Hillary, claims to have seen yeti tracks in 1946 and 1952 and spoor on glaciers often as a young boy in the Solo Khumbu. Tenzing wrote in his autobiography, "Though I cannot prove it, I am convinced that some such thing exists."

According to Tenzing, his father actually saw a yeti near Makalu. He described it to Tenzing as "a big monkey or ape, except that its eyes were deeply sunken and its head was pointed at the top. The color was grayish, and a noticeable thing was that the hair grew in two directions—from above the waist upward and from below the waist downward. It was about four feet high, and a female, with long hanging breasts; and when it ran, which was on two legs only, it held the breasts up with its hands."

Now, that's the kind of "encounter" we all dream about.

Another "sighting" occurred at Tengboche in November 1949 during a Buddhist festival. A group of Sherpas spotted a yeti twenty-five yards away through a screen of trees. Sen Tenzing, a Sherpa who later worked for Shipton, described it as five foot six standing on hind legs, with a tall, pointed head. It had reddish brown hair except on the face, which was bare and red, and no tail. Was this the first Sherpa festival without chang, the ever-present homemade rice beer?

Eric Shipton, whom I quoted in chapter 12 on his 1951 exploration of Menlungtse, came across tracks after crossing the Menlung La into Menlungtse's sanctuary. "Sen Tensing [Author's note: Sen Tensing could make a living on "yeti encounters"] was the only one of us who had no doubts as to the origin of the mysterious tracks. With complete confidence he pronounced that they had been made by yeti."

Shipton described the tracks as "some twelve inches long and five inches wide. There was a big, rounded toe, projecting a bit to one side; the next toe was well separated from this, while three small toes were grouped closely together. They could hardly have been clearer had they been made in wax."

Here's where Shipton walks off his own plank: "Hitherto I had been open-minded, perhaps a little sceptical on the subject of the Yeti; but now I became convinced, particularly by the unmistakable evidence of the toes, of the existence of a large, ape-like creature. . . . For, whatever creatures had made those tracks, they were neither bears nor human beings."

I found his description of the feet particularly amusing. In 1979, on the approach to Gauri Shankar, I photographed an old Nepali porter resting along the trail near the Tibetan border. His bare feet were as wide as they were long, and the soles callused as thick as a Vibram sole. This in itself was not uncommon, but his deformity was: like Shipton's "animal," the porter's big toes splayed at ninety-degree angles to his feet and the other toes were loosely grouped. If I had seen this man's track in the mud without seeing him, I might have photographed the prints as another example of a yeti "encounter." Could it be that as a young man this same porter, after taking a load of tsampa to Namche, took a shortcut over the Menlung La back to his village of Changbujian the day before Shipton's crossing?

The most infamous mountaineer's "sighting" was that by Englishman Don Whillans in 1970. He spotted the creature above his camp near Annapurna South Face on a cold, moonlit night. Using a monocular, he distinguished limbs on a dark spot that was bounding quickly uphill on all fours. It disappeared behind a leafless tree, only to reappear wandering from one clump of trees to the next in a shadowy portion of the hillside at the base of a kind of dune. Whillans admits, "I couldn't see it clearly."

"Once it started to move out in the moonlight, I could get a better idea of what it was. It was on all fours and it was bounding along very quickly across the snow, heading for the shelter of the cliffs." It soon disappeared, but the next morning he found tracks confirming what he had seen the day before. For the record, Whillans states, "That thing is an ape or ape-like creature."

Whillans, who was known to tip a few, is also widely quoted as replying to a reporter's question, "When do you start getting in shape for these expeditions, Mr. Whillans?" by saying, "In the last pub out of town."

In chapter 5 I wrote about a "yeti" skull and hand kept for posterity at the gomba in Pangboche. They have been studied by Western scientists, who came to the following conclusions:

According to Peter Byrne of the Slick Johnson Zoological Expedition of 1958-59, "Pangboche Gompa is the oldest of the temples of Khumbu. It is between two and three hundred years old and its founder is believed to be one Lama Sanga Dorje. The prized exhibits of the temple gomba are a 'hand and a scalp'; both are claimed to be the parts of a Yeti or an Abominable Snowman whose carcass was brought from Tibet many years ago. The scalp may actually be the head–skin and hair of some anthropoid. Extensive research today by scientists of both the U.S.A. and the U.K. has failed to prove otherwise. The hand, according to Dr. Osman Hill, Professor of the Regent Park Zoo, London, who has been able to examine radiographs by this expedition, is human."

There has been expedition after expedition led by some of the most famous explorers of our time who have sought proof of the yeti. None of them have returned with absolute proof positive, but there is the unexplained.

Bonington's 1988 Menlungtse Expedition did not find any conclusive evidence of the yeti's existence, but as it was later reported, "We did make a series of observations that are difficult to explain away":

1. John-Paul Davidson, the BBC director, saw tracks, then a figure behind a rock below base camp. It was cloudy with flurries of snow, so he was unable to identify fully the figure. [Author's note: Mystifying.]

2. Base manager Jess Stock came across tracks that seemed to be those of bipeds. He photographed these. [Author's note: More tracks?]

3. Team physician Charles Clarke and journalist Ian Walker found two fairly fresh bharal (blue sheep) skins and no bones. [Author's note: Filleted?]

4. Alan Hinkes and Andy Fanshawe found their ski poles gone from a camp high on Menlungtse even though they had been weighted down by rock. According to Bonington, "I don't think we can blame the yeti for the loss, but it was odd." [Author's note: Luckily they didn't leave a gun.]

So how does one explain the apparent lack of physical evidence? Is there or isn't there a yeti? Everyone's opinion differs.

Howard-Bury said his tracks were those of a loping wolf. A nonbeliever, our English gentleman writes, "Tibet, however, is not the only country where there exists a 'bogey man.' In Tibet he takes the form of a hairy man who lives in the snows, and little Tibetan children who are naughty and disobedient are frightened by wonderful fairy tales that are told about him. To escape from him they must run down the hill, as then his long hair falls over his eyes and he is unable to see them."

Reinhold Messner, the world's greatest mountaineer, believes the yeti "to be more a creature of fable than fact."

Sherpas feel the role of the yeti is as a divine or demonic messenger of the gods who watch over the practice of Buddhism.

Herbert Tichy, a well-known author and Himalayan explorer, considers the yeti as "Nepal's oddest and most elusive source of foreign exchange, which seldom, if ever, puts in an appearance." He doesn't expound his own beliefs. But in his book *Himalaya*, Tichy does relate a story of the capture of a yeti by Sherpas.

"Some Sherpas even claim to have once captured a yeti that came down to their village every evening and drank from the trough. The villagers were so frightened that they barricaded themselves in their houses, but after the yeti had gone, they filled the trough with strong chang. The next morning they found a completely intoxicated yeti snoring off his potations. At the sight of this pathetic spectacle their fears evaporated, and they were immediately struck by the business possibilities of the situation. Remembering how keen the white sahibs were to catch a yeti, they bound the creature's hands and feet and carried him down the valley slung on a pole. On the second day the yeti emerged from his stupor, broke his bonds, killed one of the Sherpas, and vanished into the realms of legend."

Perhaps the best explanation for the yeti came from our porter, Kusang, from Changbujian.

"Have you even seen a yeti or do you know of anyone who ever has?" I asked him.

"A yeti is a god and you cannot see a god," he replied.

We climbed to a plateau of glacial rock and alpine juniper, sat in the warm sun, and waited for the yaks to catch us. A level half-mile walk along the plateau ended at Thom Buk, Bonington's 1987 base camp, a tabletop meadow at the foot of Menlungtse's north-west glacier.

Wickwire, feeling the tug of exploration, climbed the easy yak slopes above camp that afternoon to 15,000 feet to photograph Menlungtse's north and west sides.

"There is no reasonable route," Jim said upon his return at sundown. "All the lines along the face are protected by ice cliffs. The direct North Ridge can be reached and perhaps climbed, but it is so damn steep it's a buttress."

As he finished describing the wall, the lip of a stadium-sized hanging icefall across the valley from us and beneath the West Summit broke loose, sending thousands of tons of ice down the wall as if to punctuate "no reasonable route."

"Looks like an Australian route to me," I said.

"Well, it won't be me, mate," Greg replied. "I'm getting too old."

Greg was feeling his age. He was thirty-three that day, and if he were playing tennis or football, he'd be over the hill. Wickwire and Duenwald just looked at each other and laughed. At forty-nine and forty-seven, it wasn't getting any easier for them to lug loads through deep snow and up steep rock and they knew it. "Just one more, Lord or, uh, yeti. Just one more."

Base Camp

I walked slowly beneath the seven-thousand-foot East Face of Gauri Shankar the next morning, April 13. The snow runnels, knife-edged arêtes, rock slabs, and ribs resembled an ancient Tibetan's face; a wise old face, burnt brown from the airless sky, leathery, with lines as deep as the Grand Canyon and scattered like rivulets through the Mississippi Delta.

I got that ol' familiar climbing urge looking at that face, that injection of adrenaline that sparks a bit of climber's insanity. Not a big one like years gone by. Not one like those that used to stop me dead in my tracks, pump me up, and say, "You have to climb that thing." Nope. A little urge that tapped me on the shoulder lightly and said, "Someday that face will be climbed. Maybe not by you. But by someone just as good, a little younger, and with a hell of a lot more enthusiasm."

I sat and picked out a line on the face as the yak drivers whistled their yaks forward, bouncing rocks off their butts in case one of them forgot who was herder and who was the herd. This was familiar territory to some of them. The Menlung Valley and flat meadows beneath Menlungtse and Gauri Shankar were the summer high pastures for many of our herders and their animals.

I crossed the morainal floodplain where the two rivers that drain the Menlungtse sanctuary meet to form the Menlung Chu, then gained a few hundred feet of altitude underneath the West Face. Beneath the massive walls lay small meadows dotted with old yak manure. As many as ten Changbujian families spend their summers along Menlungtse's base fattening their yaks, naks, and calves in preparation for the lean winters.

Beneath the West Rib, Kusang stopped and bent down to examine a line of prints in the snow. "Leopard," he said.

Angling across the lee side of a spring snowfield were the five-toed prints of a large cat, several of them inside boot tracks made by Duenwald on a hike the previous afternoon.

"Look at the large pad with three humps," Kusang added.

He didn't need to convince me; I knew it was a snow leopard. The prints in a fresh skiff of powder over crusty ice were sharp and distinct. A wild dog, fox, or coyote would have left claw marks. I felt strangely akin to this animal. Perhaps above us in the shadow patterns of rock and ice, it was watching, smelling, hearing a man different from those of Changbujian. Me.

With the instinct of a hunter, I focused on the hillsides seeking a movement, a nonangular curve of a tail, even a prey's dead giveaway — the eyes. He was either gone or well hidden. What did he eat? Was there a mate? Kittens? To see this elusive creature would be the highlight of my Himalayan climbing. The odds were one in a million. But this animal was close. Very close.

The yak trail disappeared into wind-packed snow on a south slope. Ang Nima, Greg, Wick, and I began breaking across the two hundred yards of inch-thick ice crust, stomping down a reasonable path so the yaks would follow. After an hour's labor, the track was all but finished. It was good — for a ways. Then cold and fatigue reduced our efforts to shovel-leaning and half-hearted stomping. Only Ang Nima had the perseverance to continue packing a reasonable track. The rest of us were too tired at 15,000 feet to do more than stand and watch. The yaks, driven from behind by the herders, reluctantly pressed forward, unsure at first of the footing underneath our packed track along the thirty-degree slope. I sensed there would be a problem and stood by with Ang Nima as the first yaks crossed the worst section.

The third yak, a massive black beast with twenty-inch horns, plunged into a hole we hadn't packed thoroughly, raised its inside leg to move again, leaned too far toward the downhill side, and fell over, pulled by his load.

He rolled on the ice—first on his side, then with all four feet skyward—skidding like a sled. He flopped over twice more as the momentum of his 150-pound load propelled him. Somehow he dug his legs into the snow and stopped seventy-five feet below. His eyes were the size of pearly white bowling balls as he surveyed his position. The herders, Ang Nima and I, leaped through the snow down the slope to calm him before his struggles could shoot him down another two hundred feet to the river.

Sheepishly, the yak stood up unhurt and lunged upward carefully back to the other yaks that had stopped in their tracks to watch their comrade. His driver chastised him like a child, carried the yak's load up to the trail with the help of two other drivers, and reloaded our gear onto the animal. The yak hung his head as if to indicate he was sorry for the commotion.

The other yaks, naks, and zopkios were more careful. An hour later our caravan of tireless yaks and herders crossed a small creek and assembled on a grassy floodplain peppered with glacial boulders. Imitating the yak herders, I clicked my tongue at each animal to stand still as I approached them from the side. They eyed me with concern, rotating their massive, pointed horns down and into a sweep, but then passively stood while I untied and pulled their hitch lines to release their loads. After seventeen days of travel by air, bus, truck, yak, and our own two feet, base camp was a little spot of heaven in a hostile world. I, for one, was ready to climb.

17

---

re·mote \ ri-′mōt \ *adj*   **1:** Providing temporary sanctuary for living things from human destruction. **2:** Menlung Valley.
(*Roskelley's First Climber's Dictionary*, 1991)

"TEA READYYYY!" Ang Nima hollered from the kitchen tent. He
didn't have to holler too loudly. Like a flock of crows on a road kill,
the team restlessly paced near the meal tent waiting for just this
moment. Breakfast of yak-scrambled eggs (thoroughly broken
during the trek), baked beans, boiled potatoes, and chapatis was
steaming on the table. He and Chering scurried back into the
kitchen tent to the warmth of two better-than-average stoves that
purred like kittens in a warm lap.

Jeff, cup in hand, paced impatiently near the chow tent. Inside,
I prepared Starbuck French roast brought from Seattle. As Con-
noisseur de la Café, it was my job to perform the coffee ritual
religiously each morning. Mrs. Olsen was never this popular.

Near the tents, Greg and Jim were shooting film at the rate an
Uzi fires bullets. Gauri Shankar, Menlungtse, and the sanctuary
peaks were striking, almost luminescent, against the bluer-than-
bluebird sky. If there was a prettier place in the Himalayas, we
would have to look long and hard to find it.

The morning was our second at base camp. We had sorted

equipment for the upper camps and organized food and personal gear the day before, and we were now ready to make our first carry to advanced base camp (ABC).

"What'll we take today, guys?" I asked.

"How about a tent, a rope, a few gas cartouches, and a stove each?" Jim suggested.

"Should be light enough for a first carry," I replied. Then I added a water bottle, lunch, camera and film, extra lenses, gloves, coat and jumpsuit, face cream, sunglasses, and a ditty bag of accessories. Had I forgotten anything? Maybe, but it wouldn't have fit anyway.

You would think after all the years and expeditions the four of us had been on that we would have eased into the hike and enjoyed the scenery. Uh-uh. Neither age nor experience had smartened us. Like puppies chasing tails, we bolted from camp like we had to be on the summit that night. Not one of us took the same path up the valley, as if it were against the law to follow a teammate.

After a mile and a half of flat trekking along the rocky flood-plain, we halted for a breather. Before us was the first steep terminal moraine. The great equalizer, altitude, slowed the troops down. There was still the semblance of a yak trail, though, and the hike was surprisingly easy. Once on top of the moraine, we meandered along the grass and scrub-brush crests of four lateral moraines, the remnants of a waning glacier waiting for another ice age. These valley pathways contoured delicately around the base of Menlungtse paralleling each other similarly to corrugated roofing. Three hundred feet below our morainal crest, and still gouging out the valley, was the Menlung Glacier, a massive jumble of rock and ice we were only too happy to avoid. Our path along the moraines paralleled Menlungtse's base, close to its immensely corniced and pinnacled ridges and avalanche-prone gullies and faces. This was the easiest approach to a Himalayan peak I'd ever been on.

The pleasant, two-mile walk ended abruptly at the Southeast Glacier, a debris feeder for the main glacier nearby. Feeding this glacier and above our heads was the ugliest, meanest avalanche-prone face that ever funneled a rock onto a climber's helmet. It spit a few boulders and snowslides toward us as we studied its character and attitude. The only route up that face led straight to heaven.

The name "Southeast Glacier" really didn't fit its personality, so I called it as I saw it, "Ugly Glacier," and living up to its name, it had gouged a deep trough a half mile wide between us and our ridge. After scrutinizing the entire west and south sides we decided the only reasonable route was our first pick of the litter, the Southeast Ridge.

We had all the choice of where to cross Ugly Glacier that a heifer has about being led to market. Reluctantly the four of us descended among loose glacial boulders and ice debris, and made our way through the ups and downs and chaos of "ice-heavals" that reminded me of the folds of skin on a Shar-Pei. Nothing was stable. Boulders the size of Toyotas moved as easily as pebbles. If one moved, they all moved.

It didn't look feasible for us to climb the morainal-debris cliffs on the other side, but on demand, face to face, the steep route off the glacier came together like Tinkertoys. We surmounted the moraine's glacial cut below the Southeast Ridge at 2 P.M., then searched and found a protected, flat advanced base camp. At our approach to camp, eleven curious but cautious bharal sheep walked slowly away from their feeding grounds at the base of the Southeast Ridge. We dropped our loads, manicured two tent sites, then ate a quick lunch.

The wind, a real biter, forced us to head for base an hour after arrival. Jeff and I scrambled across Ugly Glacier, up the other side, and down the valley to camp in an hour and a half. Jim and Greg were close on our heels. The round trip took a comfortable six and a half hours.

April 1990 was the spring of my twenty-fifth year of climbing, and I felt every foot of elevation gain and every mile of trail. My pack's harness, as padded as a pillow, still dug a furrow deep into four decades of well-used muscle, ten years past the hard, sinewy stage. In my youth, more weight on my back was just an annoyance. With age, the years of neglect, a changing pattern of life, physical misuse, and a lot of wear into the shoulders dictated a slower pace and a lot more thinking than doing.

I often wonder how many pounds have hitched rides on my frame, built more for ballet than for power lifting. An old friend of mine once said, "Roskelley, how can a skinny Thoroughbred like you do a draft-horse job?" Because I want to. Desire is all it takes. The necessity of carrying loads is the destiny of a mountaineer. There's freedom in those pounds, visions only a mountain climber will ever see. My home on my back, my next meal in a ditty sack. Mountaineering — so little climbing yet so much work.

"I'm heavier today, so take it a little slower," Jeff said.

"God, me too," I agreed. "Heavier and, I hope, a lot smarter. Truce. No more running."

"How are we going to climb with all this shit?"

"Don't know. It'll just have to work itself out."

The competitiveness among us wore out with time, then the carries to ABC became a pleasure, periods of serenity and peace. Only crossing Ugly Glacier below ABC ruined a day's effort, and then just when it snowed, leaving the loose, car-sized boulders playing a deadly game of rock 'n' roll.

Working, living, eating, breathing in one of the world's most remote valleys is only a treat for a few days. When I've stared at the West Summit of Menlungtse as many times as at the dashboard of my car or glanced at the unclimbed East Face of Gauri Shankar enough times to know it better than my wife's visage, and it starts to look less intimidating, I've been there too long. Time to move on to the next camp and learn to ignore the chances of death above.

"The ridge is looking better," Greg said one afternoon.

Time erodes even the deepest fear. After a while any route begins to look reasonable and safe.

Base camp had its little pleasures. Mornings typically were calm and clear affairs, while evenings were introduced by lightning shows to the west, thunder, warm-air-induced avalanches off Menlungtse, fiery sunsets, and intense snowstorms. The team gathered at night in the meal tent and talked of the day's activities, news on the BBC and the Voice of America, and all mountaineers' favorite subject — past climbs.

As we became part of meadow life, herds of bharal sheep (kin to both sheep and goats, but lacking the facial glands of the sheep and the rancid odor of the goats) lost their fear and pastured nearby. I watched and studied several "world record" rams that knew I was weaponless and paraded by camp daily to spite the hunter in me. Golden marmots, twenty pounds of whistle-pig, as we know them, crawled from their burrows underneath rocks to soak up a few late rays of sun, ever wary of Himalayan golden eagles and condor-sized lammergeiers. Goraks, Himalayan ravens, black as the witching hour and smarter than Rhodes scholars, picked at our garbage pit and our food bags. They were always within reach but never catchable.

My respect for goraks is endless. In 1981, below the East Face of Everest, I walked up to our temporary cache of food and equipment on the glacier below the face and was shocked at the devastation before me. Every one of the forty or so doubled, thirty-three-gallon, black plastic bags containing our expedition food was ripped open and their contents scattered. At first I thought it had to be the work of a Himalayan black bear, but upon closer inspection of tracks in the snow, I knew the vandals had been a flock of goraks. All the packages of oatmeal, hot cocoa, and tea, and boxes of any kind were pecked into. Nothing escaped their search for food.

Snow Leopard

The day before I left my family for Tibet, my seven-year-old son, Jess, and I made a short trip to town. I was feeling pretrip regret, that my time with Jess, Jordan, and Joyce was over—again. I hadn't said I loved them nearly enough; hadn't wrestled with Jess the way we used to; hadn't started the landscaping for Joyce; hadn't begun to fulfill my obligations as dad, husband, pseudo-farmer, and wage earner. Time had bested me again.

I bought each of them a stuffed animal to ease my guilt. A soft, white, forty-dollar Dakin polar bear for Joyce to remind her that I growl a hell of a lot more than I bite; a twenty-dollar battery-operated pink rabbit that squeaked and flipped for my six-month-old girl, Jordan; and a five-dollar snow leopard the size of a child's shoe for Jess. The little cat wasn't nearly as big or as talented as the other stuffed toys, but that didn't matter. It was just the right size for a boy about to lose his dad for two months.

I was proud of Jess that day. He helped me select the animals for Jordan and Joyce without once asking, "What about me?" I sent him off on an errand and looked for something special for him.

The tiny snow leopard was just one of a rack full of stuffed animals, yet I knew it was for Jess the moment I saw it. Somehow I hoped this image of a snow leopard would become my son's "totem" and impart to him its strength and purpose, its instinct to survive, its harmony with the land, and, yes, its cunning and stealth. When I gave it to him that night, Nintendos and bicycles no longer mattered. We named it Snowy, and when I kissed Jess goodnight, he had it tightly tucked under his arm. If I never returned, I knew Jess would forever keep his Snowy.

Jeff and I were burdened with fifty pounds of personal gear as we slowly made our way toward ABC to stay. Four bharal sheep grazed unconcernedly four hundred yards above us on the steep, grassy slope of Menlungtse. It was the second herd we had seen that morning. We were quiet, internalizing our thoughts, headphones over our ears, listening contentedly to our Sonys.

Snow leopard. There, fifty yards ahead and slightly to my right. Poised as if caught unaware by our approach, the cat stood broadside on a rock, crouched as if on springs, taut, bewildered, looking me straight in the eyes. He was in the feline "get-ready-to-move-in-haste" position, a front foot and a back foot forward, the other two back, body low to the ground. I could have sworn he was running, yet the leopard was rock still. His body-length tail, thick as a man's arm, never moved but drooped slightly toward the ground then turned up in a slow curve to its tip.

Tracy Chapman was on her last chorus of "For My Lover" on my Sony Walkman when I glanced up and spotted the leopard a second later than he saw me. When the leopard and I made direct eye contact, he flowed over the bank and out of sight.

The image of that predator, his grays and dark spots faultlessly hiding him among black-lichened glacial boulders, froze in my mind. He will be with me forever. I recognized his crouch: it reminded me of a very old, shiny, black porcelain panther with gold stripes that hunted for ten years beneath my parent's coffee table as I grew up.

My leopard didn't leap but turned its head forward, kept low, scooted over the rock embankment, and was gone like a shadowy illusion. But it wasn't an apparition. Nor a ghost.

I turned wide-eyed toward Jeff. "Snow leopard," I silently mouthed and pointed at the now-empty scene.

Dropping my pack, I ran for the bank while adjusting my camera. Was it luck? For the first time during our trips to ABC, I had my 43–88 mm zoom on my camera.

The leopard was in full gear, running and leaping from rock to rock far below. He sensed an urgency. The cat had watched man from a distance in the past. Smelled their fires, their sweat, even their sex. To him, man reeked of death. But something was different about the yellow, blue, and green predators on the moraine. He wanted to use his best sense, his nose, to quell his curiosity, but instinct demanded that he put miles between us — and quickly.

By the time I got him on camera, the leopard was nearly three hundred yards away. I shot him centered in the 86 mm as he loped across the glacial debris intent on crossing the Menlungtse Glacier. He reached a frozen glacial lake, stopped in the center and glanced back at Jeff and me, curiously stared at us, then turned and loped and trotted across the ice. Every few yards he did the same. Since he never had our wind, his curiosity had gotten the better of his fear.

At eight hundred yards we could still make him out. It was his tail that marked him. It flowed out behind him as if it were a kite, lighter than air, a mirage. Like a comet, it followed the cat as if indicating he had been there a minute ago but was now gone forever.

I thought of Jess after the cat disappeared across the glacier and into the blacks, creams, and grays of the land. Was Jess sending me a message? Could that image have been his spirit crossing my path one last time? Stranger incidents in my life had happened. I didn't want to think along those lines. There was nothing I could do if Jess were hurt or dead, but that was not a consolation.

No, I decided the encounter with the leopard was a good omen. I could feel it: Jess was fine.

To see that leopard so close was one of the highlights of my life. Twice before I had encountered big cats in the wild. An adult mountain lion walked onto a trail ten yards in front of me in Banff National Park, and a jungle leopard fed on a baited goat one hundred yards from my blind in Chitwan National Park in Nepal. Both encounters I can bring back in my memory as though they were just happening. The snow leopard would join these memories.

And there was another reason seeing this leopard was important to me. He was one of less than four thousand left in the world. Proof beyond a doubt that we, the caretakers of this earth, were still in moderate, if not tentative, control of our destiny. The snow leopard is an indicator, a measure, of how well the earth is doing. If we lose the snow leopard, if we remove the rain forest, if the salmon no longer run in our rivers, then we have failed in the one job we have been given as intelligent life. Our neglect and continual destruction of the earth's natural resources will reap its own reward.

18

nem·e·sis \ˈnem-ə-səs\ *n*   The fear within oneself.

(Roskelley's First Climber's Dictionary, 1991)

THE BRITISH/AMERICAN TEAM led by Chris Bonington reconnoitered the Southeast Ridge in 1988 and, according to Andy Fanshawe, found "no realistic routes to the summit other than by a traverse from the West Peak." He described the Southeast Ridge as "desperate looking." Bonington was more reserved in his judgment. In a letter to Wickwire he wrote of the Southeast Ridge that it "certainly isn't easy, but it's a beauty—hard, challenging, but probably relatively safe."

Bonington speculated on the "relatively safe" character of the ridge after having attempted alternate routes on two previous expeditions. The Southeast Ridge was obviously not as safe as they wanted. Bonington chose instead to attempt Menlungtse by a southern buttress in 1987 and the West Face in 1988, reach the lower western subpeak, then try to traverse over a mile to the main summit. Why? Cornices.

The Southeast Ridge, despite its directness and aesthetics, is crowned with unending cornices, ice frozen in gigantic waves as terrifying as the winter storm surf off the North Shore of Oahu. Their reconnaissance indicated that the West Face was the safer and more probable route to the virgin summit. Bonington wanted the first ascent of Menlungtse; the route was incidental.

The Southeast Ridge was our route of choice. From the summit of Gauri Shankar eleven years before, it had appeared to be one of the world's great routes, like Makalu's West Ridge or Dhaulagiri's Southeast Ridge. Like Bonington I wanted the summit of Menlungtse—but my way. To repeat an ascent of the British route to the West Peak then traverse to Menlungtse's summit did nothing to scratch my itch for Menlungtse itself. I wanted the Southeast Ridge and, I hoped, so did the team.

For days, as I carried to ABC, I glassed the razor-sharp ridge, studied its intricate twists, measured its span, took stock of its dangers and difficulties. I walked away absolutely convinced the ridge would be ours. The Southeast Ridge was no cakewalk; one or two of us would have to show some ingenuity, a measure of technical expertise, even a few skills honed on similar climbs. We might even have to play a little Russian roulette with the cornices. So what's new? Mountain climbing isn't a game of croquet. It's taking risks, tossing out the guidebook, and discovering talents that lie dormant within us. There are some talents in us that can't be used practicing law or medicine, in sales or teaching. These talents stem from necessity—the need to survive.

Advanced Base Camp

The four of us moved to our 17,000-foot advanced base camp on April 18, the same morning Jeff and I jumped the leopard. ABC was stocked for an attempt on the ridge with food and camp, climbing, and personal gear from four days of carrying loads from base camp. Just enough time to acclimatize but not blow out our knees or wear us down. I don't mind carrying loads when necessary, and I've carried my share in fifteen major expeditions, but I'm not a pack animal. One of the many benefits of an alpine-style ascent is eliminating loads to upper camps. I'll reap that reward any day.

"Up and at 'em, guys!" I shouted. I'm an early riser, preferring to greet the sun on the move. Rousting out Wickwire was easy. I could just bump him and rattle the pots. Greg and Jeff, in a nearby tent, took a more verbal approach.

Flawless weather invited us onto the ridge. I dressed carefully to avoid knocking down an inch-thick layer of hoarfrost on the tent's ceiling, which in our large two-man dome wasn't too difficult. I walked down to a small glacial pond below camp to fill the team's water jug, while Jim heated our breakfasts of foil-packaged spaghetti. Two chicken-sized snow cocks, over-sized chukarlike birds, *raawaakkk, raawaaakked* as they scooted uphill from me, then jumped, set their wings, and glided away like F-16s, squawking their annoyance.

Carrying light loads of climbing gear, the four of us scrambled up loose rock and grit for twelve hundred feet to a flat shoulder on the ridge, where we had cached personal gear during a previous reconnaissance. The route above marked a change in difficulty. We could take any one of ten different paths to reach the main ridge. But which one? Greg and Jim chose to follow a gully and ramp system to the left in hopes of reaching an icefield that dropped tonguelike off the ridge. Jeff and I, in our Nike hiking shoes and determined to stay that way, climbed stringers of ice and shattered rock straight above our cache. Two hundred feet up, the rock wall steepened to resemble a skyscraper. It was too late to retreat without a rappel. As Jeff belayed, I solved the broken and intricate puzzle that led to the ridge, all the while cursing myself for not following the easier ramp system Jim and Greg were walking along far below. If it looks easy, I thought, plan for the worst. After four 150-foot moderate rock pitches along the razor-sharp ridge, we reached the start of the ice. Thirty minutes later, Greg, belayed two hundred feet below by Wickwire, slowly climbed to our exposed position from the face below.

"Looks like your route is the winner, Greg," I said. "Our route was too dangerous."

"Ours was easy enough, " he replied as he reached the ridge crest. "We can fix it from where Jim is belaying."

His face contorted as he balanced on the steep ice slope. "What's the problem?" I asked.

"My hands are frozen," he said. "Got 'em wet down below."

"Here," I said, "try these." I handed him my gloves and put his on. As he windmilled his arms to get blood moving to his hands, I slammed a two-foot picket into the ice and tied him in.

Greg oooohed and aaaahed as circulation returned and with it the pain of rewarmed flesh. While he relaxed, I put on my boots and crampons, grabbed some hardware and rope from his pack, handed him back his own icy gloves, and began untangling a rope to lead along the ridge.

With a snowstorm and wind howling in from Everest, I led two long pitches along the slightly rising but narrow ridge crest, remaining ten feet below the corniced lip. Looks were deceiving again. The ridge section I was climbing had looked like an easy walk from ABC. The real thing was far more exposed as I cramponed along the pocketed, rotten, wind-packed ice.

"Do we have any more pickets?" I yelled to Jeff. "Ice screws are useless."

We didn't. In fact, six pickets made up our entire expedition inventory. The ridge looked blue, icy, and difficult from photos available to us in Seattle. I had guessed that ice screws would fulfill most of our needs. I'd guessed wrong. Only pickets worked in the loose, rotten névé ice, and we were running out.

Jeff belayed me along the ridge, then caught me at my anchors like a Slinky catches itself on a stair. We made a good team. Out of pickets and with the storm butting heads with our ridge, we retreated back to the comfort and warmth of ABC.

The next day's effort put us at the only potential site for Camp I. Under blue skies and sunshine, the four of us scrambled up the low-angled scree slope above ABC through fresh powder snow, then along Jim and Greg's ramp to the fixed line that dropped from the ridge. Ropes, hardware, tents, and personal gear made our loads heavy and awkward.

When we reached the top of the three fixed ropes, our morning weather changed abruptly. I watched as Cho Oyo's summit faded beneath a lenticular ice cloud, then felt penetrating cold and rising winds bite through my two layers of pile clothing. I wasn't prepared for the abrupt change of weather. The skies had been too clear that morning, too warm to expect a storm. My wind shell clothing was back at camp. After leading two new pitches, I had suffered enough. I dumped my load at the top anchor and descended. Greg, Jim, and Jeff, better prepared, continued for another four-hundred feet along the ridge. As Jeff belayed, Greg led the last difficult pitch to the first major obstacle on the ridge, a five-hundred-foot-high icefall.

Jim waited patiently at Jeff's belay, hacking out a campsite on the narrow, icy ridge crest. His efforts were hardly noticeable in the concrete-hard ridge. We needed a backhoe, not ice axes, to excavate Camp I.

The storm continued through the night and into the next day. The following morning, in dense cloud and under six inches of fresh snow, we descended to base camp in an all-out ground blizzard. It would be another five days before we could move back to ABC.

Revelations at Base

"John, I'm not going back up on the ridge."

I leaned up off my mattress, put down the book I was reading, and looked at Jim. He was dead serious.

"Any particular reason why?" I asked.

"I didn't realize what age could do," he replied. "I should have taken the hint from Kangchenjunga last year."

Jim's reference to the 1989 American-Indonesian Kangchenjunga Expedition, led by Lou Whittaker, brought back painful memories. He had succumbed to fatigue and illness at 21,000 feet on the North Wall and without warning decided to descend and return home. His decision and impending departure, though, helped me make a tough decision of my own.

For years I have advocated using Sherpas for base camp and trekking employment only, not for technical or dangerous climbing situations. Upon arrival at Kangchenjunga base camp, I realized that not only were Sherpas carrying expedition loads to Camp 2 below the North Face, but five technically inexperienced Sherpas, who were taught how to use jumars at base camp, were asked to carry loads up the difficult, rockfall-swept North Wall.

My respect for Lou Whittaker is endless, and his leadership is superb, but I had to make a tough decision whether to accept this use of Sherpas or withdraw from the team. My decision suddenly became clear to me.

As all the sahibs sat in base camp playing cards, the Sherpas at Camp 2 were asked to jumar loads up the wall by themselves with communication and direction limited to walkie-talkie. Not one sahib was even on the mountain! That incident made me realize this expedition was in direct conflict with my beliefs.

I had been climbing in top form. Ed Viesturs, Wickwire's and my climbing partner, just held the rope and let me burn it through his hands pitch after pitch. Of the four thousand feet of intensely demanding ice climbing up the North Wall, I led more than three thousand. Strangely, though, Jim, the Sherpas, and I, who had all worked so hard to put six of the members on top, never received any credit in expedition newsletters or slide shows for our per-formance. I'm convinced the expedition would not have succeeded without us.

Kangchenjunga was still fresh in Jim's memory. The struggle to acclimatize and keep up with the three of us on Menlungtse's ridge had taken a lot out of him.

"We're all tired at this altitude, Jim," I said.

"Yeah, but I'm mentally tired. Physically too. I don't want it anymore."

In five words he had summed it up: "I don't want it anymore." It was all I needed to understand his decision.

Through body language and occasional offhand statements on the ridge and at camp, Jim had unknowingly prepared himself and us for the inevitable. By base camp he had made up his mind not to return to the ridge.

"Mary Lou deserves to have me around in the coming years," Jim continued. "I've come to the end of a serious climbing career because I'm not the man I was five or ten years ago. The route is beyond my capabilities, at least to the degree I think the risks are justified."

I chose to listen to and agree with his reasoning. I would have taken a different approach with a younger, less-experienced climber, but not with Jim. He knew his strengths and mindset. On a climb like Menlungtse, it was to be one hundred percent; nothing more, nothing less.

Mountaineering is a high-risk activity. As age finally overcomes enthusiasm, as our priorities change and living is more important than a summit, then it's time to appreciate what's been accomplished and proceed to the next challenge in life. Jim had risked enough in thirty years of climbing. He would remain to support the three of us.

Greg and Jeff were disappointed but, like me, realized Jim had saved the expedition a yakload of problems by making his decision at base camp and not on the ridge, where it would have been too late. The three of us didn't envy his position. It's far more difficult to watch from the sidelines than to play the game.

I've considered climbing my profession since 1976. I know doubt is always in my psyche before and during a climb. It was not a factor for me on Menlungtse, however. I also know what it is to lose without trying, to perceive a risk and fail before the start. I was dead set on success this time.

I feel the same acidic drip of fear in my stomach prior to each climb. It's my first obstacle. The mountain isn't my adversary, I am. I'm my own worst enemy. The mountain is only a catalyst that starts the conflict within myself.

There is no more formidable opponent than my own doubt. Sometimes I bury it within me, other times I take it out on the route. But it's always there. At times the butterflies in my belly are so big I think I'm going to lift off the ground.

Questions as numerous as snowflakes light up my mind: "Will I survive?" "Is the ridge dangerous?" "Are there spots to bivouac?" And the toughest one of all, "Will I fail?" The answers aren't in base camp. They can't be answered by worry or talk, only by taking the first step, and the next, and the next. It's frustrating to challenge the unknown, but challenge is what the sport is about, and challenge has to be accepted on its own terms.

Jeff crumbled another pitted wall of my confidence the morning that he, Greg, and I were to head back to ABC for our first attempt. Quitting is a disease. Once it infects one, it spreads to all.

"I'm not sure I should be going with you guys," he said as we ate breakfast. "I'm afraid I'll slow you two down."

Oh, God, I thought, it's catching.

"Don't be ridiculous, Jeff," I said. "We can't lose you too."

"Yeah," Greg said, as shocked as I. "I don't want to climb as a twosome. It's much safer with three."

Jeff acquiesced. "Okay, that's the last negative thought you'll hear from me. If you think I'm useful, then I'll go."

Another drop of bile settled into my stomach. How different climbing Tawoche last year with Lowe had been. Not a negative word had been said. Not a grunt of dissension, not a whisper of regret. Just "Let's do it," "Belay on," "Great pitch."

The team is more important than any piece of equipment. Each climber must be just as positive at the base of the climb as he was at home. Self-doubt spills over to others in camp and smothers a positive perception. Children aren't the only victims of "dungeons and dragons." Even as adults our fantasies too often overshadow reality and we fail from within before one foot is lifted. The hardest step to take is the first.

The three of us departed base after breakfast. Our good-byes to the Chinese, the Sherpas, and Jim were emotional. This would be our first and, hopefully, only attempt to climb the ridge continuously to the summit.

My walk up the Menlung Valley to ABC was a lesson in erosion. Icefalls crack and thunder down mountainsides, grinding their way along slopes to explode at the bottom. Rivers become engorged with midday melt, rolling boulders along like marbles. Glaciers pop and squeak, grind and crash. Moraines cut loose tons of debris onto glacial ice that moves at the speed a tree grows. In a Himalayan mountain valley, erosion is a visual concept.

I was up at 4:45 the next morning in preparation for our climb up the ropes to reach our site for Camp I. High mares' tails streamed over the peaks. I wanted to go but was outvoted two to one. I spent a frustrating day listening to a horny snow cock chasing a hen along our hillside and watching the weather improve. Of course if we had climbed, it would have snowed. Since we stayed in camp, it was sunny. That's the way mountaineering is.

We made our first move on April 26. High cirrus clouds danced between the peaks to our west and the overall weather looked worse than it had the previous day, but our patience seemed on the verge of explosion. The three of us raced up to our cache below the ropes, changed from tennis shoes to boots, then strapped, clipped, and snapped on climbing gear. Laden with fifty pounds each, we climbed as slowly as Galapagos turtles to the fixed rope.

I went first, breaking loose the buried line, testing each anchor, while trying to stay just ahead of Jeff and Greg. I reached our intended campsite by noon. We didn't have much of a choice. The ridge swept to vertical on both sides of the narrow crest. Neither below nor above was there any semblance of a platform. We would just have to dig and chop where Jim had stood and worked the week before.

Jeff slowly pulled his way to the anchor. "Is this where you want to camp?" he asked.

"Jim started a pretty good platform here," I said. "Let's finish it and dig another just below."

Jeff began hacking away ice, while I dropped three hundred feet for the load of ropes and hardware I had left on the ridge the week before. Burdened with that load and an extra two ropes pulled up from below, I collapsed exhausted onto Jeff's platform shortly after Greg's arrival.

Strapped to the fixed line, Greg, Jeff, and I worked four hours chopping two platforms the size of deer beds in the concrete-hard ice. Greg and Jeff pitched the small two-man Bibler tent for themselves on the larger platform. Four feet below, I pitched a tiny Wild Country bivouac tent that I called the "coffin." It wasn't big enough to change my mind in, let alone sit up, but it was better than bivouacking in the open.

In the afternoon, billowing, big-breasted Pooh clouds swallowed the camp whole. Hail and snow pelted the tents, while I removed sweat-soaked clothes and crawled into my bag. I lay exhausted on my mat, eyes closed, haunted by countless trips wasted in rain or storm. "When were we going to get a break in the weather?" I wondered.

The clouds separated. It was still snowing, but the evening sun peeked below the upper level and threw golden rays on the surrounding summits. Soon the storm returned. It snowed and blew most of the night. I slept off and on, awakened continually by sunburn itch and annoying dreams. The tent was so flimsy and unsecured that I finally tied in to the fixed line in case the "coffin" decided to leave the ridge for ancient burial grounds.

Despite angry storm clouds knotted around the surrounding peaks the next morning, we decided to fix as much rope as we could above camp. It was a tough decision. If the storm continued and we were forced to descend to base camp, all our rope would be fixed above camp. Descent would necessitate retrieval of two ropes from above camp to use for rappel, and on our return for another attempt, we would have to reclimb every pitch back to Camp I.

Greg was reluctant. To him, the weather justified a standoff. He wanted to take middle ground, stay put and then flow with the weather punch—up if it cleared, down if it stormed. Jeff was for "putting in a few pitches." Not commit totally until we had sunny skies, but get our feet wet. I wanted full measure. For one thing, the icefall above us was becoming bigger than life. I was starting to see it in my sleep, imagine death by avalanche below it, dream of being crushed underneath it. To kill those thoughts, I had to climb around it. That meant fixing all six of our ropes to its top.

I jumared out from camp using the 200-foot rope Greg had fixed along the ridge crest to the foot of the overhanging icefall blocking progress above camp. It was on this obstacle my fear was centered. With Greg belaying, I dropped below the anchors and traversed beneath the wall of ice in knee-deep wind slab. The slab stayed put and nothing from above cut loose on me. I made the traverse in two 150-foot rope lengths.

Black humpies, massive cumulus clouds, moved onto our ridge, bringing with them light snowfall. I stood crouched at the belay, waiting for Greg. The ice pitch above me was steep, fifty to fifty-five degrees. I was glad it was Greg's lead.

"You're fresh," Greg said upon his arrival at my belay. "Have a go at the next lead."

What could I say? I wasn't psyched up to do the pitch. I was cold from sitting in my own sweat waiting for Greg. My new One-Sport boots had fallen apart and I had no ankle support, which by the looks of the pitch would be crucial. And the weather was getting worse, if that were possible.

"Sure," I replied. "I'll just take a few pickets and a rack of screws."

I was disappointed. The Southeast Ridge was going to take the abilities of us all, and I needed Greg, our team's only other lead climber, to show me his stuff. As much as I hated to admit it, the days were long gone when I could lead every pitch and want more.

I left the belay playing games with my psyche. Could I climb boiler-plate fifty-degree ice in boots with ripped out ankle straps? Was it up to me to lead every pitch? Two moves above Greg's belay, I put my mind into the game. Warmth returned with work and so did my concentration. I ran the rope out 160 feet in fifteen minutes, slammed in a picket, backed it up with a moderate ice screw, and yelled for Greg and Jeff. I felt like the old Roskelley, confident, smooth, ready and willing to lead them all if that's what it would take.

The next two pitches were steeply rising traverses. I contoured twenty feet below the corniced ridge, placing protection every fifty feet to prevent a long swing on the rope by Greg or Jeff if they should slip while ascending the rope with jumars. The ridge was getting hit hard by bad weather. We were in thick cloud and it was snowing with the winds gusting up to forty miles per hour. Greg, at the belay one hundred feet below, was a ghostly apparition, and Jeff was invisible.

Greg reached my belay as I untangled one of our two remaining ropes. My hands were numb and I was chilled to the bone. Jeff had returned to camp after giving Greg his load of rope at the anchor below.

"I'll take the next one," Greg offered. "Let's drag out the long eight millimeter."

"You got it," I replied.

His offer to lead instilled a breath of life back into the climb for me. My confidence in Greg, sorely beaten down below, returned. I knew he was steady and willing. He'd shown that on the way up the ropes in the storm. But I had to feel his strengths, see him perform before my vision of success on the Southeast Ridge could return.

Greg's long lead put him on top of the icefall, out of sight and hearing. I knew by the action on the rope that he was stopped and placing an anchor. Three prearranged tugs sent me robotically rappelling down the fixed lines. The storm seemed bent on blowing us off the ridge. Visibility was down to the tops of my boots.

My fingers were stiff and painful. Could I stick them in my armpits? No, too much clothing. Did I have an extra set of dry gloves? Yes, but I had given those to Greg for his lead. I concentrated on connecting my figure-eight rappeling device correctly. As I reached the traverse, Greg appeared above me in the whiteout. I was cold but excited about our progress in the teeth of the storm. We could do this ridge.

We were stuck. The storm could last days, even a week. We had provisions for four, maybe five days. If we waited out the storm at Camp I, we would consume our supplies of food and butane. If we retreated, we would have to do so with two ropes and a smidgen of hardware. The ridge up to Camp I would have to be led again after the storm. We drained our thoughts on whether to stay or descend. It's a decision faced by every expedition party.

"Let's think on it until morning," I suggested. "Maybe the storm will pass."

The storm blustered throughout the night and into the early morning hours. Hard ice pellets cratered into the tent's fabric until enough snow had accumulated on the tent to mute the hammering. The "coffin" closed in with the weight of the snow. Every few minutes I sent a fist into the wall and ceiling to knock the snow off. Twice I got up and dug the snow out from around both tents.

"Let's get the hell out of here," Greg yelled down to me that morning. "This one's here to stay."

He was right. The Himalayas were hidden within blobs of clouds thick as pancake batter. But what convinced me was an orange tinge that lit the bottoms of the clouds. For twenty-five years I've depended on one weather sign more than any other: "Red sky at night, sailors' delight. Red sky in the morning, sailors' forewarning." It works better than listening to those weather sorcerers on the nightly news. We decided to bail.

Jeff handed me a cup of lukewarm chicken soup for breakfast. I took a sip and threw it out. While they packed, I stowed my gear in a duffle, stuffed my pack with necessities I would need down below, then dropped the poles on the "coffin" so it wouldn't fly away during our absence.

I rappeled first, carrying the extra hardware to anchor the three of us onto the ridge while we pulled the ropes and set up the next rappel. We were short on rope, on usable anchors, which had been left the day before at our high point, and on confidence in ourselves and the route conditions. Like a car with only three tires, we limped down the ridge.

I disentangled myself from the last rappel, hollered to Greg, "Off rappel!" and began wading through thirty-degree, deep windslab to descend. I didn't like what I was on. Ever since I was buried in an avalanche in the Russian Pamirs in 1974, I've been paranoid about snow slopes.

I heard a long hiss like that of a dog-cornered cat, then experienced a shot of vertigo as the slope I was on moved while the surrounding rock stayed motionless. The tug on the back of my legs pitched me forward. I ran down five long strides, gained momentum, then jumped to an icy crest. The slab grew, sliced into a gully, and shot down the slope and out of sight. I was lucky.

Two hours after leaving Camp I, we reached ABC. The snow was quieter there. Snowflakes cooled my skin while I sat and ate sardines and candy before trudging to base. What a difference in weather just a few thousand feet of elevation make. The air temperature was warm, and radiant heat was already melting the few inches of snow along the moraine.

By noon we were eating Sherpa-cooked fried potatoes, boiled cabbage, and peanut butter on crackers at base camp—in the sun. The storm had dissipated. Should we have bailed? Again, doubt seeped into the corners of my mind.

19

cor·nice \ ˈkȯr-nəs, -nish \ *n*   A quick and effective means of meeting your Maker.
(Roskelley's First Climber's Dictionary, 1991)

"RELAX, ROSKELLEY," Wickwire suggested, "you'll get your chance."

Relax. Sit. Read. Eat. Arduous tasks to accept for a mountaineer, far more difficult than climbing but part of the game.

I've spent weeks trapped in tents by weather. My longest imprisonment was in 1973 when I spent ten days pinned down by wind in a two-man, A-frame tent at 24,600 feet on Dhaulagiri. I read everything from the warning label on my sleeping bag to the instructions in the film box.

The four-day storm at Menlungtse base camp passed quickly, however. I photographed the marmots and bharal sheep, walked in the meadow, read two books, and rested. Then there was my secret love, Tanya. She kept me company in the morning at seven and again at noon, radiating a sexy persona through her voice as Radio Moscow's propaganda officer. Why would anyone listen to Voice of America or the BBC when they could have a clandestine love affair with Tanya?

We awoke to clear skies May 2. A breeze filtered down the valley, and to the west were Himalayan friendlies, the remnants of our storm, caressing minor summits and playing tag in the surrounding valleys. The day was perfect for us to move back to ABC.

"I've got severe diarrhea," Jeff said. "I don't think I can go."

More discouraging words can't be said on a clear morning before an alpine-style ascent. Jeff had been trotting back and forth across the meadow to his private latrine that morning with the runs as if he were in training for the Himalayan Olympics. Nausea and diarrhea had attacked his system the night before, and he was obviously spent and weak from the illness.

"Can you go today?" Greg asked.

"I'll try," he replied, "but don't count on me."

Experience generates a whole lot more sympathy than apathy. We had all "run" this trail before. Illness at altitude opens the door to pulmonary or cerebral edema. It was a risk, but Jeff chose to try to move to ABC. A mile from base camp, Jeff's normal beastly pace slowed to a crawl. His loss of electrolytes and fluid took its toll.

"I can't go any farther," he said. "I've got a terrible headache and I'm too weak. I'll never make it to camp."

Greg and I accepted his personal evaluation. Jeff was tough. If he could have continued, he would have. The decision for Greg and me was difficult: turn back and wait at base for Jeff to recover or go for it as a two-man team.

I searched Greg's eyes for some definite answer. He was obviously upset. Jeff and he had become close friends and climbing partners. Jeff relieved us of the decision.

"You guys have to go. The weather's good and the two of you will be much faster on the ridge without a third."

I didn't agree with the "faster" part, but he was right about the weather. The route was in good condition and Greg and I were healthy and strong. Besides, the expedition's deadline to leave base was May 15. If this attempt collapsed due to weather, Jim could possibly extend our departure time enough for us to make one more shot at the ridge.

"Okay, Jeff," I said, "we're off. If you should feel better or the weather turns shitty, we'll wait for you. Thanks for your help."

I shook his hand. It wasn't enough. I pulled him to me and bear-hugged him to let him know he'd be missed, then turned and hiked up the hill. Greg did the same, the ice among men broken

and melted. Jeff sat in the meadow, his head bowed, characteristically rubbing his balding pate in concern for us and, perhaps, in
despair at the turn of one's life.

I hated the decision to leave without Jeff. I trusted him, believed in his experience, relied on his strength. The ridge was safer
with three. If anything went wrong and either Greg or I needed to
be evacuated, a third member would almost be essential. Now,
before making any decision on the ridge, we'd have to take into
consideration the chances of survival with only two men.

The loss of teammates is the most difficult situation to overcome on a climb. Greg and I suddenly became a two-horse hitch
fastened to a four-horse wagon. The ridge was going to be that
much more of a problem. Could the two of us pull it off alpine
style? On the hike to ABC, we formulated ideas and suggestions
into an adjusted plan. Most important, we convinced ourselves,
perhaps erroneously, that the ridge was still ours for the taking.

The clear, cold high-pressure system gripping the central
Himalayas was still in place the following morning. Not a whisper
of a breeze flowed across ABC, and by 6:30 A.M. we were ascending the ridge. Four hours later and twenty-five hundred feet
higher, Greg and I climbed into Camp I. We weren't alone. Small
Pooh clouds lazily drifted over our ridge, discharging gently falling snow like autumn leaves. I packed, racked, and stacked group
gear for our attempt the next morning, while Greg warmed a brew
of tea. Suspicious as always, I shot glances at the buildup of
weather near Everest and Cho Oyo. Evil was brewing a homecom-
ing for us.

Heavy weather rolled in around noon. At first I tried to be
positive, but by 6 P.M. the lightning, thunder, and continuing
snowfall were too much. Discouraged, I buried myself in my bag
and skimmed my trashy novel for sex and violence to match my
mood. Then the weather turned on us like a junkyard dog.

I was up most of the night knocking snow off the tent walls
so it wouldn't collapse. At dawn I sneaked a peek like a trapdoor
spider through the tent's vent tube toward Nepal at the angriest
sky I'd ever seen. Long, lenticular gray clouds like immense oysters

drifted slowly through an oily thick, blackened sky. Our storm had settled for an encore.

"Greg, we've got electricity in the air." I yelled. A popping and snapping oscillated through my tent. If I'm scared of avalanches and icefalls, I'm terrified of lightning. There is no more unnerving an experience than to be caught in a lightning storm in the mountains.

"We're right in the middle of an electric storm," he replied.

A steady buzz filtered through the air, then a flash lit up the inside of my tent, and without pause, thunder rolled through camp. Quarter-sized snowflakes thick as goose feathers filled the air. Another bolt of lightning hit nearby, then there was more thunder.

"Let's get the hell out of here!" I yelled.

We dressed and began rappeling within ten minutes. Visibility was less than my reach, but I could feel the slope angle and judge my distance to the ridge crest and its cornices as I rappeled. Short of anchor hardware, I placed ice screws, rock pins, deadmen, pickets, even ski poles in whatever decomposed ice or shattered rock would hold our weight. Speed outweighed safety. The buzz in the air and around our metal increased. My ice axe bit me on the leg with the intensity of an electric fence. I felt another jolt from my ice hammer. It wouldn't be long before either Greg or I would become charcoal broiled and ground fifty thousand volts. At each anchor I removed my metal tools from my harness and stuck them in the ice as far away from my body as possible.

I thought of a lady I had met the previous year in Nova Scotia. She had been hit by lightning as a child and survived horrible injury to her internal organs and at the point where the electricity exited. If hit, there was no way Greg or I would survive this far from medical help.

At Camp I and for five rappels along the ridge crest, we were at the mercy of random lightning strikes. Once we left the crest on the sixth rappel and descended down the face, the buzz ceased. I took a full breath for the first time in an hour. Our only concern now was the avalanche-prone slope at the end of the rope, and it had already sloughed.

Soaked from the wet snowfall, scared, and discouraged, we descended to ABC. Our second attempt again thwarted by weather. Menlungtse, centrally located between the hot, moist Indian plains and the cold, dry Tibetan Plateau, was a magnet for intense electrical storms and poor weather. Would we ever get a five-day clear spell?

Greg and I spent the night at ABC hoping in vain that the storm would cease and we could return to the ridge. By morning there were four to five inches of snow, and avalanches roared down the gullies on Menlungtse's Southeast Face. Our ridge was days away from being safe.

At 7 A.M., we left ABC for base. Ugly Glacier was waiting patiently for us to cross, like a lion after a gazelle. I didn't care. I boulder-hopped, slid, fell, got up, and did it again, time after time. On the other side I waited in the wind and snowfall for forty minutes for Greg to ensure his safe arrival across the glacier.

"I'll make it down slowly," he said. "Go ahead."

I leaned into the storm and semitrotted for base camp, stumbling forward with little care for my safety. I was too discouraged to worry about injury. One and a half hours later I walked into base.

Wickwire quickly put my worst fears to rest. "I promise you, John, you'll get another shot at the ridge. I'll make arrangements with Chen and the yak herders."

That's all I wanted to know.

Wickwire arranged with Mr. Chen for the yaks to arrive at Base on May 17. We had to make the departure date or risk excessive expense for our Chinese vehicles and drivers. In Nepal, an expedition leaves when the climb is completed or it is defeated. In Tibet, however, we were dependent on prearranged scheduling of transport, and our budget would not allow much leeway.

On May 8 the weather cleared and stabilized, making possible another attempt. When I had first arrived at base camp to wait out the storm, I had consoled myself that the team would again include Jeff. This was not to be the case. Like Wickwire, Jeff decided he was not up to the challenge of the ridge. He felt Greg and I would make a stronger team and a quicker ascent without a third member. I strongly disagreed, but his mind was fixed. As in Jim's case, it was better that Jeff had made his decision at base rather than high on the ridge.

Greg and I, supported by Jeff, hiked to ABC in the afternoon. I was surprised at the depth of the snow along the moraine and even more so at the sight of our route on the ridge. A foot of snow blanketed the rocks along the ridge, and the avalanche-prone slopes below Camp I continued to slough periodically.

If I were to choose one day on the expedition I would rather forget, it was this day. The deep, wet snow to ABC made the hike with loads slow and dangerous; black, boiling clouds surrounded the peaks by midafternoon; and, to make matters worse, I was having second thoughts about climbing with only Greg.

In frustration as we hiked up the valley I said, "God damn it, Jeff, you should be coming along on this attempt. I need you up there. I don't know Greg well enough to feel comfortable on that ridge."

"You'll do all right, John," he replied. "Just trust your own judgment."

Why Jeff wouldn't go with us was never clear to me. I never pressed the issue again.

Greg and I reached Camp I at one o'clock the next afternoon. I pitched the "coffin" once again for sleeping comfort and ate with Greg in his two-man Bibler tent. As we hydrated and rested, I repaired my boots, which were useless for steep ice climbing unless I could strengthen the ankle supports. Using my Swiss Army knife, I cut holes through the leather of my new five-hundred dollar boots, then inserted rubberized-nylon crampon straps. It worked. I would now be able to front-point with some security.

On the morning of May 10, a cloud battle raged to our south. A massive thunderstorm, angered by the warm, rising air in Nepal, lashed out in a frenzy of flash and fury. Mushroomlike thunderheads loomed beyond like battleships. Above us, mares' tails streamed south as if late for the encounter.

Should we go? Stay? Descend? The weather looked better than on our last attempt, but only by the breadth of a snowflake. At 7:30 A.M. we decided to go for it. If we were forced to descend, we would have to leave all our hardware as rappel anchors, making this attempt our final one.

Carrying sixty-pound packs of personal gear, food, extra hardware, the "coffin," pots, stove, and fuel, Greg and I jumared the ropes above Camp I. Greg went first, breaking trail and pulling the fixed rope free of the snow that had accumulated on top of the ridge since our reconnaissance.

In our effort to go "light," or alpine style, I had calculated back in Spokane months before that two nine-millimeter, 165-foot ropes and four longer lengths of eight-millimeter were the most we would need on the ridge. This would be enough rope to secure several areas of difficulty or danger low on the ridge, but not enough to hamper an alpine-style ascent. Now, with only two climbers, we decided to take only three ropes.

As we ascended the ropes, Greg and I each clipped an eight-millimeter rope to our harness and dragged them to the top of the fixed lines. We now had two eight-millimeter and one nine-millimeter we carried with us. We left the other three ropes in place for our descent.

The storm dissipated as we climbed. Despite the weight of our loads, we reached our previous high point by noon. Greg led the first new pitch, a long, low-angled snow slope to the bergschrund separating the upper ice face from the icefall we had fixed.

"Is there a bivy site?" I yelled.

"I don't think so," he replied. "I'm coming back down to get my load."

As I watched him descend to my belay, I sensed his reluctance to put his full weight on the rope. He seemed to be down-climbing the pitch. "How are the anchors," I asked.

"Shitty," he replied. "I put in a picket, but it's no good. Don't put any weight on it."

"What d'ya mean, don't put any weight on it? I've got to jumar the thing." If I'd had any sense I'd have turned around right there, but the ridge was too important to me. Greg's expertise was rock climbing, and he had indicated to me several times throughout the trip that he was uncomfortable on snow and ice. His critique on his ability surprised me. Now it scared me.

As Greg rested at the belay, I clipped my jumar to the line and climbed the pitch without putting my weight on the rope. At the bergschrund, a two-foot picket anchored the rope in unconsolidated depth hoar. He was right; it was a bad anchor. But I breathed a bit easier about his placement after surveying the conditions. There was nothing better.

"We'll spend the night here," I said. "There's nothing above us but steep ice and this looks like the only place to pitch a tent."

We hacked out a narrow but stable platform beneath the bergschrund's five-foot ice wall. The snow had the consistency of a sack of beans.

Bringing the "coffin" had been a mistake. It was the ideal tent — if I were with the Playmate of the Year; but with another guy, it was claustrophobic. Head to toe, we spent the night in a physical contest of "bump and turn," never once able to rest flat on our backs.

I was out of the tent before the sun hit our ledge. Greg cooked while I sorted climbing hardware and uncoiled the ropes. Off to the south, a lightning storm battered the highlands of Nepal. From Everest to Cho Oyo to Menlungste fat, round snow clouds hovered amidst the valleys, working their way ever higher, drawn to each other like drops of water.

I led a two-hundred-foot pitch up the smooth ice face on granulated, forty-five-degree ice straight above the bergschrund. Without the burden of my heavy pack, which I had left on the ledge for later retrieval, the pitch began as a happy sojourn along memories of climbs on giant ice faces in the Canadian Rockies. But as the thunk of ice tools and grind of crampon points upon the ice became repetitious, I removed my inner self to a beach on Santa Cruz Island with . . . who knows, but she was dynamite.

Greg tied into the 320-foot, eight-millimeter rope I uncoiled at the belay and climbed the next section of ice face easily, anchoring two ice screws to solid waste ice on the face. I led the third rope length of the morning on hard snow along the ridge crest to duck-walk casually up the route. We rappeled the three fixed lines, picked up our loads, and jumared back to our high point. By one o'clock, we were ready to lead again.

Greg front-pointed slowly one hundred feet to the curving ridge crest from my belay. "There's nothing but air on the other side," he yelled. "I can't seem to get any anchors in either."

"Drop until you're able to get in some good screws!"

The ridge crest was rotten ice overlain with three feet of windslab. Pickets were useless and ice screws difficult to place. Greg was eating up the clock trying to place an anchor so close to the crest. Realizing it was useless, he traversed left and up 150 feet, paralleling the crest but away from the windslab. After an hour of effort, he found solid ice and placed two good anchors 250 feet above my belay.

The sixth and last pitch of the day was mine. The ridge steepened to fifty-five degrees as I approached the 21,000-foot pinnacle, an obvious landmark beginning the main corniced ridge to the summit two thousand five hundred feet higher. Two things concerned me: finding a reasonable campsite and good anchors. Neither looked probable.

I led to within ten feet of the pinnacle's top before placing an anchor, a two-foot picket in loose snow. We weren't going any farther that day, so I concentrated on finding a bivouac site. Three feet to my right, the corniced ridge crest I climbed on disappeared into a void with enough vertical depth to create its own weather. Nothing there for a bivouac, and we certainly wouldn't be going that way in the morning. On my left, an arm's length away and five feet up, was the only possible passage around the potato-chip-thin, corniced pinnacle, but a bat would have had trouble finding a sleeping spot there.

I almost lost my self-control. I was perched on a possible cornice two hundred feet above Greg with a worthless picket for an anchor, daylight was fading, a twenty-mile-per-hour wind ripped over the ridge, a thick cloud enveloped the pinnacle, our loads were three long pitches below, and there was no obvious place to bivouac. Then I remembered seeing a hole in the ice the size of a large dog dish, thirty feet below me and on the other side of the ridge that formed the pinnacle on which I now stood. There was something odd about that hole.

"I'm going to lower off the anchor fifty feet and swing over to my left," I yelled to Greg. "There might be a spot to bivy near that rock ridge."

The scene was reminiscent of Toni Kurz on the Eiger. I could barely see Greg through the thickening cloud, and the wind howled strongly enough to make communication a shouting match. My picket slid in and out of its hole like a piston, and I was thirty feet above my last good anchor. There wasn't a spot on the entire face big enough to stand on through the night. I pictured myself, a frozen stiff hanging by the rope like Kurz for a year until the Japanese attempted the ridge in 1991 and cut me loose.

The hole was twenty-five feet to my left on steep ice near the rock ridge. Something about a black hole in an otherwise flawless ice face didn't seem natural. I pendulumed left on my front points, careful not to put too much weight on the picket. I peeked into the hole. A tunnel beyond was three feet in circumference for a short distance. Darkness within prevented me from seeing any farther. But to my left I noticed a much larger opening along the rock ridge and hidden behind a bulge in the ice.

At the mouth of the cave, I placed a rock piton, clipped in my rope, and slid feetfirst into the cavern. I could crawl in the limited space, but not sit up. A few hours of ol' chop-and-hack work would be necessary to be comfortable. Greg and I would at least have a flat, sheltered spot to bivouac. Better yet, the "coffin" would not have to be used.

As I retrieved my load, Greg jumared the line with his to the cave.

"What do you think?" I asked when I finally reached him at the cave.

"The lower cave is too small for two of us," he replied, "but I crawled into an upper tunnel through the ceiling and into the opening above and it's perfect."

I squeezed through Greg's vertical tunnel into the finest natural ice cave I'd ever seen. Like a tenement high-rise, it had two tent-sized rooms, one above the other, and smaller side rooms for our gear. The platforms were flat, frozen pools, body length or longer, and each had a ceiling at least three feet high. The small hole I had originally looked through from the face entered one of the platforms. I took the lower site, while Greg climbed two feet higher and deeper into the cave to the other fairy-tale platform. At any moment I expected Rod Serling to poke his head through the hole and say, "You have now entered the Twilight Zone." I would have believed him.

May 12, 1990

"Looks worse than yesterday morning," I said, peeking out the hole. "Heavy clouds are everywhere and the wind's picking up."

"What'cha think?" he asked.

"Let's fix our three ropes along the ridge and come back here to spend the night," I suggested. "Then go like hell with light loads for the summit the next day."

Greg chewed on the idea awhile, then okayed it. The half mile of corniced ridge beyond the pinnacle looked technical. It would be slow traversing around and along the thin, dangerous cornices to the summit pyramid. Three fixed pitches would, in effect, slingshot us along the ridge the following morning.

At 7:30 A.M. I slipped from the cave, jumared to my anchors along the ridge, and sorted and racked our hardware. As I coiled the last of the rope, Greg traversed to my position from the cave, then to the picket at my high point of the previous night.

"I can see the ridge," he said. "It's difficult but climbable."

Five minutes later I was at his side. The ridge was socked in and hidden. "Do you want to lead?" I asked.

"You go ahead, this is your kind of climbing," he replied.

I tied into an eight-millimeter rope, grabbed the lead rack and our only remaining picket, then waited as Greg prepared the belay.

"Give 'er 'ell, mate," he said.

From the apex of our ice face, I traversed over a snow lip and onto the main ridge. The Southeast Face dropped away beneath my boots thousands of feet, while the wafer-thin, fifteen-foot-high cornice crested like a wave above me ready to break on the opposite side of the ridge. Twenty-five feet from Greg, I reached a foot-wide rock ledge covered by fresh powder snow. Delicately I placed the picks of my ice tools into the névé ice of the cornice as I inched sideways. The rock ledge ended fifty feet from Greg. I couldn't step across the fifteen-foot chasm between me and the safety of a bulge in the ridge. My only choice was to climb onto the cornice, traverse along its crest, and drop onto the ridge twenty feet away.

I sixth-sensed danger. My intuition is my greatest asset as a mountaineer, and I've used it more times than the Pope has used his rosary. Greg's belay anchor was pretty much cosmetic. I knew that because I had placed it. True, he was anchored to bomber ice screws thirty feet below, but still, if I flew he might be pulled off his stance and drop me another ten feet, which would put me into rock horns and ledges below. I was willing to take that chance.

I drove a picket into firm névé ice on the cornice at chest level for protection, and swung my ice tools into the Styrofoam névé ice, and stepped up. Nothing. My feet collapsed through the snow. The bottom two feet of the cornice was Rice Krispy-like sugar snow formed by the sun-warmed rock beneath the cornice and colder ice above. The fifteen-foot-high, wavelike cornice, ten feet wide at its base, perched on the rock ridge crest had the same stability as freshly fallen powder snow on a fence rail. The cornice was a time bomb, and it just might be my weight that would serve as a detonator.

I had no choice but to climb the cornice. It was the only way along the ridge. I reset my tools in the ice above me and pulled up slowly and carefully onto the cornice. Two more feet up, and I was ready to traverse sideways. I stepped to my left. Again, nothing. There was no support from the snow. I swung my left ice tool into the cornice to my side. My arm disappeared to the elbow. With the axe handle, I jabbed into the cornice, felt a vacuum where solid ice should have been, then pulled it out. I was looking through the cornice at Cho Oyo.

I knew then that I was riding a sheet of ice that was set to fly at any moment with me attached to it by my ice tools and a picket. "Picture this, John," I thought, "Greg having to stop you and a ton of ice hooked together. If the rope doesn't break, if you aren't turned into what looks like a road kill, if you survive the ride and fall, how will Greg get you down the mountain all broken to pieces like you're going to be?" He couldn't.

With only the two of us, there was no doubt in my mind that if I wasn't directly ripped away by the cornice, I would hang by the rope over the northeast side of the ridge until the goraks pecked enough of me away to cut my body loose from my harness. As experienced and technical as Greg was, he was no superman. An accident here, even a minor one, would cost me my life. I knew it and Greg knew it. This was a chance I was not willing to take. I backed down to the rock ledge.

"It's too risky. I can't get across here."

"Any way of going across the rock?" Greg yelled.

He couldn't see the chasm from his angle. "I'll try," I replied.

I scraped at the slab with my crampons, then with my axe. It was smooth as a mirror and just as steep. The cornice was the only way, and I was unwilling to take that risk.

"I don't like this totally on my head," I yelled to Greg. "You want to try?"

By now it was snowing hard and Greg was a shadow in the cloud that covered the pinnacle. I could barely make him out, but his reply was clear and final.

"No. Your judgment is good enough for me," he said. "If it's this bad here, it can't get much better along the rest of the ridge."

With a half mile of similar ridge ahead of us, I agreed with him; but turning around without even getting to see the rest of the ridge devastated me. Poor visibility, along with the snow hump thirty feet ahead, obstructed my view of the long, corniced ridge to the summit. Dejected, I returned to Greg's belay.

"Well, that's it then," I said.

"That's it," Greg replied.

_____ E p i l o g u e _____

ep·ic \ 'ep-ik \ *n* A prelude to disaster result-
ing from poor judgment or lack of self-esteem.
(*Roskelley's First Climber's Dictionary*, 1991)

OUR DEFEAT ON Menlungtse's Southeast Ridge can be viewed as a token success. I don't think of it in that way, but my mother does. Perhaps Greg and I avoided what I term a "creative epic," better known as a potential disaster. These don't just happen; they are created.

Himalayan mountaineers have a proclivity toward creative epics, not because the Himalayas are more dangerous than other mountain ranges — that's relative — but because many climbers leave their fates at the mercy of others or of uncontrollable events. I eliminated creative epics from my repertoire in 1974 after Gary Ullin's death on Peak XIX in the Russian Pamirs. From that trip forward, I took control of my own destiny.

To do so takes fortitude, conviction, and, sometimes, a healthy disregard for authority. I question everything — my climbing part-ners' decisions, their anchors, their techniques, their routes — all regardless of who they are or what their reputations. Furthermore, I expect them to do the same with me. I've gone to the mat with Jim Whittaker, Willi Unsoeld, and other climbing "immortals" concerning decisions affecting the welfare of the rest of us on the team—and stood my ground.

Conviction doesn't come cheap. I absorbed bad press, enjoyed verbal abuse, and acquired a reputation as a renegade, but after the avalanche settled, I was still here, digging myself out.

"All right, Roskelley," you say, "you can eliminate most human error, but what about "objective" dangers, such as avalanche, rock-fall, and high-altitude disease?"

Take a good look at my ascents; they speak for themselves. Don't just casually glance, but inspect. Examine Makalu's West Ridge, Uli Biaho, Tawoche, Trango, and Gauri Shankar—bold, intense personal and team endeavors that have defined excellence in the sport. But upon close scrutiny, they are relatively safe and as free from objective danger as one could hope. Skill, not luck, determined our success.

Too many mountaineers turn their lives over to chance—fate if you will—for the opportunity to climb on an expedition. I have learned through experience to pick and choose my peaks and routes for esoteric rewards, not for fame or fortune.

For instance, I have been asked on a number of Sagarmatha (Everest) expeditions attempting the South Col route. I have not accepted one. Luck, Sherpas, and bottled oxygen determine who summits Sagarmatha up the South Col route, not mountaineering skill.

My attitude toward the use of Sherpas and bottled oxygen is already on record. So what does luck have to do with climbing Sagarmatha?

Protecting the South Col route is the Khumbu Icefall. Expeditions negotiate this jumbled mass of moving ice to reach the upper mountain. Route-finding problems are inevitable, and it's roped and laddered like poor Gulliver by the Lilliputians. Survival in the icefall is absolute luck. No skill, experience, or technical ability can save my tail. Despite my probability of reaching the summit, leaving my destiny to chance does not justify the risk.

Mountain climbing is a risky sport, there is no denying it. Each person has to decide how much risk is acceptable to him or her. Besides skill, acceptable risk is the one variable among climbers.

On Menlungtse, I would have lost control of my own destiny to an objective danger: cornices. The level of climbing skill needed to climb the ridge was inconsequential. Both Greg and I were easily up to the standard necessary to climb the ridge. But neither of us was willing to accept the risk of a half mile of delicately corniced ridge.

Tawoche presented different risks, such as hypothermia, rock-fall, frostbite, radical equipment failure, zero chance of rescue, and more. Jeff Lowe and I accepted these risks. Why? Perhaps because of our confidence in each other; perhaps because we calculated the risks to be justifiable with our skill, experience, time of year, and route. Whatever, I never once felt that I handed my fate to chance.

I considered my expeditions to Tawoche and Menlungtse my last days in the Himalayas. I lied to myself. Tawoche threw dry wood on a flicker of desire and set it burning strong again. Menlungtse fanned that flame with defeat, and I can't quit knowing I'll have to repeat over and over, "I failed on my last Himalayan attempt." I'm going out a winner or I'm not going.

The Himalayas are a strong part of me. They have ruled my life in one way or another for more than eighteen years, and I'm not about to kick them out now. If I thought for a moment that I could walk away to an eight-hour day, kids, and bills, I must have been a minute short of insanity.

I came to my senses a half hour's walk from Menlungtse base camp as we left for home. Rising eight thousand feet from where I stood to its magnificent summit was Gauri Shankar's unclimbed East Face. I picked out a line through the lower ice wall, around the imposing rock cliff at midheight, and straight up the ice fluting to the summit. It had Roskelley written all over it.

"I wonder if Lowe is busy next fall?" I thought.

G l o s s a r y

advanced base camp (ABC). The second camp on an expedition; usually placed prior to the mountain's difficulties.

aid (artificial climbing). A climbing technique that relies on aids such as pitons, chocks, étriers, etc., to hold part or all of the climber's weight.

alpine wall. A mixed rock and ice mountain face of any height.

alpinist. A mountaineer with rock, ice, and alpine climbing skills.

anchor. A solid chock (nut), piton, or natural object such as a tree or rock horn used as a supporting point at a belay. An anchor should be "bombproof"—strong enough to hold any possible force subjected to the belayer by a falling climber. Multiple anchors at a belay is standard.

avalanche cone. An accumulation of snow, ice, and/or rock debris at the base of a gully or canyon.

baby angle (piton). An alloy hammer-driven piton shaped in a V used in cracks from three-eighths inch to one-half inch.

bail. To descend.

belay. The device and technique employed by a climber using a rope and who is anchored to safeguard his/her partner(s) from the effect of a fall.

bergshrund. The crevasse formed between a moving glacier and an upper snowfield.

Bhotia. A tribe of people in Nepal of Tibetan ancestry; known for their long-distance trading.

bivouac (bivy). An unplanned overnight stay, usually with a minimum of comfort.

cache. Temporary storage.

carabiner. An oval or D-shaped metal snap-link, one side of which opens by means of a spring clip. It is used for belays, runners, rappeling, etc., and is the universal attachment mechanism of climbing.

cerebral edema (CE). Swelling of the brain probably caused by increased blood flow to the brain and swelling of the brain cells from hypoxia. The most effective treatment is immediate descent to lower altitude. Constant administration of bottled oxygen is a secondary alternative.

chang. Sherpa beer made from fermented barley.

chapati (Indian). Disc-shaped unleavened bread similar to pita bread.

chimney. A vertical fissure in a rock face, wider than a crack but narrower than a gully. Generally a climber can get his body into a chimney.

chockstone. A rock obstruction within a chimney or gully.

chuba (Tibetan). Man's or woman's robe usually of homespun wool cloth.

clean (the pitch). To remove chocks, pitons, and other protective devices placed by the lead climber.

col. A dip in a ridge, usually between two peaks.

cornice. Deposit of wind-drifted snow on the lee edge of a ridge or other exposed terrain feature.

crampon. A steel framework with usually twelve spikes that fits over the sole of a boot and are held in place by straps or a binding; for use on snow and ice. Two of the sharp spikes protrude from the toe of the boot either in an arc or at about forty-five degrees.

crevasse. A crack in the surface of a glacier of any width, length, or depth.

crux. The most difficult section of a pitch. The "crux pitch" is the most difficult pitch on a route.

dehydration. The loss of natural body fluids.

dzong (Tibetan). Fortress.

étrier (French). A lightweight portable ladder of two to four small steps made with webbing or small diameter rope and alloy steps. Étriers are used for artificial climbing or in conjunction with ascenders (*see* jumar).

Everest. The world's highest mountain (29,028 feet), which straddles the Nepal-Tibet border. It is named after Sir George Everest, a former Surveyor General of India. Nepal officially recognizes the peak as Sagarmatha, meaning "The One Whose Forehead Reaches up to the Sky," or, in Sanskrit, "Churning of the Ocean." China's official name for the mountain is Chomolangma, a word of Tibetan origin meaning "Lady of the Wind" or "Goddess of the Place."

eyebrow. An eyebrow-shaped ice field of any size.

figure-8. A friction control device made of metal rod bent in the form of the numeral eight. The rope is placed through the larger hole and looped over the top of the 8, then held by the climber's brake hand to create friction while descending.

fixed rope. Length of rope left in place and anchored to the mountain for ascending or descending a section of the climb more than once.

free-climb. To climb a rock problem using only hands, feet, fingers, or any part of the body. As opposed to artificial climbing.

Friend. A spring-activated camming device (*see* nuts) that comes in an assortment of sizes and is used as a chock in cracks. Friends are versatile and can be used in parallel-sided cracks, flaring cracks and in overhangs as well as in conventional uses.

front-pointing. The technique of climbing steep snow or ice using the two front points of a crampon that angle sharply outward.

frostbite. The deterioration and infection of tissue cells due to ice crystals that form between the cells and cut down the supply of oxygen to minor blood vessels.

ghee or **ghiu** (Nepali). Clarified butter.

glacier. The permanent ice associated with high or arctic mountain regions.

gomba (Tibetan). Monastery.

hammock. A special lightweight support suspended from anchors by webbing. Used on big walls for sleeping.

hauling. A method of raising equipment by using a pulley, rope, and jumar at the anchor.

Himalaya. A mountain range embodying the highest mountains on the earth's surface, lying between India in the south and Tibet in the north. It stretches one thousand five hundred miles from the Indus River in the west to the Brahmaputra in the east and has a width of about one hundred miles. The Himalayas lie in the countries of India, Tibet, Nepal, Pakistan, and Bhutan. The name comes from the Sanskrit words *hima* (snow) and *alaya* (abode).

hypothermia. The cooling of the body's core.

icefall. An area of crevasses and seracs (large ice blocks) created by a glacier flowing over a steep decline.

ice hammer. A short-handled tool consisting of a combination ice pick/hammer head, a shaft, and a ferruled spike. Usually used as a pair or with one ice axe with an adze.

ice screw. A threaded, alloy, hollow-core tube used to protect or anchor on hard ice.

jam crack. A fissure in the rock small enough to insert a finger or large enough for balled fists or boots.

jumar (ascender). A camming device with a handle that, when attached to a fixed rope, enables a climber to ascend the rope but prevents the climber from sliding down. Jumars are normally used as a pair. The word is frequently used as a verb, "to jumar," meaning to ascend using jumars or any similar device.

Karakoram. A vast complex of high mountains in the trans-Himalaya chain lying east of the Indus and west of the Shaksgam from the Aghil Mountains. The range is about 250 miles long and has nineteen peaks over 25,000 feet, including K2, the world's second highest mountain.

Kathmandu. Nepal's capital city with a population of over 350,000 people.

khukari. A large Gurkha-made knife with a curved blade.

Limbu. A tribe of people in Nepal's easternmost middle hills.

moraine. A ridge of glacial till dumped around the margin of a glacier. Lateral moraines are located to the sides of the glacier; medial moraines are found within the body of the glacier where two or more glaciers come together; terminal moraines are at the glacier's receding end.

nak. Female yak.

Nepal. A small, independent kingdom (54,362 square miles) located between India in the south and Tibet in the north, with a population of over fifteen million.

névé ice. Old snow similar in characteristics to dense Styrofoam having structural and crystalline changes due to metamorphism.

nuts (chocks). Pieces of metal of various shapes and sizes attached to loops of rope, webbing, or cable, then attached to the climber's rope with a carabiner and used as protection by wedging them into cracks.

perlon. The tightly woven nylon outer sheath of a core-and-sheath climbing rope.

picket. A two- to three-foot length of extruded aluminum T-bar used as an anchor or for protection in hard snow.

pitch. The distance between two belays a climber has to travel. A pitch can vary from a few feet to the full length of a rope.

pitons. Tapered metal spikes of a variety of sizes and shapes that can be hammered into cracks in rock or directly into ice.

Pooh. Large, heavy cumulus clouds named after the pudgy cartoon bear, Winnie the Pooh.

protection. Chocks, pitons, Friends, slings, or other hardware used to protect the lead climber on a pitch.

pulmonary edema (HAPE—High Altitude Pulmonary Edema). Leakage of blood plasma into the lungs, which renders the air sacs ineffective in exchanging oxygen and carbon dioxide in the blood. The most effective treatment is immediate descent to lower altitude. Constant administration of oxygen is a secondary alternative.

rappel. To descend using a rope.

rockfall. Falling rock debris cut loose by erosion, wildlife, or climbers.

roof. Overhanging rock formation.

runner. A short length of rope or webbing tied or sewn into a loop.

rupee. Currency used in Nepal; 12 Rs are equivalent to $1.

sahib (Nepali). Loosely means "sir."

Sherpa. A race of people of Tibetan origin originally from Kham in eastern Tibet. They are Mayahana Bhuddists, speak a dialect of Tibetan, and have no written language.

Sherpa tea. A customary drink left over from the British Raj now served by a Sherpa staff to their trek and mountaineering groups. The tea is made with inordinate amounts of milk and sugar.

sirdar (Nepali). The leader or headman of a team of Sherpas or porters.

sling. A loop of nylon webbing or rope used for belays, rappeling, climbing, or other uses.

solo. A climb attempted alone.

Tibetan tea. A distinctly Tibetan drink made with tea, yak butter, and salt.

tsampa (Tibetan). Roasted barley four.

tumpline. A length of rawhide, rope, or wool cord with a forehead patch used to carry loads. The patch is placed near the top of the head while the line circles the load enabling the carrier to use the strength of the neck muscles rather than the shoulders.

yak. A large, long-haired, wild or domesticated ox of Tibet and adjacent elevated parts of central Asia.

zhum (Tibetan). A female crossbreed betwen yak and cattle.

zopkio (Tibetan). A male, infertile crossbreed between yak and cattle.